Mediterranean
DIET COOKBOOK FOR BEGINNERS

30-DAYS
Meal Plan Included
to enjoy a new healthy lifestyle

You don't need to enter any details

except your e-mail

GET YOUR FREE BONUS PASSWORD ON **PAGE 16**

TABLE OF CONTENTS

Chapter- 6: Poultry and Meats 75

Introduction

The Mediterranean diet is more than a diet; it's a way of eating that celebrates food, unity, and well-being. It is a popular eating plan that is flexible and easy to follow.

The populations of the Mediterranean are, on average, fitter and live longer. Are Italians, Spaniards, and Greeks always on a diet? No way. They simply have healthier eating habits and traditions. And the fascinating thing is that they also eat in a tastier way, with more refined and flavorful dishes than Americans. It's no coincidence that year after year, the Mediterranean diet tops the annual ranking of the best diets in the *U.S. News and World Report*.

Let's enjoy a nice plate of spaghetti with sauce or a Margherita pizza with tomato and mozzarella. Or a grilled steak and a salad dressed with extra virgin olive oil, also accompanied by a perfect red wine (which must never be missing at the table).

It doesn't seem like giving up anything, yet this is a typical menu of the Mediterranean diet. It is a way of eating healthily, without ever losing the pleasure of flavors.

In the 1950s, an American nutritionist named Ancel Keys noticed that people in the Mediterranean region seemed to get sick less often than Americans.

He thought that maybe the Mediterranean diet, which includes things like fruits, vegetables, fish, and olive oil, might help people live longer and healthier lives.

Ancel Keys went back to the United States and spent many years studying this idea. His research resulted in a book called *Eat Well and Stay Well, the Mediterranean Way*. In this book, he talked about his large study, the "Seven Countries Study," where he looked at the diets and health of 12,000 people from different countries, like Japan, the USA, the Netherlands, Yugoslavia, Finland, and Italy.

The study confirmed his idea that the Mediterranean diet could be really good for health and could help prevent diseases.

So, from the 1970s onwards, people started trying to encourage Americans to eat more like people in the Mediterranean. They suggested eating more grains, vegetables, fruits, fish, and olive oil instead of a diet that's too high in fats, proteins, and sugars.

In the 1990s, a straightforward food pyramid was introduced to outline the key principles of the Mediterranean diet and connect with the public. At the pyramid's base were the foods to be eaten more frequently throughout the day, while at the top were the foods to be consumed in moderation.

HEALTHY EATING PYRAMID

- Healthy Fats
- Meat, Fish, Eggs, Nuts, Milk, Yoghurt, Cheese
- Grains
- Fruit, Vegetables & Legumes

The Mediterranean Food Guide Pyramid is built upon the eating habits of the Greek island of Crete, as well as other regions of Greece and southern Italy, around 1960. During this time, chronic diseases like heart disease and cancer were less prevalent.

At the base of the food pyramid, you'll find plenty of vegetables, a bit of fruit, and preferably whole grains. Moving up, there are low-fat dairy products (like yogurt) recommended in 2-3 servings of 4 ounces each.

Extra virgin olive oil, the preferred condiment, should mainly be used raw (about 3-4 tablespoons per day), along with garlic, onion, spices, and herbs, instead of salt, making them the best seasonings for Mediterranean-style dishes. Other healthy fats, in addition to those from olive oil, come from nuts and olives, in one or two servings of 2 tablespoons.

Towards the top of the food pyramid, you'll find foods to be consumed not every day but on a weekly basis. These are primarily sources of protein, among which we should favor fish and legumes, with at least two servings of each per week, poultry with 2-3 servings, eggs from 1 to 4 per week, and cheeses, not exceeding a couple of servings of 3.5 ounces, or 1.7 ounces if they are aged.

At the very top of the pyramid, there are foods to be consumed sparingly: two servings or less per week for red meats (3.5 ounces), while processed meats (such as cold cuts, sausages, etc.) should be consumed even more sparingly (one serving per week of 1.7 ounces or even less). Finally, sweets should be consumed as little as possible.

One of the most important concepts of the Mediterranean diet pattern is consuming an abundance of plant foods such as fruits, vegetables, legumes (such as beans, lentils, and peas), and whole grains like bulgur wheat or barley. In fact, people in the Mediterranean region commonly incorporate five to ten servings of fruits and vegetables into their daily meals, often including two to three vegetable servings with each meal. Legumes and whole grains are also fundamental components of their daily diet. Foods in these categories are naturally low in calories and rich in nutrients, making them highly effective for weight management and overall health.

Here is a variety of plant-based foods that are prominently grown in the Mediterranean and play a significant role in the Mediterranean diet:

- **Legumes**: Peas, lentils, chickpeas
- **Fruits**: Grapes, olives, figs, pomegranates, persimmons, mandarin oranges, lemons
- **Grains**: Wheat, rice, barley, corn
- **Nuts**: Almonds, walnuts, hazelnuts, pine nuts
- **Vegetables**: Tomatoes, eggplant, garlic, onions, artichokes, broccoli, green beans, cabbage, asparagus, broccoli rabe.

Eat Fish

Fish and seafood are essential parts of the Mediterranean diet on a weekly basis.
One of the reasons is that seafood is an excellent source of those highly sought-after omega-3 fatty acids.

Reducing your consumption of red meat:

Many people automatically think of protein-rich foods like beef, poultry, pork, and fish as the main course. However, in the Mediterranean diet, beef is typically served only once or twice a month, rather than several times a week as often seen in many American households.
Additionally, when beef is included, it's usually in smaller portions (2 to 3 ounces) as a side dish rather than a substantial 8-plus-ounce main course.
This practice helps maintain a moderate intake of saturated fats and omega-6 fatty acids, contributing to a balanced and healthier diet.

Remember that the Mediterranean diet doesn't require you to completely eliminate all red meat. The goal is simply to reduce your intake of animal protein and increase your consumption of plant-based protein.

Fortunately, you can easily substitute a portion of your usual meat serving with lentils or beans to incorporate plant-based protein into your meals. For instance, instead of an 8-ounce steak, you might opt for a 3- or 4-ounce portion alongside a lentil salad or by sprinkling some nuts on a salad.

This approach also helps you increase your vegetable intake, filling your plate with more greens.

Dairy in Moderation

Dairy is indeed a daily part of the Mediterranean diet, and cheese (along with yogurt) serves as a common source of calcium. However, the secret lies in moderation. Incorporate two to three servings of dairy products into your daily routine. One serving may consist of an 8-ounce glass of milk, 8 ounces of yogurt, or 1 ounce of cheese. Opt for low-fat versions of milk and yogurt to reduce your saturated fat intake. Given the limited quantity consumed, you can choose regular cheese if you prefer.

Boosting Flavor and Health with Herbs and Spices

Fresh herbs and spices not only elevate the taste of your dishes but also harbor numerous concealed health advantages. Take, for instance, oregano and basil in your spaghetti sauce – they do more than just impart an authentic Italian flavor. These herbs are also plants, brimming with various health benefits that can significantly impact your overall well-being. Basic seasonings like ginger and oregano contain phytochemicals, natural substances known to promote health and safeguard against conditions such as cancer and heart disease.

You might be surprised to learn that herbs and spices are also rich in healthy omega-3 fatty acids, which play a role in reducing inflammation in the body. Explore some of the specific health benefits associated with commonly used herbs and spices:

- **Basil** offers more than just flavor; it boasts anti-inflammatory properties that can be particularly beneficial for individuals dealing with chronic inflammation conditions like arthritis or inflammatory bowel disease. Additionally, basil serves as a protective shield against harmful bacteria and is a rich source of vitamin A, which plays a vital role in reducing free radical-induced damage to the body.

- **Cinnamon** isn't just a delightful spice for baking or a comforting addition to tea; it also helps regulate blood sugar levels by slowing down digestion, preventing rapid spikes in blood sugar.

- **Oregano** is a spice packed with essential nutrients, including fiber, iron, manganese, calcium, vitamin C, vitamin A, and omega-3 fatty acids. This versatile spice has been linked to antibacterial and antioxidant properties, making it a valuable addition to your culinary repertoire.

- **Parsley** is a treasure trove of antioxidants, boasting ample amounts of vitamin A and vitamin C. These antioxidants play a vital role in shielding the body from the risks of heart disease and cancer. (Who would've thought that nibbling on that parsley garnish was a wise move?)

- **Turmeric**, on the other hand, wields its power as a potent anti-inflammatory and antioxidant agent, lending a hand in defending against conditions like arthritis, heart disease, and specific types of cancer.

Sipping wine during meals

Having a glass of wine with your dinner is a widespread tradition in Mediterranean areas. Red wine contains unique nutrients that have been proven to promote heart health. However, it's crucial to exercise moderation. It's a good idea to include red wine in your routine a few times a week for the sake of your heart, but it's advisable to consult with your doctor to ensure it's suitable for your individual health circumstances.

SCAN

https://sites.google.com/view/freebonusbooks

Your password to open pdf bonus book is:

pdfbonus4u

Chapter 1
Breakfasts

Spinach and Egg Breakfast Wraps

Prep time: 10 minutes | Cook time: 7 minutes | Serves 2

1 tablespoon olive oil
¼ cup minced onion
3 to 4 tablespoons minced
sun-dried tomatoes in
olive oil and herbs

3 large eggs, whisked
1½ cups packed baby spinach
1 ounce (28 g) crumbled feta
cheese
Salt, to taste
2 (8-inch) whole-wheat tortillas

1. Heat the olive oil in a large skillet over medium-high heat.
2. Sauté the onion and tomatoes for about 3 minutes, stirring occasionally, until softened.
3. Reduce the heat to medium. Add the whisked eggs and stir-fry for 1 to 2 minutes.
4. Stir in the baby spinach and scatter with the crumbled feta cheese. Season as needed with salt.
5. Remove the egg mixture from the heat to a plate. Set aside.
6. Working in batches, place 2 tortillas on a microwave-safe dish and microwave for about 20 seconds to warm them.
7. Spoon half of the egg mixture into each tortilla. Fold them in half and roll up, then serve.

Per Serving
calories: 434 | fat: 28.1g | protein: 17.2g | carbs: 30.8g | fiber: 6.0g | sodium: 551mg

Mediterranean Eggs (Shakshuka)

Prep time: 5 minutes | Cook time: 20 minutes | Serves 4

2 tablespoons extra-virgin
olive oil
1 cup chopped shallots
1 teaspoon garlic powder
1 cup finely diced potato
1 cup chopped red bell
peppers

1 (14.5-ounce/ 411-g) can diced
tomatoes, drained
¼ teaspoon ground cardamom
¼ teaspoon paprika
¼ teaspoon turmeric
4 large eggs
¼ cup chopped fresh cilantro

1. Preheat the oven to 350ºF (180ºC).
2. Heat the olive oil in an ovenproof skillet over medium-high heat until it shimmers.
3. Add the shallots and sauté for about 3 minutes, stirring occasionally, until fragrant.
4. Fold in the garlic powder, potato, and bell peppers and stir to combine.
5. Cover and cook for 10 minutes, stirring frequently. Add the tomatoes, cardamon, paprika, and turmeric and mix well.
6. When the mixture begins to bubble, remove from the heat and crack the eggs into the skillet.
7. Transfer the skillet to the preheated oven and bake for 5 to 10 minutes, or until the egg whites are set and the yolks are cooked to your liking.
8. Remove from the oven and garnish with the cilantro before serving.

Per Serving
calories: 223 | fat: 11.8g | protein: 9.1g | carbs: 19.5g | fiber: 3.0g | sodium: 277mg

Pumpkin Pie Parfait

Prep time: 5 minutes | Cook time: 0 minutes | Serves 4

1 (15-ounce / 425-g) can pure
pumpkin purée
4 teaspoons honey
1 teaspoon pumpkin pie spice

¼ teaspoon ground
cinnamon
2 cups plain Greek yogurt
1 cup honey granola

1. Combine the pumpkin purée, honey, pumpkin pie spice, and cinnamon in a large bowl and stir to mix well.
2. Cover the bowl with plastic wrap and chill in the refrigerator for at least 2 hours.
3. Make the parfaits: Layer each parfait glass with ¼ cup pumpkin mixture in the bottom.
4. Top with ¼ cup of yogurt and scatter each top with ¼ cup of honey granola. Repeat the layers until the glasses are full. Serve immediately.

Per Serving
calories: 263 | fat: 8.9g | protein: 15.3g | carbs: 34.6g | fiber: 6.0g | sodium: 91mg

Ricotta Toast with Strawberries

Prep time: 10 minutes | Cook time: 0 minutes | Serves 2

½ cup crumbled ricotta cheese
1 tablespoon honey, plus
additional as needed
Pinch of sea salt, plus additional
as needed

4 slices of whole-grain bread,
toasted
1 cup sliced fresh strawberries
4 large fresh basil leaves,
sliced into thin shreds

1. Mix together the cheese, honey, and salt in a small bowl until well incorporated.
2. Taste and add additional salt and honey as needed. Spoon 2 tablespoons of the cheese mixture onto each slice of bread and spread it all over.
3. Sprinkle the sliced strawberry and basil leaves on top before serving.

Per Serving
calories: 274 | fat: 7.9g | protein: 15.1g | carbs: 39.8g | fiber: 5.0g | sodium: 322mg

Morning Overnight Oats with Raspberries

Prep time: 5 minutes | Cook time: 0 minutes | Serves 2

⅔ cup unsweetened
almond milk
¼ cup raspberries
⅓ cup rolled oats
1 teaspoon honey

¼ teaspoon turmeric
⅛ teaspoon ground
cinnamon
Pinch ground cloves

1. Place the almond milk, raspberries, rolled oats, honey, turmeric, cinnamon, and cloves in a mason jar. Cover and shake to combine. Transfer to the refrigerator for at least 8 hours, preferably 24 hours. Serve chilled.

Per Serving
calories: 81 | fat: 1.9g | protein: 2.1g | carbs: 13.8g | fiber: 3.0g | sodium: 97mg

Cinnamon Oatmeal with Dried Cranberries

Prep time: 5 minutes | Cook time: 8 minutes | Serves 2

1 cup almond milk
1 cup water
Pinch sea salt

1 cup old-fashioned oats
½ cup dried cranberries
1 teaspoon ground cinnamon

1. In a medium saucepan over high heat, bring the almond milk, water, and salt to a boil.
2. Stir in the oats, cranberries, and cinnamon. Reduce the heat to medium and cook for 5 minutes, stirring occasionally.
3. Remove the oatmeal from the heat. Cover and let it stand for 3 minutes.
4. Stir before serving.

Per Serving
calories: 107 | fat: 2.1g | protein: 3.2g | carbs: 18.2g | fiber: 4.1g | sodium: 122mg

Basil Scrambled Eggs

Prep time: 5 minutes | Cook time: 8 minutes | Serves 2

4 large eggs
2 tablespoons grated Gruyère cheese
2 tablespoons finely chopped fresh basil

1 tablespoon plain Greek yogurt
1 tablespoon olive oil
2 cloves garlic, minced
Sea salt and freshly ground pepper, to taste

1. In a large bowl, beat together the eggs, cheese, basil, and yogurt with a whisk until just combined.
2. Heat the oil in a large, heavy nonstick skillet over medium-low heat. Add the garlic and cook until golden, about 1 minute.
3. Pour the egg mixture into the skillet over the garlic. Work the eggs continuously and cook until fluffy and soft.
4. Season with sea salt and freshly ground pepper to taste. Divide between 2 plates and serve immediately.

Per Serving
calories: 243 | fat: 19.7g | protein: 15.6g | carbs: 3.4g | fiber: 0.1g | sodium: 568mg

Creamy Breakfast Bulgur with Berries

Prep time: 2 minutes | Cook time: 10 minutes | Serves 2

½ cup medium-grain bulgur wheat
1 cup water
Pinch sea salt
¼ cup unsweetened almond milk

1 teaspoon pure vanilla extract
¼ teaspoon ground cinnamon
1 cup fresh berries of your choice

1. Put the bulgur in a medium saucepan with the water and sea salt, and bring to a boil.
2. Cover, remove from heat, and let it stand for 10 minutes until water is absorbed.
3. Stir in the milk, vanilla, and cinnamon until fully incorporated. Divide between 2 bowls and top with the fresh berries to serve.

Per Serving
calories: 173 | fat: 1.6g | protein: 5.7g | carbs: 34.0g | fiber: 6.0g | sodium: 197mg

Kale and Apple Smoothie

Prep time: 5 minutes | Cook time: 0 minutes | Serves 2

2 cups shredded kale
1 cup unsweetened almond milk
¼ cup 2 percent plain Greek yogurt

½ Granny Smith apple, unpeeled, cored and chopped
½ avocado, diced
3 ice cubes

1. Put all ingredients in a blender and blend until smooth and thick.
2. Pour into two glasses and serve immediately.

Per Serving
calories: 177 | fat: 6.8g | protein: 8.2g | carbs: 22.0g | fiber: 4.1g | sodium: 112mg

Mediterranean Omelet

Prep time: 8 minutes | Cook time: 15 minutes | Serves 2

2 teaspoons extra-virgin olive oil, divided
1 garlic clove, minced
½ yellow bell pepper, thinly sliced
½ red bell pepper, thinly sliced
¼ cup thinly sliced red onion

2 tablespoons chopped fresh parsley, plus extra for garnish
2 tablespoons chopped fresh basil
½ teaspoon salt
½ teaspoon freshly ground black pepper
4 large eggs, beaten

1. In a large, heavy skillet, heat 1 teaspoon of the olive oil over medium heat. Add the garlic, peppers, and onion to the skillet and sauté, stirring frequently, for 5 minutes.
2. Add the parsley, basil, salt, and pepper, increase the heat to medium-high, and sauté for 2 minutes. Slide the vegetable mixture onto a plate and return the skillet to the heat.
3. Heat the remaining 1 teaspoon of olive oil in the skillet and pour in the beaten eggs, tilting the pan to coat evenly. Cook the eggs just until the edges are bubbly and all but the center is dry, 3 to 5 minutes.
4. Spoon the vegetable mixture onto one-half of the omelet and use a spatula to fold the empty side over the top. Slide the omelet onto a platter or cutting board. To serve, cut the omelet in half and garnish with extra fresh parsley.

Per Serving
calories: 206 | fat: 14.2g | protein: 13.7g | carbs: 7.2g | fiber: 1.2g | sodium: 729mg

Apple-Tahini Toast

Prep time: 5 minutes | Cook time: 0 minutes | Serves 1

2 slices whole-wheat bread, toasted
2 tablespoons tahini

1 small apple of your choice, cored and thinly sliced
1 teaspoon honey

1. Spread the tahini on the toasted bread.
2. Place the apple slices on the bread and drizzle with the honey. Serve immediately.

Per Serving
calories: 458 | fat: 17.8g | protein: 11.0g | carbs: 63.5g | fiber: 10.5g | sodium: 285mg

Feta and Spinach Frittata

Prep time: 10 minutes | Cook time: 15 minutes | Serves 2

4 large eggs, beaten
2 tablespoons fresh chopped herbs, such as rosemary, thyme, oregano, basil or 1 teaspoon dried herbs
¼ teaspoon salt
Freshly ground black pepper, to taste
4 tablespoons extra-virgin olive oil, divided

1 cup fresh spinach, arugula, kale, or other leafy greens
4 ounces (113 g) quartered artichoke hearts, rinsed, drained, and thoroughly dried
8 cherry tomatoes, halved
½ cup crumbled soft goat cheese

1. Preheat the broiler to Low.
2. In a small bowl, combine the beaten eggs, herbs, salt, and pepper and whisk well with a fork. Set aside.
   In an ovenproof skillet, heat 2 tablespoons of olive oil over medium heat. Add the spinach, artichoke hearts, and cherry tomatoes and sauté until just wilted, 1 to 2 minutes.
3. Pour in the egg mixture and let it cook undisturbed over medium heat for 3 to 4 minutes, until the eggs begin to set on the bottom.
4. Sprinkle the goat cheese across the top of the egg mixture and transfer the skillet to the oven.
5. Broil for 4 to 5 minutes, or until the frittata is firm in the center and golden brown on top.
6. Remove from the oven and run a rubber spatula around the edge to loosen the sides. Slice the frittata in half and serve drizzled with the remaining 2 tablespoons of olive oil.

Per Serving
calories: 529 | fat: 46.5g | protein: 21.4g | carbs: 7.1g | fiber: 3.1g | sodium: 762mg

Feta and Olive Scrambled Eggs

Prep time: 5 minutes | Cook time: 5 minutes | Serves 2

4 large eggs
1 tablespoon unsweetened almond milk
Sea salt and freshly ground pepper, to taste
1 tablespoon olive oil

¼ cup crumbled feta cheese
10 Kalamata olives, pitted and sliced
Small bunch fresh mint, chopped, for garnish

1. Beat the eggs in a bowl until just combined. Add the milk and a pinch of sea salt and whisk well.
2. Heat a medium nonstick skillet over medium-high heat and add the olive oil.
3. Pour in the egg mixture and stir constantly, or until they just begin to curd and firm up, about 2 minutes. Add the feta cheese and olive slices, and stir until evenly combined.
4. Season to taste with salt and pepper. Divide the mixture between 2 plates and serve garnished with the fresh chopped mint.

Per Serving
calories: 244 | fat: 21.9g | protein: 8.4g | carbs:3.5g | fiber: 0.6g | sodium: 339mg

Tomato and Egg Breakfast Pizza

Prep time: 5 minutes | Cook time: 15 minutes | Serves 2

2 (6- to 8-inch-long) slices of whole-wheat naan bread
2 tablespoons prepared pesto

1 medium tomato, sliced
2 large eggs

1. Heat a large nonstick skillet over medium-high heat.
2. Place the naan bread in the skillet and let warm for about 2 minutes on each side, or until softened. Spread 1 tablespoon of the pesto on one side of each slice and top with tomato slices.
3. Remove from the skillet and place each one on its own plate. Crack the eggs into the skillet, keeping them separated, and cook until the whites are no longer translucent and the yolks are cooked to desired doneness.
4. Using a spatula, spoon one egg onto each bread slice. Serve warm.

Per Serving
calories: 429 | fat: 16.8g | protein: 18.1g | carbs: 12.0g | fiber: 4.8g | sodium: 682mg

Avocado and Egg Toast

Prep time: 5 minutes | Cook time: 8 minutes | Serves 2

2 tablespoons ground flaxseed
½ teaspoon baking powder
2 large eggs, beaten
1 teaspoon salt, plus additional for serving
½ teaspoon freshly ground black pepper, plus additional for serving

½ teaspoon garlic powder, sesame seed, caraway seed, or other dried herbs (optional)
3 tablespoons extra-virgin olive oil, divided
1 medium ripe avocado, peeled, pitted, and sliced
2 tablespoons chopped ripe tomato

1. In a small bowl, combine the flaxseed and baking powder, breaking up any lumps in the baking powder. Add the beaten eggs, salt, pepper, and garlic powder (if desired) and whisk well.
2. Let it sit for 2 minutes.
3. In a small nonstick skillet, heat 1 tablespoon of olive oil over medium heat. Pour the egg mixture into the skillet and let cook undisturbed until the egg begins to set on bottom, 2 to 3 minutes.
4. Using a rubber spatula, scrape down the sides to allow uncooked egg to reach the bottom. Cook for an additional 2 to 3 minutes.
5. Once almost set, flip like a pancake and allow the top to fully cook, another 1 to 2 minutes.
6. Remove from the skillet and allow to cool slightly, then slice into 2 pieces.
7. Top each piece with avocado slices, additional salt and pepper, chopped tomato, and drizzle with the remaining 2 tablespoons of olive oil. Serve immediately.

Per Serving
calories: 297 | fat: 26.1g | protein: 8.9g | carbs: 12.0g | fiber: 7.1g | sodium: 1132mg

Savory Breakfast Oatmeal

Prep time: 5 minutes | Cook time: 15 minutes | Serves 2

½ cup steel-cut oats
1 cup water
1 medium cucumber, chopped
1 large tomato, chopped
1 tablespoon olive oil

Pinch freshly grated Parmesan cheese
Sea salt and freshly ground pepper, to taste
Flat-leaf parsley or mint, chopped, for garnish

1. Combine the oats and water in a medium saucepan and bring to a boil over high heat, stirring continuously, or until the water is absorbed, about 15 minutes.
2. Divide the oatmeal between 2 bowls and scatter the tomato and cucumber on top. Drizzle with the olive oil and sprinkle with the Parmesan cheese.
3. Season with salt and pepper to taste. Serve garnished with the parsley.

Per Serving
calories: 197| fat: 8.9g | protein: 6.3g | carbs: 23.1g | fiber: 6.4g | sodium: 27mg

Avocado Smoothie

Prep time: 2 minutes | Cook time: 0 minutes | Serves 2

1 large avocado
1½ cups unsweetened coconut milk

2 tablespoons honey

1. Place all ingredients in a blender and blend until smooth and creamy.
2. Serve immediately.

Per Serving
calories: 686 | fat: 57.6g | protein: 6.2g | carbs: 35.8g | fiber: 10.7g | sodium: 35mg

Marinara Poached Eggs

Prep time: 5 minutes | Cook time: 15 minutes | Serves 6

1 tablespoon extra-virgin olive oil
1 cup chopped onion
2 garlic cloves, minced
2 (14.5-ounce / 411-g) cans no-salt-added

Italian diced tomatoes, undrained
6 large eggs
½ cup chopped fresh flat-leaf parsley

1. Heat the olive oil in a large skillet over medium-high heat.
2. Add the onion and sauté for 5 minutes, stirring occasionally. Add the garlic and cook for 1 minute more.
3. Pour the tomatoes with their juices over the onion mixture and cook for 2 to 3 minutes until bubbling.
4. Reduce the heat to medium and use a large spoon to make six indentations in the tomato mixture. Crack the eggs, one at a time, into each indentation.
5. Cover and simmer for 6 to 7 minutes, or until the eggs are cooked to your preference.
6. Serve with the parsley sprinkled on top.

Per Serving
calories: 89 | fat: 6.0g | protein: 4.0g | carbs: 4.0g | fiber: 1.0g | sodium: 77mg

Breakfast Pancakes with Berry Sauce

Prep time: 5 minutes | Cook time: 10 minutes | Serves 4

Pancakes:
1 cup almond flour
1 teaspoon baking powder
¼ teaspoon salt
6 tablespoon extra-virgin olive oil, divided
2 large eggs, beaten

Zest and juice of 1 lemon
½ teaspoon vanilla extract
Berry Sauce:
1 cup frozen mixed berries
1 tablespoon water, plus more as needed
½ teaspoon vanilla extract

Make the Pancakes

1. In a large bowl, combine the almond flour, baking powder, and salt and stir to break up any clumps.
2. Add 4 tablespoons olive oil, beaten eggs, lemon zest and juice, and vanilla extract and stir until well mixed.
3. Heat 1 tablespoon of olive oil in a large skillet. Spoon about 2 tablespoons of batter for each pancake. Cook until bubbles begin to form, 4 to 5 minutes. Flip and cook for another 2 to 3 minutes. Repeat with the remaining 1 tablespoon of olive oil and batter.

Make the Berry Sauce

4. Combine the frozen berries, water, and vanilla extract in a small saucepan and heat over medium-high heat for 3 to 4 minutes until bubbly, adding more water as needed. Using the back of a spoon or fork, mash the berries and whisk until smooth. Serve the pancakes with the berry sauce.

Per Serving
calories: 275 | fat: 26.0g | protein: 4.0g | carbs: 8.0g | fiber: 2.0g | sodium: 271mg

Sautéed Kale with Garlic and Lemon

Prep time: 10 minutes | Cook time: 7 minutes | Serves 4

1 tablespoon olive oil
3 bunches kale, stemmed and roughly chopped
2 teaspoons chopped garlic

¼ teaspoon kosher salt
1 tablespoon freshly squeezed lemon juice

1. Heat the oil in a 10-inch skillet over medium-high heat. Once the oil is shimmering, add as much kale as will fit in the pan. You will probably only fit half the leaves into the pan at first.
2. Mix the kale with tongs so that the leaves are coated with oil and start to wilt. As the kale wilts, keep adding more of the raw kale, continuing to use tongs to mix.
3. Once all the kale is in the pan, add the garlic and salt and continue to cook until the kale is tender. Total cooking time from start to finish should be about 7 minutes.
4. Mix the lemon juice into the kale. Add additional salt and/or lemon juice if necessary.
   Place 1 cup of kale in each of 4 containers and refrigerate.
5. STORAGE: Store covered containers in the refrigerator for up to 5 days.

Per Serving
calories: 396 | fat: 10.6g | protein: 7.3g | carbs: 68.0g | fiber: 4.8g | sodium: 307mg

Warm Bulgur Breakfast Bowls with Fruits

Prep time: 5 minutes | Cook time: 15 minutes | Serves 6

*2 cups unsweetened
almond milk
1 ½ cups uncooked bulgur
1 cup water
½ teaspoon ground
cinnamon*

*2 cups frozen (or fresh, pitted)
dark sweet cherries
8 dried (or fresh) figs, chopped
½ cup chopped almonds
¼ cup loosely packed fresh
mint, chopped*

1. Combine the milk, bulgur, water, and cinnamon in a medium saucepan, stirring, and bring just to a boil.
2. Cover, reduce the heat to medium-low, and allow to simmer for 10 minutes, or until the liquid is absorbed.
3. Turn off the heat, but keep the pan on the stove, and stir in the frozen cherries (no need to thaw), figs, and almonds. Cover and let the hot bulgur thaw the cherries and partially hydrate the figs, about 1 minute.
4. Fold in the mint and stir to combine, then serve.

Per Serving
calories: 207 | fat: 6.0g | protein: 8.0g | carbs: 32.0g | fiber: 4.0g | sodium: 82mg

Eggs with Sun-dried Tomatoes

Cook time: 15 minutes | Serves 5

*5 large eggs
3 tablespoons prepared
pesto
¼ teaspoon white vinegar*

*2 tablespoons low-fat (2%)
plain Greek yogurt
5 teaspoons sliced
sun-dried tomatoes*

1. Place the eggs in a saucepan and cover with water. Bring the water to a boil. As soon as the water starts to boil, place a lid on the pan and turn the heat off. Set a timer for 15 minutes.
2. When the timer goes off, drain the hot water and run cold water over the eggs to cool.
3. Peel the eggs, slice in half vertically, and scoop out the yolks.
4. Place the yolks in a medium mixing bowl and add the pesto, vinegar, and yogurt. Mix well, until creamy.
5. Scoop about 1 tablespoon of the pesto-yolk mixture into each egg half. Top each with ½ teaspoon of sun-dried tomatoes. Place 2 stuffed egg halves in each of separate containers. STORAGE: Store covered containers in the refrigerator for up to 5 days.

Per Serving
Calories: 124; Total fat: 9g; Saturated fat: 2g; Sodium: 204mg; Carbohydrates: 2g; Fiber: <1g; Protein: 8g

Feta and Pepper Frittata

Prep time: 10 minutes | Cook time: 20 minutes | Serves 4

*Olive oil cooking spray
8 large eggs
1 medium red bell pepper,
diced
½ teaspoon salt*

*½ teaspoon black pepper
1 garlic clove, minced
½ cup feta, divided*

1. Preheat the air fryer to 360ºF (182ºC). Lightly coat the inside of a 6-inch round cake pan with olive oil cooking spray.
2. In a large bowl, beat the eggs for 1 to 2 minutes, or until well combined.
3. Add the bell pepper, salt, black pepper, and garlic to the eggs, and mix together until the bell pepper is distributed throughout. Fold in ¼ cup of the feta cheese.
4. Pour the egg mixture into the prepared cake pan, and sprinkle the remaining ¼ cup of feta over the top. Place into the air fryer and bake for 18 to 20 minutes, or until the eggs are set in the center.
5. Remove from the air fryer and allow to cool for 5 minutes before serving.

Per Serving
calories: 204 | fat: 14g | protein: 16g | carbs: 4g | fiber : 1g | sodium: 606mg

Oatmeal and Buckwheat Cookies

Prep time: 15 minutes | Cook time: 20 minutes | Serves 2

*3.5 cups (500g) all-purpose flour
1/2 cup (80g) ground oat flakes
2.3 oz (65g) buckwheat flour
3/4 cup (180g) unsalted butter,
softened
Pinch of salt*

*4.25 oz (120g) brown sugar
2.8 oz (90g) granulated
sugar
1 large egg
2.8 oz (80g) fresh milk
1 tablespoon baking
powder*

1. Mix the butter with the sugars until a well-whipped cream is obtained.
2. Add all the other ingredients, leaving the flours, ground oat flakes, and yeast for last.
3. Stir slowly until a homogeneous mixture is obtained.
4. Roll out the dough to 7mm thickness and cut the cookies with a cookie cutter or glass. Sprinkle with brown sugar.
5. Bake at 350°F for 20 minutes on a previously buttered pan.

Per Serving
Calories: 145 | Carbs: 20.3g | Protein: 2.1g | Fat: 6.3g | Fiber: 0.8g | Sodium: 65mg

Vanilla Raspberry Oats

Prep time: 10 minutes | Cook time: 0 minutes | Serves 2

*⅔ cup vanilla, unsweetened
almond milk
⅓ cup rolled oats
¼ cup raspberries
1 teaspoon honey*

*¼ teaspoon turmeric
⅛ teaspoon ground
cinnamon
Pinch ground cloves*

1. In a mason jar, combine the almond milk, oats, raspberries, honey, turmeric, cinnamon, and cloves and shake well.
2. Store in the refrigerator for 8 to 24 hours, then serve cold or heated.

Per Serving
calories: 82 | fat: 2g | protein: 2g | carbs: 14g | fiber : 3g | sodium: 98mg

Green Smoothie

Prep time: 10 minutes | Cook time: 0 minutes | Serves 1

1 small very ripe avocado,
peeled and pitted
1 cup almond milk or water,
plus more as needed
1 cup tender baby spinach
leaves, stems removed
½ medium cucumber, peeled
and seeded

1 tablespoon extra-virgin
olive oil or avocado oil
8 to 10 fresh mint leaves,
stems removed
1 to 2 tablespoons juice of
lime

1. In a blender or a large wide-mouth jar, if using an immersion blender, combine the avocado, almond milk, spinach, cucumber, olive oil, mint, and lime juice and blend until smooth and creamy, adding more almond milk or water to achieve your desired consistency.

Per Serving
calories: 330 | fat: 30g | protein: 4g | carbs: 19g | fiber : 8g | sodium: 36mg

Frittata

Prep time: 10 minutes | Cook time: 7 minutes | Serves 2

4 large eggs
2 tablespoons fresh chopped
herbs, such as rosemary,
thyme, oregano, basil or 1
teaspoon dried herbs
¼ teaspoon salt
Freshly ground black
pepper, to taste
8 cherry tomatoes, halved
½ cup crumbled soft goat
cheese

4 tablespoons extra-virgin
olive oil, divided
1 cup fresh spinach, arugula,
kale, or other leafy greens
4 ounces (113 g) quartered
artichoke hearts, rinsed,
drained, and thoroughly
dried

1. Preheat the broiler.
2. In small bowl, combine the eggs, herbs, salt, and pepper and whisk well with a fork. Set aside.
3. In a 4- to 5-inch oven-safe skillet or omelet pan, heat 2 tablespoons olive oil over medium heat. Add the spinach, artichoke hearts, and cherry tomatoes and sauté until just wilted, 1 to 2 minutes.
4. Pour in the egg mixture and let it cook undisturbed over medium heat for 3 to 4 minutes, until the eggs begin to set on the bottom.
5. Sprinkle the goat cheese across the top of the egg mixture and transfer the skillet to the oven.
6. Broil for 4 to 5 minutes, or until the frittata is firm in the center and golden brown on top.
7. Remove from the oven and run a rubber spatula around the edge to loosen the sides. Invert onto a large plate or cutting board and slice in half. Serve warm and drizzled with the remaining 2 tablespoons olive oil.

Per Serving
calories: 527 | fat: 47g | protein: 21g | carbs: 10g | fiber : 3g | sodium: 760mg

Roasted Cherry Tomatoes

Cook time: 40 minutes | Serves 2 Cups

2 pints cherry tomatoes
(20 ounces total)
2 teaspoons olive oil, plus 3
tablespoons

½ teaspoon chopped garlic
¼ cup fresh basil leaves
¼ teaspoon kosher salt

1. Preheat the oven to 350°F. Line a sheet pan with a silicone baking mat or parchment paper.
2. Place the tomatoes on the lined sheet pan and toss with 2 teaspoons of oil. Roast for 40 minutes, shaking the pan halfway through.
3. While the tomatoes are still warm, place them in a medium mixing bowl and add the salt, the garlic, and the remaining 3 tablespoons of oil. Mash the tomatoes with the back of a fork. Stir in the fresh basil.
4. Scoop the sauce into a container and refrigerate. STORAGE: Store the covered container in the refrigerator for up to days.

Per Serving :(.1 cup)
141; Total fat: 13g; Saturated fat: 2g; Sodium: 158mg; Carbohydrates: 7g; Fiber: 2g; Protein: 1g

Sweet Potato Toast

Prep time: 5 minutes | Cook time: 15 minutes | Serves 4

2 plum tomatoes, halved
6 tablespoons extra-virgin
olive oil, divided
Salt and freshly ground
black pepper, to taste
2 large sweet potatoes,
sliced lengthwise
1 cup fresh spinach
8 medium asparagus,
trimmed

4 large cooked eggs or egg
substitute (poached,
scrambled, or fried)
1 cup arugula
4 tablespoons pesto
4 tablespoons shredded
Asiago cheese

1. Preheat the oven to 450ºF (235ºC).
2. On a baking sheet, brush the plum tomato halves with 2 tablespoons of olive oil and season with salt and pepper. Roast the tomatoes in the oven for approximately 15 minutes, then remove from the oven and allow to rest.
3. Put the sweet potato slices on a separate baking sheet and brush about 2 tablespoons of oil on each side and season with salt and pepper. Bake the sweet potato slices for about 15 minutes, flipping once after 5 to 7 minutes, until just tender. Remove from the oven and set aside.
4. In a sauté pan or skillet, heat the remaining 2 tablespoons of olive oil over medium heat and sauté the fresh spinach until just wilted. Remove from the pan and rest on a paper towel-lined dish. In the same pan, add the asparagus and sauté, turning throughout.
5. Transfer to a paper towel-lined dish.
6. Place the slices of grilled sweet potato on serving plates and divide the spinach and asparagus evenly among the slices. Place a prepared egg on top of the spinach and asparagus. Top this with ¼ cup of arugula.
7. Finish by drizzling with 1 tablespoon of pesto and sprinkle with 1 tablespoon of cheese. Serve with 1 roasted plum tomato.

Per Serving
calories: 441 | fat: 35g | protein: 13g | carbs: 23g | fiber : 4g | sodium: 481mg

Banana Corn Fritters

Prep time: 5 minutes | Cook time: 10 minutes | Serves 2

½ cup yellow cornmeal ¼ cup flour
2 small ripe bananas, peeled and mashed
2 tablespoons unsweetened almond milk
1 large egg, beaten

½ teaspoon baking powder
¼ to ½ teaspoon ground chipotle chili
¼ teaspoon ground cinnamon
¼ teaspoon sea salt
1 tablespoon olive oil

1. Stir together all ingredients: except for the olive oil in a large bowl until smooth.
2. Heat a nonstick skillet over medium-high heat. Add the olive oil and drop about 2 tablespoons of batter for each fritter. Cook for 2 to 3 minutes until the bottoms are golden brown, then flip. Continue cooking for 1 to 2 minutes more, until cooked through. Repeat with the remaining batter.
3. Serve warm.

Per Serving
calories: 396 | fat: 10g | protein: 7g | carbs: 68g | fiber: 4g | sodium: 307mg

Bruschetta with Prosciutto

Prep time: 10 minutes | Cook time: 20 minutes | Serves 4

¼ teaspoon kosher or sea salt
6 cups broccoli rabe, stemmed and chopped (about 1 bunch)
1 tablespoon extra-virgin olive oil
2 garlic cloves, minced (about 1 teaspoon)
1 ounce (28 g) prosciutto, cut or torn into ½-inch pieces
¼ teaspoon crushed red pepper
Nonstick cooking spray
3 large eggs

1 tablespoon unsweetened almond milk
¼ teaspoon freshly ground black pepper
4 teaspoons grated Parmesan or Pecorino Romano cheese
1 garlic clove, halved
8 (¾-inch-thick) slices baguette-style whole-grain bread or 4 slices larger Italian-style whole-grain bread

1. Bring a large stockpot of water to a boil. Add the salt and broccoli rabe, and boil for 2 minutes. Drain in a colander.
2. In a large skillet over medium heat, heat the oil. Add the garlic, prosciutto, and crushed red pepper, and cook for 2 minutes, stirring often. Add the broccoli rabe and cook for an additional 3 minutes, stirring a few times. Transfer to a bowl and set aside.
3. Place the skillet back on the stove over low heat and coat with nonstick cooking spray.
4. In a small bowl, whisk together the eggs, milk, and pepper. Pour into the skillet. Stir and cook until the eggs are soft scrambled, 3 to 5 minutes. Add the broccoli rabe mixture back to the skillet along with the cheese. Stir and cook for about 1 minute, until heated through. Remove from the heat.
5. Toast the bread, then rub the cut sides of the garlic clove halves onto one side of each slice of the toast. (Save the garlic for another recipe.) Spoon the egg mixture onto each piece of toast and serve.

Per Serving
calories: 313 | fat: 10g | protein: 17g | carbs: 38g | fiber: 8g | sodium: 559mg

Veggie Sandwiches

Prep time: 10 minutes | Cook time: 0 minutes | Serves 4

8 slices whole-grain or whole-wheat bread
1 ripe avocado, halved and pitted
¼ teaspoon freshly ground black pepper
¼ teaspoon kosher or sea salt

4 romaine lettuce leaves, torn into 8 pieces total
1 large, ripe tomato, sliced into 8 rounds
2 ounces (57 g) prosciutto, cut into 8 thin slices

1. Toast the bread and place on a large platter.
2. Scoop the avocado flesh out of the skin into a small bowl. Add the pepper and salt. Using a fork or a whisk, gently mash the avocado until it resembles a creamy spread. Spread the avocado mash over all 8 pieces of toast.
3. To make one sandwich, take one slice of avocado toast, and top it with a lettuce leaf, tomato slice, and prosciutto slice.
4. Top with another slice each of lettuce, tomato, and prosciutto, then cover with a second piece of avocado toast (avocado-side down on the prosciutto). Repeat with the remaining ingredients: to make three more sandwiches and serve.

Per Serving
calories: 262 | fat: 12g | protein: 8g | carbs: 35g | fiber: 10g | sodium: 162mg

Portobello Mushrooms with Breadcrumbs

Prep time: 10 minutes | Cook time: 50 minutes | Serves 4

2 Portobello mushrooms
3 Ripe Tomatoes
Mozzarella
Basil

Salt
Crushed red pepper
Breadcrumbs
Extra virgin olive oil

1. Wash the mushrooms and remove the stems. Dry them and bake them in the oven at 400°F to remove the water. Turn them a few times and remove when they look dry; they will appear much smaller than the original.
2. Cover them with the previously chopped tomatoes and add a drizzle of olive oil. Sprinkle with salt and place them back in the oven for 10 minutes or until the tomatoes are cooked.
3. Sprinkle with chopped basil and crushed red pepper. Add the mozzarella and sprinkle with a pinch of breadcrumbs.
4. Place them back in the oven and remove when the mozzarella is melted.

Per Serving
Calories: 36 | Carbs: 2.6g | Protein: 1.7g | Fat: 2g | Fiber: 0.5g | Sodium: 88mg

Chapter 2
Sides, Salads, and Soups

Sumptuous Greek Vegetable Salad

Prep time: 20 minutes | Cook time: 0 minutes | Serves 6

Salad:
1 (15-ounce / 425-g) can chickpeas, drained and rinsed
1 (14-ounce / 397-g) can artichoke hearts, drained and halved
1 head Bibb lettuce, chopped (about 2½ cups)
1 cucumber, peeled deseed-ed, and chopped (about 1½ cups)
1½ cups grape tomatoes, halved
¼ cup chopped basil leaves
½ cup sliced black olives

½ cup cubed feta cheese
Dressing:
1 tablespoon freshly squeezed lemon juice (from about ½ small lemon)
¼ teaspoon freshly ground black pepper
1 tablespoon chopped fresh oregano
2 tablespoons extra-virgin olive oil
1 tablespoon red wine vinegar
1 teaspoon honey

1. Combine the ingredients for the salad in a large salad bowl, then toss to combine well.
2. Combine the ingredients for the dressing in a small bowl, then stir to mix well.
3. Dress the salad and serve immediately.

Per Serving
calories: 165 | fat: 8.1g | protein: 7.2g | carbs: 17.9g | fiber: 7.0g | sodium: 337mg

Greek Chicken, Tomato, and Olive Salad

Prep time: 10 minutes | Cook time: 0 minutes | Serves 2

Salad:
2 grilled boneless, skinless chicken breasts, sliced (about 1 cup)
10 cherry tomatoes, halved
8 pitted Kalamata olives, halved
½ cup thinly sliced red onion
Dressing:
¼ cup balsamic vinegar
1 teaspoon freshly squeezed lemon juice

¼ teaspoon sea salt
¼ teaspoon freshly ground black pepper
2 teaspoons extra-virgin olive oil
For Serving:
2 cups roughly chopped romaine lettuce
½ cup crumbled feta cheese

1. Combine the ingredients for the salad in a large bowl. Toss to combine well. Combine the dressing ingredients in a small bowl. Stir to mix well. Pour the dressing the bowl of salad, then toss to coat well. Cover with plastic wrap and refrigerate for at least 2 hours.
2. Remove the bowl from the refrigerator. Spread the lettuce on a large plate, then top with marinated salad. Scatter the salad with feta cheese and serve immediately.

Per Serving
calories: 328 | fat: 16.9g | protein: 27.6g | carbs: 15.9g | fiber: 3.1g| sodium: 1102mg

Marinated Mushrooms and Olives

Prep time: 1 hour 10 minutes | Cook time: 0 minutes | Serves 8

1 pound (454 g) white button mushrooms, rinsed and drained
1 pound (454 g) fresh olives
½ tablespoon crushed fennel seeds
1 tablespoon white wine vinegar

2 tablespoons fresh thyme leaves
Pinch chili flakes
Sea salt and freshly ground pepper, to taste
2 tablespoons extra-virgin olive oil

1. Combine all the ingredients in a large bowl. Toss to mix well.
2. Cover with plastic wrap and refrigerate for at least 1 hour to marinate.
3. Remove the bowl from the refrigerator and let it sit at room temperature for 10 minutes, then serve.

Per Serving
calories: 111 | fat: 9.7g | protein: 2.4g | carbs: 5.9g | fiber: 2.7g | sodium: 44 9mg

Moroccan Lentil, Tomato, and Cauliflower Soup

Prep time: 15 minutes | Cook time: 4 hours | Serves 6

1 cup chopped carrots
1 cup chopped onions
3 cloves garlic, minced
½ teaspoon ground coriander
1 teaspoon ground cumin
1 teaspoon ground turmeric
¼ teaspoon ground cinnamon
¼ teaspoon freshly ground black pepper
1 cup dry lentils

28 ounces (794 g) tomatoes, diced, reserve the juice
1½ cups chopped cauliflower
4 cups low-sodium vegeta-ble soup
1 tablespoon no-salt-added tomato paste
1 teaspoon extra-virgin olive oil
1 cup chopped fresh spinach
¼ cup chopped fresh cilantro
1 tablespoon red wine vinegar (optional)

1. Put the carrots and onions in the slow cooker, then sprinkle with minced garlic, coriander, cumin, turmeric, cinnamon, and black pepper.
2. Stir to combine well. Add the lentils, tomatoes, and cauliflower, then pour in the vegetable soup and tomato paste. Drizzle with olive oil. Stir to combine well.
3. Put the slow cooker lid on and cook on high for 4 hours or until the vegetables are tender.
4. In the last 30 minutes of the cooking time, open the lid and stir the soup, then fold in the spinach.
5. Pour the cooked soup in a large serving bowl, then spread with cilantro and drizzle with vinegar. Serve immediately.

Per Serving
calories: 131 | fat: 2.1g | protein: 5.6g | carbs: 25.0g | fiber: 5.5g | sodium: 364mg

Cucumber Gazpacho

Prep time: 10 minutes | Cook time: 0 minutes | Serves 4

2 cucumbers, peeled, deseeded, and cut into chunks
½ cup mint, finely chopped
2 cups plain Greek yogurt
2 garlic cloves, minced

2 cups low-sodium vegetable soup
1 tablespoon no-salt-added tomato paste
3 teaspoons fresh dill
Sea salt and freshly ground pepper, to taste

1. Put the cucumber, mint, yogurt, and garlic in a food processor, then pulse until creamy and smooth.
2. Transfer the puréed mixture to a large serving bowl, then add the vegetable soup, tomato paste, dill, salt, and ground black pepper. Stir to mix well.
3. Keep the soup in the refrigerator for at least 2 hours, then serve chilled.

Per Serving
calories: 133 | fat: 1.5g | protein: 14.2g | carbs: 16.5g | fiber: 2.9g | sodium: 331mg

Baby Potato and Olive Salad

Prep time: 10 minutes | Cook time: 20 minutes | Serves 6

2 pounds (907 g) baby potatoes, cut into 1-inch cubes
1 tablespoon low-sodium olive brine
3 tablespoons freshly squeezed lemon juice (from about 1 medium lemon)

¼ teaspoon kosher salt
3 tablespoons extra-virgin olive oil
½ cup sliced olives
2 tablespoons torn fresh mint
1 cup sliced celery (about 2 stalks)
2 tablespoons chopped fresh oregano

1. Put the potatoes in a saucepan, then pour in enough water to submerge the potatoes about 1 inch. Bring to a boil over high heat, then reduce the heat to medium-low. Simmer for 14 minutes or until the potatoes are soft. Meanwhile, combine the olive brine, lemon juice, salt, and olive oil in a small bowl. Stir to mix well. Transfer the cooked tomatoes to a colander, then rinse with running cold water.
2. Pat dry with paper towels. Transfer the tomatoes to a large salad bowl, then drizzle with olive brine mixture. Spread with remaining ingredients and toss to combine well. Serve immediately.

Per Serving
calories: 220 | fat: 6.1g | protein: 4.3g | carbs: 39.2g | fiber: 5.0g | sodium: 231mg

Cherry, Plum, Artichoke, and Cheese Board

Prep time: 15 minutes | Cook time: 0 minutes | Serves 4

2 cups rinsed cherries
2 cups rinsed and sliced plums
2 cups rinsed carrots, cut into sticks

1 cup canned low-sodium artichoke hearts, rinsed and drained
1 cup cubed feta cheese

1. Arrange all the ingredients in separated portions on a clean board or a large tray, then serve with spoons and forks.

Per Serving
calories: 417 | fat: 13.8g | protein: 20.1g | carbs: 56.2g | fiber: 3.0g | sodium: 715mg

Barley, Parsley, and Pea Salad

Prep time: 10 minutes | Cook time: 10 minutes | Serves 4

2 cups water
1 cup quick-cooking barley
1 small bunch flat-leaf parsley, chopped (about 1 to 1½ cups)
2 cups sugar snap pea pods

Juice of 1 lemon
½ small red onion, diced
2 tablespoons extra-virgin olive oil
Sea salt and freshly ground pepper, to taste

1. Pour the water in a saucepan. Bring to a boil. Add the barley to the saucepan, then put the lid on.
2. Reduce the heat to low. Simmer the barley for 10 minutes or until the liquid is absorbed, then let sit for 5 minutes.
3. Open the lid, then transfer the barley in a colander and rinse under cold running water.
4. Pour the barley in a large salad bowl and add the remaining ingredients. Toss to combine well.
5. Serve immediately.

Per Serving
calories: 152 | fat: 7.4g | protein: 3.7g | carbs: 19.3g | fiber:

4.7g | sodium: 20mg

Cheesy Peach and Walnut Salad

Prep time: 10 minutes | Cook time: 0 minutes | Serves 1

1 ripe peach, pitted and sliced
¼ cup chopped walnuts, toasted
¼ cup shredded Parmesan cheese

1 teaspoon raw honey Zest of 1 lemon
1 tablespoon chopped fresh mint

1. Combine the peach, walnut, and cheese in a medium bowl, then drizzle with honey. Spread the lemon zest and mint on top.
2. Toss to combine everything well. Serve immediately.

Per Serving
calories: 373 | fat: 26.4g | protein: 12.9g | carbs: 27.0g | fiber: 4.7g | sodium: 453mg

Arugula and Fig Salad

Prep time: 15 minutes | Cook time: 0 minutes | Serves 2

3 cups arugula
4 fresh, ripe figs (or 4 to 6 dried figs), stemmed and sliced
2 tablespoons olive oil

¼ cup lightly toasted pecan halves
2 tablespoons crumbled blue cheese
1 to 2 tablespoons balsamic glaze

1. Toss the arugula and figs with the olive oil in a large bowl until evenly coated. Add the pecans and blue cheese to the bowl. Toss the salad lightly.
2. Drizzle with the balsamic glaze and serve immediately.

Per Serving
calories: 517 | fat: 36.2g | protein: 18.9g | carbs: 30.2g | fiber: 6.1g | sodium: 481mg

Green Beans with Tahini-Lemon Sauce

Prep time: 5 minutes | Cook time: 10 minutes | Serves 2

1 pound (454 g) green beans, washed and trimmed	Grated zest and juice of 1 lemon
2 tablespoons tahini 1 garlic clove, minced	Salt and black pepper, to taste
	1 teaspoon toasted black or white sesame seeds (optional)

1. Steam the beans in a medium saucepan fitted with a steamer basket (or by adding ¼ cup water to a covered saucepan) over medium-high heat. Drain, reserving the cooking water.
2. Mix the tahini, garlic, lemon zest and juice, and salt and pepper to taste. Use the reserved cooking water to thin the sauce as desired. Toss the green beans with the sauce and garnish with the sesame seeds, if desired. Serve immediately.

Per Serving
calories: 188 | fat: 8.4g | protein: 7.2g | carbs: 22.2g | fiber: 7.9g | sodium: 200mg

Cheesy Roasted Broccolini

Prep time: 5 minutes | Cook time: 10 minutes | Serves 2

1 bunch broccolini (about 5 ounces / 142 g)	¼ teaspoon salt
1 tablespoon olive oil	2 tablespoons grated Romano cheese
½ teaspoon garlic powder	

1. Preheat the oven to 400ºF (205ºC). Line a sheet pan with parchment paper.
2. Slice the tough ends off the broccolini and put the rest in a medium bowl. Add the olive oil, garlic powder, and salt and toss to coat well. Arrange the broccolini on the prepared sheet pan.
3. Roast in the preheated oven for 7 minutes, flipping halfway through the cooking time.
4. Remove the pan from the oven and sprinkle the cheese over the broccolini. Using tongs, carefully flip the broccolini over to coat all sides.
5. Return the pan to the oven and cook for an additional 2 to 3 minutes, or until the cheese melts and starts to turn golden. Serve warm.

Per Serving
calories: 114 | fat: 9.0g | protein: 4.0g | carbs: 5.0g | fiber: 2.0g | sodium: 400mg

Sweet Potato Salad

Preparation and Cooking Time 30 minutes | Servings 4

Honey - 2 tbsp. Sumac spice - 1 tsp.	Dried mint - 1 tsp.
Sweet potato - 2, finely sliced	Balsamic vinegar – 1 tbsp.
Extra virgin olive oil - 3 tbsp.	Salt and pepper - to taste
	Pomegranate - 1, seeded
	Mixed greens - 3 cups

1. Place sweet potato slices on a plate and add sumac, mint, salt and pepper on both sides. Next, drizzle oil and honey over both sides.
2. Add oil to a grill pan and heat. Grill sweet potatoes on medium heat until brown on both sides.
3. Put sweet potatoes in a salad bowl and top with pomegranate and mixed greens.
4. Stir and eat right away.

Broccoli Salad with Caramelized Onions

Servings 4 | Preparation and Cooking Time 25 minutes

Extra virgin olive oil - 3 tbsp. Red onions - 2, sliced Dried thyme - 1 tsp.	Balsamic vinegar - 2 tbsp. vinegar Broccoli - 1 lb., cut into florets Salt and pepper - to taste

1. Heat extra virgin olive oil in a pan over high heat and add in sliced onions.
2. Cook for approximately 10 minutes or until the onions are caramelized. Stir in vinegar and thyme and then remove from stove.
3. Mix together the broccoli and onion mixture in a bowl, adding salt and pepper if desired.
4. Serve and eat salad as soon as possible.

Tuna Salad

Preparation Time 15 minutes | Servings 4

Green olives - 1 4 cup, sliced	Lemon – 1, juiced
Tuna in water - 1 can, drained Pine nuts - 2 tbsp.	Arugula - 2 leaves
Artichoke hearts – 1 jar, drained and chopped	Dijon mustard - 1 tbsp.
Extra virgin olive oil - 2 tbsp.	Salt and pepper - to taste

1. Mix mustard, oil and lemon juice in a bowl to make a dressing. Combine the artichoke hearts, tuna, green olives, arugula and pine nuts in a salad bowl.
2. In a separate salad bowl, mix tuna, arugula, pine nuts, artichoke hearts and tuna.
3. Pour dressing mix onto salad and serve fresh.

Yogurt Lettuce Salad

Cooking Time: 20 minutes | Servings: 4

Shredded Romaine lettuce: 1 head	Extra virgin olive oil: 2 tablespoon
Sliced cucumbers: 2	Lemon juice: 1 tablespoon
2 minced garlic cloves	Chopped dill: 2 tablespoon
Greek yogurt: 1/2 cup Dijon mustard: 1 teaspoon Chili powder: 1 pinch	4 chopped mint leaves
	Pepper and salt to taste

1. In a salad bowl, combine the lettuce and the cucumbers. Add
2. the yogurt, chili, mustard, lemon juice, dill, mint, garlic and oil in a mortar with pepper and salt as desired. Then, mix well into paste; this is the dressing for the salad.
3. Top the salad with the dressing then serve fresh.

Cabbage Salad

Prep Time 25 minutes | Servings 4

Mint - 1 tbsp. chopped Ground coriander - 1 2 tsp.	Extra virgin olive oil - 2 tbsp. Carrot - 1, grated
Savoy cabbage - 1, shredded	Red onion – 1, sliced
Greek yogurt - 1/2 cup	Honey - 1 tsp.
Cumin seeds - 1/4 tsp.	Lemon zest - 1 tsp.
	Lemon juice - 2 tbsp.
	Salt and pepper - to taste

1. In a salad bowl, mix all ingredients.
2. Add salt and pepper to suit your taste and then mix again. This
3. salad is best when cool and freshly made.

Orange Salad

Cooking Time: 15 minutes | Servings: 4

4 sliced endives
2 sliced red onion
2 oranges already cut into segments

Extra virgin olive oil: 2 tablespoon
Pepper and salt to taste

1. Mix all ingredients: in a salad bowl
2. Sprinkle pepper and salt to taste.
3. Serve the salad immediately.

Blue Cheese and Portobello Salad

Cooking Time: 15 minutes | Servings: 2

½ cup croutons
1 tbsp merlot wine
1 tbsp water
1 tsp minced garlic
1 tsp olive oil
1 large Portobello mushrooms, stemmed, wiped clean and cut into bite sized pieces

2 pieces roasted red peppers (canned), sliced
2 tbsp balsamic vinegar
2 tbsp crumbled blue cheese
4 slices red onion
6 asparagus stalks cut into 1-inch sections
6 cups Bibb lettuce, chopped
Ground pepper to taste

1. Heat oil over medium fire in a saucepan. Once hot, add onions and mushrooms. For 4 to 6 minutes, sauté until tender. Add garlic and
2. for a minute continue sautéing.
3. Pour in wine and cook for a minute.
4. Bring an inch of water to a boil in a pot with steamer basket. Once boiling, add asparagus and cover; steam for two to three minutes or until crisp and tender, while covered.
5. Once cooked, remove basket from pot and set aside. In a small bowl, thoroughly whisk black pepper, water, balsamic vinegar, and blue cheese.
6. To serve, place 3 cups of lettuce on each plate. Add 1 roasted pepper, ½ of asparagus, ½ of mushroom mixture, and whisk blue cheese dressing before drizzling equally on to plates. Garnish with croutons; serve and enjoy.

Per Serving
Calories : 660.8; Protein: 38.5g; Carbs: 30.4g; Fat: 42.8g

Red Pepper Hummus

Prep time: 10 minutes | Cook time: 0 minutes | Serves 6

6 ounces roasted red peppers, peeled and chopped
16 ounces canned chickpeas, drained and rinsed
¼ cup Greek yogurt

3 tablespoons tahini paste
Juice of 1 lemon
3 garlic cloves, minced
1 tablespoon olive oil
A pinch of salt and black pepper
1 tablespoon parsley, chopped

1. In your food processor, combine all the ingredients except the oil and the parsley and pulse well.
2. Add the oil, pulse again, divide into cups, sprinkle the parsley on top, and serve as a party spread.

Per Serving
Calories 255; Fat 11.4 g; Fiber 4.5 g; Carbs 17.4 g; Protein 6.5 g

Artichoke Flatbread

Prep time: 10 minutes | Cook time: 15 minutes | Serves 4

5 tablespoons olive oil
2 garlic cloves, minced
1 tablespoons parsley, chopped
2 round whole-wheat flatbreads
4 tablespoons parmesan, grated

14 ounces canned artichokes, drained and quartered
1 cup baby spinach, chopped
½ cup cherry tomatoes, halved
½ teaspoon basil, dried Salt and black pepper to the taste
½ cup mozzarella cheese, grated

1. In a bowl, mix the parsley with the garlic and 4 tablespoons oil, whisk well, and spread this over the flatbreads.
2. Sprinkle the mozzarella and half of the parmesan.
3. In a bowl, mix the artichokes with the spinach, tomatoes, basil, salt, pepper, and the rest of the oil; toss and divide over the flatbreads as well.
4. Spread the rest of the parmesan on top, arrange the flatbreads on a baking sheet lined with parchment paper and bake at 425° F for 15 minutes.
5. Serve as an appetizer.

Per Serving
Calories 223; Fat 11.2 g; Fiber 5.34 g, Carbs 15.5 g; Protein 7.4 g

Wrapped Plums

Prep time: 5 minutes | Cook time: 0 minutes | Serves 8

2 ounces prosciutto, cut into 16 pieces
4 plums, quartered tablespoon chives, chopped

A pinch of red pepper flakes, crushed

Wrap each plum quarter in a prosciutto slice, arrange them all on a platter, sprinkle the chives and pepper flakes all over, and serve.

Per Serving
Calories 30; Fat 1 g; Fiber 0 g; Carbs 4 g; Protein 2 g

Cucumber Rolls

Prep time: 5 minutes | Cook time: 0 minutes | Serves 6

1 large cucumber, sliced lengthwise
1 tablespoon parsley, chopped

8 ounces canned tuna, drained and mashed
Salt and black pepper to the taste
1 teaspoon lime juice

1. Arrange cucumber slices on a working surface, divide the rest of the ingredients, and roll.
2. Arrange all the rolls on a platter and serve as an appetizer.

Per Serving
Calories 200; Fat 6 g; Fiber 3.4 g; Carbs 7.6 g; Protein 3.5 g

White Bean Dip

Prep time: 10 minutes | Cook time: 0 minutes | Serves 4

15 ounces canned white beans, drained and rinsed
6 ounces canned artichoke hearts, drained and quartered
4 garlic cloves, minced

1 tablespoon basil, chopped
2 tablespoons olive oil
Juice of ½ lemon
Zest of ½ lemon, grated
Salt and black pepper to the taste

1. In your food processor, combine the beans with the artichokes and the rest of the ingredients except the oil and pulse well.
2. Add the oil gradually, pulse the mix again, divide into cups, and serve as a party dip.

Per Serving
Calories 274; Fat 11.7 g; Fiber 6.5 g; Carbs 18.5 g; Protein 16.5 g

Yogurt Dip

Prep time: 10 minutes | Cook time: 0 minutes | Serves 6

2 cups Greek yogurt
1 tablespoons pistachios, toasted and chopped
A pinch of salt and white pepper
2 tablespoons mint, chopped

1 tablespoon kalamata olives, pitted and chopped
¼ cup za'atar spice
¼ cup pomegranate
1/3 cup of olive oil

1. In a bowl, combine the yogurt with the pistachios and the rest of the ingredients, whisk well, divide into small cups and serve with pita chips on the side.

Per Serving
Calories 294; Fat 18 g; Fiber 1 g; Carbs 21 g; Protein 10 g

Bulgur Lamb Meatballs

Prep time: 10 minutes | Cook time: 15 minutes | Serves 6

1 and ½ cups Greek yogurt
½ teaspoon cumin ground
1 cup cucumber, shredded
½ teaspoon garlic, minced
A pinch of salt and pepper
1 cup bulgur

2 cups of water
1 pound lamb, ground
¼ cup parsley, chopped
¼ cup shallots, chopped
½ teaspoon allspice, ground
½ teaspoon cinnamon powder
1 tablespoon olive oil

1. In a bowl, combine the bulgur and water, cover the bowl, set aside for 10 minutes, drain and transfer to a different bowl.
2. Add the meat, the yogurt, and the rest of the ingredients except the oil, stir well and shape medium meatballs out of this mix.
3. Heat a pan with the oil over medium-high heat, add the meatballs, cook them for 7 minutes on each side, arrange them all on a platter and serve as an appetizer.

Per Serving
Calories 300; Fat 9.6 g; Fiber 4.6 g; Carbs 22.6 g; Protein 6.6 g

Veggie Fritters

Prep time: 10 minutes | Cook time: 10 minutes | Serves 8

2 garlic cloves, minced
2 yellow onions, chopped
4 scallions, chopped
2 carrots, grated
2 teaspoons cumin, ground
½ tsp turmeric powder
Salt and black pepper to the taste
¼ teaspoon coriander, ground

2 tablespoons parsley, chopped
¼ teaspoon lemon juice
½ cup almond flour beets, peeled and grated
two eggs, whisked
¼ cup tapioca flour
tablespoons olive oil

1. In a bowl, combine all the ingredients except the oil, stir well and shape medium patties out of this mix.
2. Heat a pan with the oil over medium-high heat, add the patties, cook for 5 minutes on each side, arrange on a platter, and serve.

Per Serving
Calories 209; Fat 11.2 g; Fiber 3 g; Carbs 4.4 g; Protein 4.8 g

Chili Mango and Watermelon Salsa

Prep time: 5 minutes | Cook time: 0 minutes | Serves 12

1 red tomato, chopped
Salt, and black pepper to the taste
1 cup watermelon, seedless, peeled and cubed
1 red onion, chopped

12 mangos, peeled and chopped
2 chili peppers, chopped
¼ cup cilantro, chopped
3 tablespoons lime juice Pita chips for serving

In a bowl, mix all ingredients except the pita chips and toss well. Divide the mix into small cups and serve with pita chips on the side.

Per Serving
Calories 62; Fat g; Fiber 1.3 g; Carbs 3.9 g; Protein 2.3 g

Creamy Spinach and Shallots Dip

Prep time: 10 minutes | Cook time: 0 minutes | Serves 4

1 pound spinach, roughly chopped
2 shallots, chopped
2 tablespoons mint, chopped

¾ cup cream cheese, soft
Salt and black pepper to the taste

In a blender, combine the spinach with the shallots and the rest of the ingredients, and pulse well. Divide into small bowls and serve as a party dip.

Per Serving
Calories 204; Fat 11.5 g; Fiber 3.1 g; Carbs 4.2 g; Protein 5.9 g

Eggplant Dip

Prep time: 10 minutes | Cook time: 40 minutes | Serves 4

1 eggplant, poked with a fork
2 tablespoons tahini paste
2 tablespoons lemon juice
2 garlic cloves, minced

1 tablespoon olive oil
Salt and black pepper to the taste
1 tablespoon parsley, chopped

1. Put the eggplant in a roasting pan, bake at 400° F for 40 minutes, cool down, peel, and transfer to your food processor.
2. Add all the ingredients except the parsley, pulse well, divide into small bowls and serve as an appetizer with the parsley sprinkled on top.

Per Serving
Calories 121; Fat 4.3 g; Fiber 1 g; Carbs 1.4 g; Protein 4.3 g

Feta Artichoke Dip

Prep time: 10 minutes | Cook time: 30 minutes | Serves 8

8 ounces artichoke hearts, drained and quartered ¾ cup basil, chopped

¾ cup green olives, pitted and chopped
1 cup parmesan cheese, grated
5 ounces feta cheese, crumbled

1. In your food processor, mix the artichokes with the basil and the rest of the ingredients, pulse well, and transfer to a baking dish.
2. Bake in the oven at 375° F for 30 minutes and serve as a party dip.

Per Serving
Calories 186; Fat 12.4 g; Fiber 0.9 g; Carbs 2.6 g; Protein 1.5 g

Meatballs Platter

Prep time: 10 minutes | Cook time: 15 minutes | Serves 4

1 pound beef meat, ground
¼ cup panko breadcrumbs
A pinch of salt and black pepper
3 tablespoons red onion, grated
¼ cup parsley, chopped
2 garlic cloves, minced
tablespoons lemon juice
Zest of 1 lemon, grated

½ teaspoon cumin, ground
½ teaspoon coriander, ground
¼ teaspoon cinnamon powder
2 ounces feta cheese, crumbled

1. In a bowl, mix the beef with the breadcrumbs, salt, pepper, and the rest of the ingredients except the cooking spray, stir well and shape medium balls out of this mix.
2. Arrange the meatballs on a baking sheet lined with parchment paper, grease them with cooking spray and bake at 450° F for 15 minutes.
3. Put the meatballs on a platter and serve as an appetizer.

Per Serving
Calories 300; Fat 15.4 g; Fiber 6.4 g, Carbs 22.4 g; Protein 35 g

Chicken Leek Soup with White Wine

Servings: 3

Olive oil (1/2 cup)
Two pounds of chicken breasts
One large leek
Four celery sticks, chopped

One small cabbage, cut into thick slices
White wine (1 cup)
Four green onions (scallions), chopped
Paprika (1/2 teaspoon)
Pinch of nutmeg water (3 cups)

1. Cut chicken breasts into one-inch pieces.
2. Cut the leek into rounds.
3. Warm the oil in a deep skillet. Toss in chicken, cooking until done on the outside. Add in the leeks, onions, and celery. Sauté for one minute.
4. Add in cabbage, cooking for about two minutes, until fork-tender. Add the wine, paprika, nutmeg, and water. Combine mixture well.
5. Cook on low heat for 45 minutes and serve.

Italian Turkey Meatball Soup Recipe

Servings: 4

For the meatballs:
Grated parmesan cheese (1/2 cup)
Dried oregano (1 teaspoon)
Ground turkey (One pound)
Black pepper (½ teaspoon)
Fresh parsley, minced (2 tablespoons)
One egg Olive oil (3 tablespoons)
Sea salt (1/2 teaspoon) For the soup:
Chicken broth or beef broth (2 quarts)
Tomato paste (3 tablespoons)

One onion
Two bay leaves
Four sprigs of fresh thyme
Whole black peppercorns (½ teaspoon)
If desired: Fresh parmesan cheese, grated
Fresh basil leaves, torn (1-2 tablespoons)
Salt and pepper
Fresh parsley (1-2 tablespoons)

1. Dice onion.
2. Except for the oil, combine all meatball ingredients and mix with hands in a large bowl.
3. Work meat into small balls about an inch to two inches wide.
4. Heat olive oil in a skillet, then add meatballs, browning them for a few minutes turning and browning the other side.
5. Remove the meatballs and set them to the side. Add onion to skillet, cooking for a couple of minutes.
6. Add remaining soup ingredients, then boil. Cover and allow to simmer for between five and ten minutes. Add meatballs and simmer again for a couple of more minutes.
7. Divide into serving bowls and if desired, sprinkle lightly with salt and pepper.
8. You can also add fresh parsley, basil, and Parmesan cheese.

Orange Lentil Soup

Servings: 4

Extra virgin olive oil (1 cup)
One pound washed lentils
Two cloves garlic
Tomato paste (2 tablespoons)
One onion

Water (6 cups)
Three carrots
Two orange slices
One bay leaf

1. Mince garlic cloves. Grate onion and carrots. Peel orange slices.
2. Boil lentils and six cups water in a skillet for fifteen minutes.
3. Drop in the remainder of the ingredients and reduce temperature to a low boil for a half hour or until the lentils are soft.

Gorgeous Kale Soup Made with the White Beans

Servings: 8

Drained white beans – 1 can Shredded kale – 1 bunch Chopped shallot – 1 Water – 6 cups Chopped garlic cloves – 2 Diced carrots - 2

Lemon juice – 2 tbsps Diced tomatoes – 1 can Chopped red pepper - 1 Vegetable stock – 2 cups Pepper and salt to taste Olive oil – 2 tbsps Diced celery stalk - 1

1. Heat oil in a large saucepan, then stir in celery, garlic, carrots, shallot, and red pepper. Cook for two minutes, until soft.
2. Add other Ingredients: and season with pepper and salt.
3. Simmer soup for 30 minutes on low heat.
4. Serve warm or chilled.

Mediterranean Chicken Soup

Servings: 5

2 sliced cloves
2 peeled and sliced tomatoes
A bay leaf
1 juiced lemon
1 sweet onion; diced
1 cubed zucchini
Water; 4 cups
½ teaspoon of capers; sliced

½ teaspoon of oregano; dried
Dried basil; 1 teaspoon
½ cup of orzo
Chicken stock; 2 cups
1 pound of chicken drumsticks
1 chopped and cored green bell pepper
1 chopped and cored red bell pepper
Pepper and salt to taste

1. In a large stockpot, stir together vegetables, stock, herbs, chicken, bay leaf, and water, then add pepper and salt to taste and cook on low heat for 25 minutes.
2. Now add your lemon juice and cook again for 5
3. minutes. Serve and enjoy your warm soup.

Special Orzo Soup

Servings: 8

Orzo – ¼ cup
Vegetable stock – 2 cups
Lemon juice – 2 tbsps
Cored and diced yellow bell pepper - 1
Extra virgin olive oil – 2 tbsps Chopped shallots - 2

Baby spinach – 4 cups
Green peas – 1 cup
Cored and diced green bell pepper - 1
Water – 4 cups
Chopped garlic cloves – 2
Pepper and salt to taste

1. Heat the oil in the stockpot, then stir in the garlic and shallots.
2. Add other ingredients after cooking it for 2 minutes and season with pepper and salt.
3. Simmer for 25 minutes over low heat.
4. Best served chilled or warm.

Tuscan White Bean Stew

Servings: 4

Olive oil (1 tablespoon)
Two cloves garlic
One slice of whole-grain bread
For the soup: Dried cannellini beans (2 cups)
Black pepper (1/4 teaspoon)
One bay leaf

Salt (1/2 teaspoon)
Yellow onion (1 cup)
Three carrots
Olive oil (2 tablespoons)
Six cloves garlic
Water (6 cups)
Chopped fresh rosemary (1 tablespoon)
vegetable stock or broth (1 1/2 cups)

1. Quarter garlic. Cut whole-grain bread into half-inch cubes.
2. Rinse and drain beans.
3. Chop onion, carrots, and six cloves of garlic. Quarter two cloves of garlic for croutons.
4. Heat the oil in a large pan over medium heat. Drop in the quartered garlic, cooking for about one minute.
5. Remove the pan from the heat, letting it stand for ten minutes. Remove all cooked garlic pieces and throw them away. Preheat a skillet over medium heat.
6. Stirring frequently, drop-in bread cubes, and cook for three to five minutes. Pour into a small bowl; set aside.
7. Combine the water, beans, a quarter teaspoon of salt, and the bay leaf. Use a medium-sized skillet.
8. Bring to a boil, then cover and reduce heat to low. Allow to simmer until beans are nice and tender, which should take about 60 to 75 minutes. Drain all the beans, saving about half a cup of liquid from the beans. Throw away the bay leaf.
9. Put beans into a bowl.
10. Combine saved bean liquid and a half cup of the cooked beans in a small-sized bowl. Mash into a textured cream. Stir the cooked beans together with the bean paste.
11. Return the cooking skillet to the stovetop, adding olive oil, and cook over medium heat.
12. Add in onions and carrots, cooking for five to six minutes.
13. Drop in the garlic. Stir in the rest of the salt, stock, rosemary, pepper, bean mixture, and boil. Reduce heat and allow to simmer until heated through.
14. Pour into serving bowls; add croutons and garnish if desired.

Easy Mediterranean Salad

Time: 10 minutes | Serves: 4

2 cups diced cherry tomatoes
1 diced yellow bell pepper
1 cup diced red onion
½ cup sliced black olives
1 sliced medium-sized cucumber
3 tablespoons of crumbled feta cheese
3 tablespoons julienne cut sun-dried tomatoes

3 tablespoons extra virgin olive oil
1 teaspoon minced garlic
1 tablespoon lemon juice
1 teaspoon salt
1 teaspoon black pepper
1 tablespoon chopped fresh parsley

1. Using a large bowl, add the cherry tomatoes, yellow bell pepper, red onions, black olives, cucumber, feta cheese, sun- dried tomatoes and toss together until combined.
2. In a smaller bowl, mix olive oil, garlic, lemon juice, salt and pepper, using a whisk to make the salad dressing.
3. Pour your salad dressing over your salad, and toss to combine.
4. Finish it off with some fresh parsley and serve.

Per Serving
Net Carbs: 22.67g | Fiber: 3.6 g | Protein: 4.75g Fat: 8.99 g | Kcal (per serving): 199

Balela Salad

Time: 15 minutes | Serves:6

3½ cups cooked chickpeas
½ chopped green bell-pepper
1 optional finely chopped jalapeno
2 ½ cups cherry tomatoes
3 – 5 green onions, chopped
½ cup sun dried tomatoes
⅓ cup pitted Kalamate olives
¼ cup pitted green olives
½ cup chopped fresh parsley

½ cup chopped fresh mint leaves
¼ cup extra virgin olive oil
2 tablespoons white wine vinegar
2 tablespoons lemon juice
1 minced garlic clove
Generous pinches salt and pepper
1 teaspoon of ground sumac
½ teaspoon of Aleppo pepper

1. Using a large mixing bowl, mix the chickpeas, vegetables, olives and fresh herbs all together.
2. Using a smaller mixing bowl, add together the dressing ingredients: namely the olive oil, white wine vinegar, lemon juice, minced garlic, salt, pepper, sumac and Aleppo pepper.
3. Once your dressing is combined, drizzle it over the salad and gently mix to coat everything.
4. Set aside for at least 30 minutes before serving.
5. If you're preparing it long before serving, cover and put in the fridge until ready to serve.
6. Before serving, give the salad a quick stir and a taste. Add some salt if required.

Per Serving
Net Carbs: 39.5 g | Fiber: 10 g | Protein: 12.4 g Fat: 7.6g | Kcal (per serving): 267

Lettuce Cups Egg Salad

Time: 10 minutes | Serves:3

5 eggs, hard boiled and peeled
1 tablespoon of finely diced red onion
1 thinly sliced green onion
¼ cup of diced cucumber
¼ cup of chopped mixed olives
¼ cup of crumbled feta cheese

5 oz of plain Greek yogurt
¼ cup chopped roasted red-peppers
1 teaspoon of pepper
1 teaspoon of salt
6 Romaine lettuce leaves

1. Using a large bowl, add the Greek yogurt, cucumber, red onion, green onion, olives, and feta cheese. Mix thoroughly to combine.
2. Slice the eggs; add to the mixture and mix.
3. Taste and add salt and pepper if desired.
4. Add the roasted red peppers and mix until combined.
5. Use a Romaine lettuce leaf in place of a bowl/plate (i.e as an edible plate!) and scoop some salad into it. Continue until all 6 lettuce leaves are filled.

Per Serving
Net Carbs: 6.18 g | Fiber: 0.7 g | Protein: 22 g Fat: 20 g | Kcal (per serving): 298

Pasta and Hummus Salad

Time: 20 minutes | Serves:5

12 oz penne rotini (or any small pasta of your choosing)
2 cups broccoli florets
1 chopped medium-sized pepper
1 chopped onion
½ cup kalamata olives
¼ cup parmesan cheese

2/3 cup hummus
1 tablespoon olive oil
1 tablespoon water
1 teaspoon pepper
1 teaspoon of salt
½ teaspoon lemon juice

1. Cook your penne (or your choice of small pasta) according to the package instructions, and let it cool.
2. Using a mixing bowl, add the hummus, water, olive oil, some salt and pepper to taste and stir well to make the salad dressing.
3. In another bowl, add the broccoli, pepper, onion, kalamata olives, cheese, and some salt and pepper and stir to combine.
4. Add the cooked pasta, dressing and mix.

Per Serving
Net Carbs: 27.65 g | Fiber: 4.2 g | Protein: 7.67 g Fat: 9.66 g | Kcal (per serving): 223

Chapter 3
Sandwiches, Pizzas, and Wraps

Mashed Grape Tomato Pizzas

Prep time: 10 minutes | Cook time: 20 minutes | Serves 6

3 cups grape tomatoes, halved
1 teaspoon chopped fresh thyme leaves
2 garlic cloves, minced
¼ teaspoon kosher salt
¼ teaspoon freshly ground black pepper
1 tablespoon extra-virgin olive oil
¾ cup shredded Parmesan cheese
6 whole-wheat pita breads

1. Preheat the oven to 425ºF (220ºC).
2. Combine the tomatoes, thyme, garlic, salt, ground black pepper, and olive oil in a baking pan.
3. Roast in the preheated oven for 20 minutes. Remove the pan from the oven, mash the tomatoes with a spatula and stir to mix well halfway through the cooking time.
4. Meanwhile, divide and spread the cheese over each pita bread, then place the bread in a separate baking pan and roast in the oven for 5 minutes or until golden brown and the cheese melts.
5. Transfer the pita bread onto a large plate, then top with the roasted mashed tomatoes. Serve immediately.

Per Serving
calories: 140 | fat: 5.1g | protein: 6.2g | carbs: 16.9g | fiber: 2.0g | sodium: 466mg

Vegetable and Cheese Lavash Pizza

Prep time: 15 minutes | Cook time: 11 minutes | Serves 4

2 (12 by 9-inch) lavash breads
2 tablespoons extra-virgin olive oil
10 ounces (284 g) frozen spinach, thawed and squeezed dry
1 cup shredded fontina cheese
1 tomato, cored and cut into ½-inch pieces
½ cup pitted large green olives, chopped
¼ teaspoon red pepper flakes
3 garlic cloves, minced
¼ teaspoon sea salt
¼ teaspoon ground black pepper
½ cup grated Parmesan cheese

1. Preheat oven to 475ºF (246ºC).
2. Brush the lavash breads with olive oil, then place them on two baking sheets. Heat in the preheated oven for 4 minutes or until lightly browned. Flip the breads halfway through the cooking time.
3. Meanwhile, combine the spinach, fontina cheese, tomato pieces, olives, red pepper flakes, garlic, salt, and black pepper in a large bowl. Stir to mix well. Remove the lavash bread from the oven and place them on two large plates, spread them with the spinach mixture, then scatter with the Parmesan cheese on top.
4. Bake in the oven for 7 minutes or until the cheese melts and is well browned. Slice and serve warm.

Per Serving
calories: 431 | fat: 21.5g | protein: 20.0g | carbs: 38.4g | fiber: 2.5g | sodium: 854mg

Artichoke and Cucumber Hoagies

Prep time: 10 minutes | Cook time: 15 minutes | Makes 1

1 (12-ounce / 340-g) whole grain baguette, sliced in half horizontally
1 cup frozen and thawed artichoke hearts, roughly chopped
1 cucumber, sliced
2 tomatoes, sliced
1 red bell pepper, sliced
⅓ cup Kalamata olives, pitted and chopped
¼ small red onion, thinly sliced
Sea salt and ground black pepper, to taste
2 tablespoons pesto
Balsamic vinegar, to taste

1. Arrange the baguette halves on a clean work surface, then cut off the top third from each half. Scoop out some insides of the bottom half out and reserve as bread-crumbs.
2. Toast the baguette in a baking pan in the oven for 1 minute to brown lightly. Put the artichokes, cucumber, tomatoes, bell pepper, olives, and onion in a large bowl. Sprinkle with salt and ground black pepper. Toss to combine well.
3. Spread the bottom half of the baguette with the vegetable mixture and drizzle with balsamic vinegar, then smear the cut side of the baguette top with pesto. Assemble the two baguette halves. Wrap the hoagies in parchment paper and let sit for at least an hour before serving.

Per Serving
1263 | fat: 37.7g | protein: 56.3g | carbs: 180.1g | fiber: 37.8g |

sodium: 2137mg

Classic Socca

Prep time: 10 minutes | Cook time: 10 minutes | Serves 4

1½ cups chickpea flour
½ teaspoon ground turmeric
½ teaspoon sea salt
½ teaspoon ground black pepper
2 tablespoons plus 2 teaspoons extra-virgin olive oil
1½ cups water

1. Combine the chickpea flour, turmeric, salt, and black pepper in a bowl. Stir to mix well, then gently mix in 2 tablespoons of olive oil and water. Stir to mix until smooth.
2. Heat 2 teaspoons of olive oil in an 8-inch nonstick skillet over medium-high heat until shimmering. Add half cup of the mixture into the skillet and swirl the skillet so the mixture coats the bottom evenly. Cook for 5 minutes or until lightly browned and crispy. Flip the socca halfway through the cooking time. Repeat with the remaining mixture. Slice and serve warm.

Per Serving
calories: 207 | fat: 10.2g | protein: 7.9g | carbs: 20.7g | fiber: 3.9g | sodium: 315mg

Alfalfa Sprout and Nut Rolls

Prep time: 40 minutes | Cook time: 0 minutes |
Makes 16 bite-size pieces

1 cup alfalfa sprouts
2 tablespoons Brazil nuts
½ cup chopped fresh
cilantro
2 tablespoons flaked
coconut
1 garlic clove, minced
2 tablespoons ground
flaxseeds

Zest and juice of 1 lemon
Pinch cayenne pepper
Sea salt and freshly ground
black pepper, to taste
1 tablespoon melted coconut
oil
2 tablespoons water
2 whole-grain wraps

1. Combine all ingredients, except for the wraps, in a food processor, then pulse to combine well until smooth.
2. Unfold the wraps on a clean work surface, then spread the mixture over the wraps.
3. Roll the wraps up and refrigerate for 30 minutes until set.
4. Remove the rolls from the refrigerator and slice into 16 bite-sized pieces, if desired, and serve.

Per Serving
calories: 67 | fat: 7.1g | protein: 2.2g | carbs: 2.9g | fiber: 1.0g | sodium: 61mg

Mushroom and Caramelized Onion Musakhan

Prep time: 20 minutes | Cook time: 1 hour 5 minutes | Serves 4

2 tablespoons sumac, plus
more for sprinkling
1 teaspoon ground allspice
½ teaspoon ground
cardamom
½ teaspoon ground cumin
3 tablespoons extra-virgin
olive oil, divided
2 pounds (907 g) portobello

mushroom caps, gills
removed, caps halved and
sliced ½ inch thick
3 medium white onions,
coarsely chopped
¼ cup water
Kosher salt, to taste
1 whole-wheat Turkish
flatbread
¼ cup pine nuts
1 lemon, wedged

1. Preheat the oven to 350ºF (180ºC).
2. Combine 2 tablespoons of sumac, allspice, cardamom, and cumin in a small bowl. Stir to mix well.
3. Heat 2 tablespoons of olive oil in an oven-proof skillet over medium-high heat until shimmering.
4. Add the mushroom to the skillet and sprinkle with half of the umac mixture. Sauté for 8 minutes or until the mushrooms are tender. You may need to work in batches to avoid overcrowding.
5. Transfer the mushrooms to a plate and set side.
6. Heat 1 tablespoon of olive oil in the skillet over medium-high heat until shimmering.
7. Add the onion and sauté for 20 minutes or until caramelized.
8. Sprinkle with remaining sumac mixture, then cook for 1 more minute.
9. Pour in the water and sprinkle with salt. Bring to a simmer. Turn off the heat and put the mushroom back to the skillet.
10. Place the skillet in the preheated oven and bake for 30 minutes. Remove the skillet from the oven and let the mushroom sit for 10 minutes until cooled down.
11. Heat the Turkish flatbread in a baking dish in the oven for 5 minutes or until warmed through.
12. Place the bread on a large plate and top with mushrooms, onions, and roasted pine nuts. Squeeze the lemon wedges over and sprinkle with more sumac. Serve immediately.

Per Serving
calories: 336 | fat: 18.7g | protein: 11.5g | carbs: 34.3g | fiber: 6.9g | sodium: 369mg

Mini Pork and Cucumber Lettuce Wraps

Prep time: 20 minutes | Cook time: 0 minutes | Makes 12 wraps

8 ounces (227 g) cooked
ground pork
1 cucumber, diced
1 tomato, diced
1 red onion, sliced
1 ounce (28 g) low-fat feta
cheese, crumbled

Juice of 1 lemon
1 tablespoon extra-virgin
olive oil
Sea salt and freshly ground
pepper, to taste
12 small, intact iceberg
lettuce leaves

1. Combine the ground pork, cucumber, tomato, and onion in a large bowl, then scatter with feta cheese.
2. Drizzle with lemon juice and olive oil, and sprinkle with salt and pepper. Toss to mix well.
3. Unfold the small lettuce leaves on a large plate or several small plates, then divide and top with the pork mixture.
4. Wrap and serve immediately.

Per Serving
calories: 78 | fat: 5.6g | protein: 5.5g | carbs: 1.4g | fiber: 0.3g | sodium: 50mg

Greek Vegetable Salad Pita

Prep time: 10 minutes | Cook time: 0 minutes | Serves 4

½ cup baby spinach leaves
½ small red onion, thinly
sliced
½ small cucumber, deseeded
and chopped
1 tomato, chopped
1 cup chopped romaine
lettuce
1 tablespoon extra-virgin
olive oil

½ tablespoon red wine
vinegar
1 teaspoon Dijon mustard
1 tablespoon crumbled feta
cheese
Sea salt and freshly ground
pepper, to taste
1 whole-wheat pita

1. Combine all the ingredients, except for the pita, in a large bowl. Toss to mix well. Stuff the pita with the salad, then serve immediately.

Per Serving
calories: 137 | fat: 8.1g | protein: 3.1g | carbs: 14.3g | fiber: 2.4g | sodium: 166mg

Roasted Tomato Panini

Prep time: 15 minutes | Cook time: 3 hours 6 minutes |
Serves 2

2 teaspoons olive oil
4 Roma tomatoes, halved
4 cloves garlic
1 tablespoon Italian
seasoning

Sea salt and freshly ground
pepper, to taste
4 slices whole-grain bread
4 basil leaves
2 slices fresh mozzarella cheese

1. Preheat the oven to 250ºF (121ºC). Grease a baking pan with olive oil.
2. Place the tomatoes and garlic in the baking pan, then sprinkle with Italian seasoning, salt, and ground pepper. Toss to coat well.
3. Roast in the preheated oven for 3 hours or until the tomatoes are lightly wilted.
4. Preheat the panini press.
5. Make the panini: Place two slices of bread on a clean work surface, then top them with wilted tomatoes. Sprinkle with basil and spread with mozzarella cheese. Top them with remaining two slices of bread.
6. Cook the panini for 6 minutes or until lightly browned and the cheese melts. Flip the panini halfway through the cooking. Serve immediately.

Per Serving
calories: 323 | fat: 12.0g | protein: 17.4g | carbs: 37.5g | fiber: 7.5g | sodium: 603mg

Samosas in Potatoes

Prep time: 20 minutes | Cook time: 30 minutes | Makes 8

4 small potatoes
1 teaspoon coconut oil
1 small onion, finely
chopped
1 small piece ginger,
minced
2 garlic cloves, minced
2 to 3 teaspoons curry
powder

Sea salt and freshly ground
black pepper, to taste
¼ cup frozen peas, thawed
2 carrots, grated
¼ cup chopped fresh cilantro

1. Preheat the oven to 350ºF (180ºC).
2. Poke small holes into potatoes with a fork, then wrap with aluminum foil.
3. Bake in the preheated oven for 30 minutes until tender.
4. Meanwhile, heat the coconut oil in a nonstick skillet over medium-high heat until melted.
5. Add the onion and sauté for 5 minutes or until translucent.
6. Add the ginger and garlic to the skillet and sauté for 3 minutes or until fragrant.
7. Add the curry powder, salt, and ground black pepper, then stir to coat the onion. Remove them from the heat.
8. When the cooking of potatoes is complete, remove the potatoes from the foil and slice in half.
9. Hollow two potato halves with a spoon, then combine the potato fresh with sautéed onion, peas, carrots, and cilantro in a large bowl. Stir to mix well.
10. Spoon the mixture back to the potato skins and serve immediately.

Per Serving (1 samosa)
calories: 131 | fat: 13.9g | protein: 3.2g | carbs: 8.8g | fiber: 3.0g | sodium: 111mg

Spicy Black Bean and Poblano Dippers

Prep time: 20 minutes | Cook time: 21 minutes | Serves 8

2 tablespoons avocado oil,
plus more for brushing the
dippers
1 (15 ounces / 425 g) can
black beans, drained and
rinsed
1 poblano, deseeded and
quartered
1 jalapeño, halved and
deseeded

½ cup fresh cilantro, leaves
and tender stems
1 yellow onion, quartered
2 garlic cloves
1 teaspoon chili powder
1 teaspoon ground cumin
1 teaspoon sea salt
24 organic corn tortillas

1. Preheat the oven to 400ºF (205ºC). Line a baking sheet with parchment paper and grease with avocado oil.
2. Combine the remaining ingredients, except for the tortillas, in a food processor, then pulse until finely chopped and the mixture holds together. Make sure not to purée the mixture.
3. Warm the tortillas on the baking sheet in the preheated oven for 1 minute or until softened.
4. Add a tablespoon of the mixture in the middle of each tortilla.
5. Fold one side of the tortillas over the mixture and tuck to roll them up tightly to make the dippers. Arrange the dippers on the baking sheet and brush them with avocado oil.
6. Bake in the oven for 20 minutes or until well browned. Flip the dippers halfway through the cooking time. Serve immediately.

Per Serving
calories: 388 | fat: 6.5g | protein: 16.2g | carbs: 69.6g | fiber: 13.5g | sodium: 340mg

Italian Club Sandwich

Prep time: 20 minutes | Cook time: 10 minutes | Serves 2

6 slices of white sandwich
bread
4 slices of bacon (2 oz / 60
g total)
10.5 oz (300 g) sliced
turkey

7 oz (200 g) vine-ripened
tomatoes
4 leaves of lettuce
3.5 tbsp (50 g) mayonnaise
1 tbsp (15 g) butter

1. Butter 6 slices of bread and briefly toast in a pan. Set aside.
2. Toast bacon in the pan for 3 mins per side. Let it cool on paper towels. Cook turkey slices for 2-3 mins per side. Allow them to cool.
3. Slice tomatoes thinly. Wash and dry lettuce leaves.
4. Spread mayo on one side of each bread slice. Place lettuce on one slice, add turkey, tomatoes, and half a bacon slice.
5. Close the sandwich with another bread slice (mayo side facing bacon). Spread mayo on the top bread slice. Repeat for the second sandwich.
6. Secure sandwich corners with toothpicks. Cut diagonally into two halves. Serve with chips and sauces.

Per Serving
Calories: 622.9 | Carbs: 34.5 g | Proteins: 46.8 g | Fats: 33 g | Fiber: 13.2 g | Sodium: 318.2 mg

Eggplant, Spinach, and Feta Sandwiches

Prep time: 10 minutes | Cook time: 6 to 8 minutes | Serves 2

1 medium eggplant, sliced
into ½-inch-thick slices
2 tablespoons olive oil
Sea salt and freshly ground
pepper, to taste

5 to 6 tablespoons hummus
4 slices whole-wheat bread,
toasted
1 cup baby spinach leaves
2 ounces (57 g) feta cheese,
softened

1. Preheat the grill to medium-high heat.
2. Salt both sides of the sliced eggplant, and let it sit for 20 minutes to draw out the bitter juices.
3. Rinse the eggplant and pat dry with a paper towel.
4. Brush the eggplant slices with olive oil and season with sea salt and freshly ground pepper to taste.
5. Grill the eggplant until lightly charred on both sides but still slightly firm in the middle, about 3 to 4 minutes per side.
6. Spread the hummus on the bread slices and top with the spinach leaves, feta cheese, and grilled eggplant. Top with the other slice of bread and serve immediately.

Per Serving
calories: 493 | fat: 25.3g | protein: 17.1g | carbs: 50.9g | fiber:
14.7g | sodium: 789mg

Grilled Caesar Salad Sandwiches

Prep time: 5 minutes | Cook time: 5 minutes | Serves 2

¾ cup olive oil, divided
2 romaine lettuce hearts,
left intact
3 to 4 anchovy fillets Juice
of 1 lemon
2 to 3 cloves garlic, peeled
1 teaspoon Dijon mustard

¼ teaspoon Worcestershire
sauce
Sea salt and freshly ground
pepper, to taste
2 slices whole-wheat bread,
toasted
Freshly grated Parmesan
cheese, for serving

1. Preheat the grill to medium-high heat and oil the grates.
2. On a cutting board, drizzle the lettuce with 1 to 2 tablespoons of olive oil and place on the grates.
3. Grill for 5 minutes, turning until lettuce is slightly charred on all sides. Let the lettuce cool enough to handle. In a food processor, combine the remaining olive oil with the anchovies, lemon juice, garlic, mustard, and Worcestershire sauce.
4. Pulse the ingredients until you have a smooth emulsion.
5. Season with sea salt and freshly ground pepper to taste. Chop the lettuce in half and place on the bread.
6. Drizzle with the dressing and serve with a sprinkle of Parmesan cheese.

Per Serving
calories: 949 | fat: 85.6g | protein: 12.9g | carbs: 34.1g | fiber:
13.9g | sodium: 786mg

Pizza Pockets

Prep time: 10 minutes | Cook time: 0 minutes | Serves 2

½ cup tomato sauce
½ teaspoon oregano
½ teaspoon garlic powder
½ cup chopped black olives

2 canned artichoke hearts,
drained and chopped
2 ounces (57 g) pepperoni,
chopped
½ cup shredded mozzarella
cheese
1 whole-wheat pita, halved

1. In a medium bowl, stir together the tomato sauce, oregano, and garlic powder.
2. Add the olives, artichoke hearts, pepperoni, and cheese. Stir to mix.
3. Spoon the mixture into the pita halves and serve.

Per Serving
calories: 375 | fat: 23.5g | protein: 17.1g | carbs: 27.1g | fiber:
6.1g | sodium: 1080mg

Veg Mix and Blackeye Pea Burritos

Prep time: 15 minutes | Cook time: 40 minutes |
Makes 6 burritos

1 teaspoon olive oil
1 red onion, diced
2 garlic cloves, minced
1 zucchini, chopped
1 tomato, diced
1 bell pepper, any color,
deseeded and diced

1 (14-ounce / 397-g) can
blackeye peas
2 teaspoons chili powder
Sea salt, to taste
6 whole-grain tortillas

1. Preheat the oven to 325ºF (160ºC).
2. Heat the olive oil in a nonstick skillet over medium heat or until shimmering.
3. Add the onion and sauté for 5 minutes or until translucent.
4. Add the garlic and sauté for 30 seconds or until fragrant.
5. Add the zucchini and sauté for 5 minutes or until tender.
6. Add the tomato and bell pepper and sauté for 2 minutes or until soft.
7. Fold in the black peas and sprinkle them with chili powder and salt. Stir to mix well.
8. Place the tortillas on a clean work surface, then top them with sautéed vegetables mix.
9. Fold one ends of tortillas over the vegetable mix, then tuck and roll them into burritos.
10. Arrange the burritos in a baking dish, seam side down, then pour the juice remains in the skillet over the burritos.
11. Bake in the preheated oven for 25 minutes or until golden brown.
12. Serve immediately.

Per Serving
calories: 335 | fat: 16.2g | protein: 12.1g | carbs: 8.3g | fiber:
8.0g | sodium: 214mg

Dulse, Avocado, and Tomato Pitas

Prep time: 10 minutes | Cook time: 30 minutes | Makes 4 pitas

2 teaspoons coconut oil
½ cup dulse, picked
through and separated
Ground black pepper, to
taste
2 avocados, sliced
2 tablespoons lime juice
¼ cup chopped cilantro

2 scallions, white and light
green parts, sliced
Sea salt, to taste
4 (8-inch) whole wheat
pitas, sliced in half
4 cups chopped romaine
4 plum tomatoes, sliced

1. Heat the coconut oil in a nonstick skillet over medium heat until melted. Add the dulse and sauté for 5 minutes or until crispy. Sprinkle with ground black pepper and turn off the heat. Set aside. Put the avocado, lime juice, cilantro, and scallions in a food processor and sprinkle with salt and ground black pepper. Pulse to combine well until smooth.
2. Toast the pitas in a baking pan in the oven for 1 minute until soft.
3. Transfer the pitas to a clean work surface and open. Spread the avocado mixture over the pitas, then top with dulse, romaine, and tomato slices. Serve immediately.

Per Serving (1 pita)
calories: 412 | fat: 18.7g | protein: 9.1g | carbs: 56.1g | fiber: 12.5g | sodium: 695mg

Mediterranean Greek Salad Wraps

Prep time: 15 minutes | Cook time: 0 minutes | Serves 4

1½ cups seedless cucumber,
peeled and chopped
1 cup chopped tomato
½ cup finely chopped fresh
mint
¼ cup diced red onion
1 (2.25-ounce / 64-g) can
sliced black olives, drained
2 tablespoons extra-virgin
olive oil

1 tablespoon red wine
vinegar
¼ teaspoon kosher salt
¼ teaspoon freshly ground
black pepper
½ cup crumbled goat cheese
4 whole-wheat flatbread
wraps or soft whole-wheat
tortillas

1. In a large bowl, stir together the cucumber, tomato, mint, onion and olives.
2. In a small bowl, whisk together the oil, vinegar, salt, and pepper. Spread the dressing over the salad. Toss gently to combine.
3. Lay the wraps on a clean work surface. Divide the goat cheese evenly among the wraps. Scoop a quarter of the salad filling down the center of each wrap.
4. Fold up each wrap: Start by folding up the bottom, then fold one side over and fold the other side over the top. Repeat with the remaining wraps.
5. Serve immediately.

Per Serving
calories: 225 | fat: 12.0g | protein: 12.0g | carbs: 18.0g | fiber: 4.0g | sodium: 349mg

Za'atar Pizza

Prep time: 10 minutes | Cook time: 10 to 12 minutes | Serves 4 to 6

1 sheet puff pastry
¼ cup extra-virgin olive oil

⅓ cup za'atar seasoning

1. Preheat the oven to 350ºF (180ºC). Line a baking sheet with parchment paper.
2. Place the puff pastry on the prepared baking sheet. Cut the pastry into desired slices.
3. Brush the pastry with the olive oil. Sprinkle with the za'atar seasoning.
4. Put the pastry in the oven and bake for 10 to 12 minutes, or until edges are lightly browned and puffed up.
5. Serve warm.

Per Serving
calories: 374 | fat: 30.0g | protein: 3.0g | carbs: 20.0g | fiber: 1.0g | sodium: 166mg

Mushroom-Pesto Baked Pizza

Prep time: 5 minutes | Cook time: 15 minutes | Serves 2

1 teaspoon extra-virgin
olive oil
½ cup sliced mushrooms
½ red onion, sliced
Salt and freshly ground
black pepper

¼ cup store-bought pesto
sauce
2 whole-wheat flatbreads
¼ cup shredded Mozzarella
cheese

1. Preheat the oven to 350ºF (180ºC). In a small skillet, heat the oil over medium heat. Add the mushrooms and onion, and season with salt and pepper. Sauté for 3 to 5 minutes until the onion and mushrooms begin to soften. Spread 2 tablespoons of pesto on each flatbread. Divide the mushroom-onion mixture between the two flatbreads. Top each with 2 tablespoons of cheese. Place the flatbreads on a baking sheet and bake for 10 to 12 minutes until the cheese is melted and bubbly. Serve warm.

Per Serving
calories: 348 | fat: 23.5g | protein: 14.2g | carbs: 28.1g | fiber: 7.1g | sodium: 792mg

Tuna and Olive Salad Sandwiches

Prep time: 10 minutes | Cook time: 0 minutes | Serves 4

3 tablespoons freshly
squeezed lemon juice
2 tablespoons extra-virgin
olive oil
1 garlic clove, minced
½ teaspoon freshly ground
black pepper

2 (5-ounce / 142-g) cans
tuna, drained
1 (2.25-ounce / 64-g) can
sliced olives, any green or
black variety
½ cup chopped fresh fennel,
including fronds
8 slices whole-grain crusty
bread

1. In a medium bowl, whisk together the lemon juice, oil, garlic, and pepper. Add the tuna, olives and fennel to the bowl. Using a fork, separate the tuna into chunks and stir to incorporate all the ingredients.
2. Divide the tuna salad equally among 4 slices of bread. Top each with the remaining bread slices.
3. Let the sandwiches sit for at least 5 minutes so the zesty filling can soak into the bread before serving.

Per Serving
calories: 952 | fat: 17.0g | protein: 165.0g | carbs: 37.0g | fiber: 7.0g | sodium: 2572mg

Mozzarella in Carrozza

Prep time: 20 minutes | Cook time: 8 minutes | Serves 4

12 slices of white bread (about 600 g)
1.1 lbs (500 g) Mozzarella di Bufala cheese (preferably from the day before)
Fine salt, to taste

5 large eggs
1 cup (100 g) flour
2 ½ cups (300 g) breadcrumbs
4 ¼ cups (1 l) sunflower seed oil
Fine salt, to taste

1. Begin by cutting the buffalo mozzarella into 1/2" (1 cm) thick slices. Place them on a tray lined with paper towels and cover with more paper towels. Gently press the mozzarella to remove excess water. If necessary, use additional paper towels until completely dry.
2. Lay slices of bread on a cutting board. Place mozzarella slices on top to cover the entire surface without letting any stick out. Sprinkle with salt and cover with another slice of bread.
3. Gently press with your hands to pack it together. Continue for all slices until the mozzarella is used up. Trim the slices with a knife to remove the outer crust. Cut the mozzarella in the bread either by making a cross for squares or diagonally for triangles. Prepare the breading by dipping each piece into flour, then beaten eggs, and finally breadcrumbs. Transfer to a cutting board and press lightly with a knife to even out the breadcrumbs. Repeat if necessary and transfer to a baking sheet lined with parchment paper. Refrigerate for about 30 mins.
4. After the mozzarella has set, start the second breading. Dip in egg, remove excess, and dip in breadcrumbs. Transfer to a baking sheet lined with parchment paper and refrigerate for another 30 minutes. Heat oil in a frying pan until it shimmers. Fry a few pieces at a time for 1-2 minutes, turning with a skimmer. Once well-browned, drain on absorbent paper to remove excess oil. Fry the remaining pieces and serve.

Per Serving
calories: 93 | fat: 2.0g | protein: 10.0g | carbs: 8.0g | fiber: 2.0g | sodium: 313mg

Open-Faced Margherita Sandwiches

Prep time: 10 minutes | Cook time: 5 minutes | Serves 4

2 (6- to 7-inch) whole-wheat submarine or hoagie rolls, sliced open horizontally
1 tablespoon extra-virgin olive oil
1 garlic clove, halved
1 large ripe tomato, cut into 8 slices

¼ teaspoon dried oregano
1 cup fresh Mozzarella, sliced
¼ cup lightly packed fresh basil leaves, torn into small pieces
¼ teaspoon freshly ground black pepper

1. Preheat the broiler a rack 4 inches under the heating element. Put the sliced bread on a large, rimmed baking sheet and broil for 1 minute, or until the bread is just lightly toasted. Remove from the oven.
2. Brush each piece of the toasted bread with the oil, and rub a garlic half over each piece. Put the toasted bread back on the baking sheet. Evenly divide the tomato slices on each piece. Sprinkle with the oregano and top with the cheese.
3. Place the baking sheet under the broiler. Set the timer for 1½ minutes, but check after 1 minute. When the cheese is melted and the edges are just starting to get dark brown, remove the sandwiches from the oven. Top each sandwich with the fresh basil and pepper before serving.

Per Serving
calories: 93 | fat: 2.0g | protein: 10.0g | carbs: 8.0g | fiber: 2.0g | sodium: 313mg

Chickpea Lettuce Wraps

Prep time: 15 minutes | Cook time: 0 minutes | Serves 2

1 (15-ounce / 425-g) can chickpeas, drained and rinsed well
1 celery stalk, diced
½ shallot, minced
1 green apple, cored and diced
3 tablespoons tahini (sesame paste)

2 teaspoons freshly squeezed lemon juice
1 teaspoon raw honey
1 teaspoon Dijon mustard
Dash salt
Filtered water, to thin
4 romaine lettuce leaves

1. In a medium bowl, stir together the chickpeas, celery, shallot, apple, tahini, lemon juice, honey, mustard, and salt. If needed, add some water to thin the mixture. Place the romaine lettuce leaves on a plate. Fill each with the chickpea filling, using it all.
2. Wrap the leaves around the filling. Serve immediately.

Per Serving
calories: 397 | fat: 15.1g | protein: 15.1g | carbs: 53.1g | fiber: 15.3g | sodium: 409mg

Roasted Vegetable Panini

Prep time: 10 minutes | Cook time: 15 minutes | Serves 4

2 tablespoons extra-virgin olive oil, divided
1½ cups diced broccoli
1 cup diced zucchini
¼ cup diced onion
¼ teaspoon dried oregano
⅛ teaspoon kosher or sea salt
⅛ teaspoon freshly ground black pepper

1 (12-ounce / 340-g) jar roasted red peppers, drained and finely chopped
2 tablespoons grated Parmesan or Asiago cheese 1 cup fresh mozzarella (about 4 ounces / 113 g), sliced
1 (2-foot-long) whole-grain Italian loaf, cut into 4 equal lengths Cooking spray

1. Place a large, rimmed baking sheet in the oven. Preheat the oven to 450ºF (235ºC) with the baking sheet inside.
2. In a large bowl, stir together 1 tablespoon of the oil, broccoli, zucchini, onion, oregano, salt and pepper. Remove the baking sheet from the oven and spritz the baking sheet with cooking spray. Spread the vegetable mixture on the baking sheet and roast for 5 minutes, stirring once halfway through cooking. Remove the baking sheet from the oven. Stir in the red peppers and Parmesan cheese. In a large skillet over medium-high heat, heat the remaining 1 tablespoon of the oil.
3. Cut open each section of bread horizontally, but don't cut all the way through. Fill each with the vegetable mix (about ½ cup), and layer 1 ounce (28 g) of sliced mozzarella cheese on top.
4. Close the sandwiches, and place two of them on the skillet. Place a heavy object on top and grill for 2½ minutes. Flip the sandwiches and grill for another 2½ minutes. Repeat the grilling process with the remaining two sandwiches. Serve hot.

Per Serving
calories: 116 | fat: 4.0g | protein: 12.0g | carbs: 9.0g | fiber: 3.0g | sodium: 569mg

Spinach Arugula Pizza

Prep time: 10 minutes | Cook time: 20 minutes | Serves 4

1 pound (454 g) refrigerated fresh pizza dough
2 tablespoons extra-virgin olive oil, divided
½ cup thinly sliced onion
2 garlic cloves, minced
3 cups baby spinach
3 cups arugula
1 tablespoon water
¼ teaspoon freshly ground black pepper
1 tablespoon freshly squeezed lemon juice
½ cup shredded Parmesan cheese
½ cup crumbled goat cheese
Cooking spray

1. Preheat the oven to 500ºF (260ºC). Spritz a large, rimmed baking sheet with cooking spray.
2. Take the pizza dough out of the refrigerator.
3. Heat 1 tablespoon of the oil in a large skillet over medium heat. Add the onion to the skillet and cook for 4 minutes, stirring constantly. Add the garlic and cook for 1 minute, stirring constantly.
4. Stir in the spinach, arugula, water and pepper. Cook for about 2 minutes, stirring constantly, or until all the greens are coated with oil and they start to cook down. Remove the skillet from the heat and drizzle with the lemon juice.
5. On a lightly floured work surface, form the pizza dough into a 12-inch circle or a 10-by-12-inch rectangle, using a rolling pin or by stretching with your hands.
6. Place the dough on the prepared baking sheet. Brush the dough with the remaining 1 tablespoon of the oil. Spread the cooked greens on top of the dough to within ½ inch of the edge. Top with the Parmesan cheese and goat cheese.
7. Bake in the preheated oven for 10 to 12 minutes, or until the crust starts to brown around the edges.
8. Remove from the oven and transfer the pizza to a cutting board. Cut into eight pieces before serving.

Per Serving
calories: 521 | fat: 31.0g | protein: 23.0g | carbs: 38.0g | fiber: 4.0g | sodium: 1073mg

Bread Machine Pizza Dough

Servings: 6

1 cup of beer
2 tablespoons butter
2 tablespoons sugar
1 teaspoon of salt
2 1/2 cups of all-purpose flour
2 1/4 teaspoons of yeast

1. Place beer, butter, sugar, salt, flour, and yeast in a bread maker in the order recommended by the manufacturer. Select the Paste setting and press Start.
2. Remove the dough from the bread maker once the cycle is complete. Roll or press the dough to cover a prepared pizza pan. Brush lightly with olive oil. Cover and let it stand for 15 minutes.
3. Preheat the oven to 250 degrees (400 degrees F). Spread the sauce and garnish on the dough.
4. Bake until the crust is a little brown and crispy on the outside, about 24 minutes.

Valentine Pizza

Servings: 12

3 cups of bread flour
1 (0.25 oz) active dry yeast cover
1 1/4 cup of warm water
3 tablespoons chopped fresh rosemary
3 tablespoons extra virgin olive oil, divided
1 can of pizza sauce (14 oz)
3 cups grated mozzarella cheese
2 ripe tomatoes
15 slices of vegetarian pepperoni
1 can (2.25 oz) sliced black olives, sliced
1 zucchini, sliced

1. Place the bread flour, yeast, water, and 2 tablespoons of olive oil in the bread maker in the order recommended by the manufacturer. Select the Paste setting. Press Start. When the dough is ready, knead the rosemary into the dough.
2. Divide the dough into three servings. Shape each into a heart about 1/2" thick. Brush with remaining olive oil, then spread a thin layer of pizza sauce on each pizza. Sprinkle cheese over pizza sauce and arrange on top with tomatoes, zucchini, pepperoni, and sliced olives.
3. Bake for about 15 to 20 minutes.

Grilled Buffalo Chicken Pizza

Servings: 2

boneless chicken fillet
2 pinches of steak herbs
1 tablespoon hot pepper sauce
2 pieces of naan tandoori bread
1 teaspoon of olive oil
½ cup of blue cheese dressing
2 tablespoons diced red onion
0.6 ounce of grated cheddar cheese
½ cup of grated iceberg lettuce
1 Roma tomato, seeded and minced

1. Season the chicken fillet with Montreal Steak Seasoning. Pour 1/3 cup of hot pepper sauce into the plastic zipper bag. Close the bag and rub the hot sauce into the chicken.
2. Place the bag in the refrigerator and marinate for 12 hours. Preheat an outside grill over medium heat and lightly oil the grill.
3. Discard the marinade. Cook the chicken on the preheated grill until it is no longer pink in the middle and the juice is clear, 5 to 7 minutes on each side. An instant-read thermometer in the center must indicate at least 165° F (74° C). Put the chicken on a cutting board and let it sit for 5 to 10 minutes.
4. Cut the chilled chicken into bite-sized pieces. Mix chicken and remaining hot sauce in a bowl.
5. Brush every naan with olive oil; bake on the grill until golden brown and grilled on one side for 3 to 5 minutes. Reduce the heat to medium-low and place the pieces of toasted bread on a baking sheet. Spread blue cheese vinaigrette on the grilled side of each naan. Garnish each with diced chicken and red onion. Sprinkle with cheddar cheese. Place the naan on the grill and cook until the cheese has melted and the bottom is grilled and golden brown, another 5 to 10 minutes. Remove from the grill, cut into pieces and garnish with lettuce and tomato.

Chapter 4
Beans, Grains, and Pastas

Curry Apple Couscous with Leeks and Pecans

Prep time: 10 minutes | Cook time: 8 minutes | Serves 4

2 teaspoons extra-virgin olive oil
2 leeks, white parts only, sliced
1 apple, diced
2 cups cooked couscous
2 tablespoons curry powder
½ cup chopped pecans

1. Heat the olive oil in a skillet over medium heat until shimmering.
2. Add the leeks and sauté for 5 minutes or until soft.
3. Add the diced apple and cook for 3 more minutes until tender.
4. Add the couscous and curry powder. Stir to combine.
5. Transfer to a large serving bowl, then mix in the pecans and serve.

Per Serving
calories: 254 | fat: 11.9g | protein: 5.4g | carbs: 34.3g | fiber: 5.9g | sodium: 15mg

Slow Cooked Turkey and Brown Rice

Prep time: 20 minutes | Cook time: 3 hours 10 minutes | Serves 6

1 tablespoon extra-virgin olive oil
1½ pounds (680 g) ground turkey
2 tablespoons chopped fresh sage, divided
2 tablespoons chopped fresh thyme, divided
1 teaspoon sea salt
½ teaspoon ground black pepper
2 cups brown rice
1 (14-ounce / 397-g) can stewed tomatoes, with the juice
¼ cup pitted and sliced Kalamata olives
3 medium zucchini, sliced thinly
¼ cup chopped fresh flat-leaf parsley
1 medium yellow onion, chopped
1 tablespoon plus 1 teaspoon balsamic vinegar
2 cups low-sodium chicken stock
2 garlic cloves, minced
½ cup grated Parmesan cheese, for serving

1. Heat the olive oil in a nonstick skillet over medium-high heat until shimmering.
2. Add the ground turkey and sprinkle with 1 tablespoon of sage, 1 tablespoon of thyme, salt and ground black pepper.
3. Sauté for 10 minutes or until the ground turkey is lightly browned.
4. Pour them in the slow cooker, then pour in the remaining ingredients, except for the Parmesan. Stir to mix well.
5. Put the lid on and cook on high for 3 hours or until the rice and vegetables are tender.
6. Pour into a large serving bowl, then sprinkle with Parmesan cheese before serving.

Per Serving
calories: 499 | fat: 16.4g | protein: 32.4g | carbs: 56.5g | fiber: 4.7g | sodium: 758mg

Baked Rolled Oats with Pears and Pecans

Prep time: 15 minutes | Cook time: 30 minutes | Serves 6

2 tablespoons coconut oil, melted, plus more for greasing the pan
3 ripe pears, cored and diced
2 cups unsweetened almond milk
1 tablespoon pure vanilla extract
¼ cup pure maple syrup
2 cups gluten-free rolled oats
½ cup raisins
¾ cup chopped pecans
¼ teaspoon ground nutmeg
1 teaspoon ground cinnamon
½ teaspoon ground ginger
¼ teaspoon sea salt

1. Preheat the oven to 350ºF (180ºC). Grease a baking dish with melted coconut oil, then evenly spread the pears in a single layer on the baking dish evenly.
2. Combine the almond milk, vanilla extract, maple syrup, and coconut oil in a bowl. Stir to mix well.
3. Combine the remaining ingredients in a separate large bowl.
4. Stir to mix well. Fold the almond milk mixture into the bowl, then pour the mixture over the pears.
5. Place the baking dish in the preheated oven and bake for 30 minutes or until lightly browned and set. Serve immediately.

Per Serving
calories: 479 | fat: 34.9g | protein: 8.8g | carbs: 50.1g | fiber: 10.8g | sodium: 113mg

Lemony Farro and Avocado Bowl

Prep time: 5 minutes | Cook time: 25 minutes | Serves 4

1 tablespoon plus 2 teaspoons extra-virgin olive oil, divided
½ medium onion, chopped
1 carrot, shredded
2 garlic cloves, minced
1 cup pearled farro
2 cups low-sodium vegetable broth
2 avocados, peeled, pitted, and sliced
Zest and juice of 1 small lemon
¼ teaspoon sea salt

1. Heat 1 tablespoon of olive oil in a saucepan over medium-high heat until shimmering.
2. Add the onion and sauté for 5 minutes or until translucent.
3. Add the carrot and garlic and sauté for 1 minute or until fragrant.
4. Add the farro and pour in the vegetable broth. Bring to a boil over high heat. Reduce the heat to low. Put the lid on and simmer for 20 minutes or until the farro is al dente.
5. Transfer the farro to a large serving bowl, then fold in the avocado slices. Sprinkle with lemon zest and salt, then drizzle with lemon juice and 2 teaspoons of olive oil.
6. Stir to mix well and serve immediately.

Per Serving
calories: 210 | fat: 11.1g | protein: 4.2g | carbs: 27.9g | fiber: 7.0g | sodium: 152mg

Spaghetti with Pine Nuts and Cheese

Prep time: 10 minutes | Cook time: 11 minutes | Serves 4 to 6

8 ounces (227 g) spaghetti
4 tablespoons almond
butter
1 teaspoon freshly ground
black pepper

½ cup pine nuts
1 cup fresh grated
Parmesan cheese, divided

1. Bring a large pot of salted water to a boil. Add the pasta and cook for 8 minutes.
2. In a large saucepan over medium heat, combine the butter, black pepper, and pine nuts. Cook for 2 to 3 minutes, or until the pine nuts are lightly toasted. Reserve ½ cup of the pasta water.
3. Drain the pasta and place it into the pan with the pine nuts.
4. Add ¾ cup of the Parmesan cheese and the reserved pasta water to the pasta and toss everything together to evenly coat the pasta.
5. Transfer the pasta to a serving dish and top with the remaining ¼ cup of the Parmesan cheese. Serve immediately.

Per Serving
calories: 542 | fat: 32.0g | protein: 20.0g | carbs: 46.0g | fiber: 2.0g | sodium: 552mg

Triple-Green Pasta with Cheese

Prep time: 5 minutes | Cook time: 14 to 16 minutes | Serves 4

8 ounces (227 g) uncooked
penne
1 tablespoon extra-virgin
olive oil
2 garlic cloves, minced
¼ teaspoon crushed red
pepper
2 cups chopped fresh flat-
leaf parsley, including stems
5 cups loosely packed baby
spinach

¼ teaspoon ground nutmeg
¼ teaspoon kosher salt
¼ teaspoon freshly ground
black pepper
⅓ cup Castelvetrano olives,
pitted and sliced
⅓ cup grated Parmesan
cheese

1. In a large stockpot of salted water, cook the pasta for about 8 to 10 minutes. Drain the pasta and reserve ¼ cup of the cooking liquid.
2. Meanwhile, heat the olive oil in a large skillet over medium heat. Add the garlic and red pepper and cook for 30 seconds, stirring constantly.
3. Add the parsley and cook for 1 minute, stirring constantly. Add the spinach, nutmeg, salt, and pepper, and cook for 3 minutes, stirring occasionally, or until the spinach is wilted.
4. Add the cooked pasta and the reserved ¼ cup cooking liquid to the skillet. Stir in the olives and cook for about 2 minutes, or until most of the pasta water has been absorbed.
5. Remove from the heat and stir in the cheese before serving.

Per Serving
calories: 262 | fat: 4.0g | protein: 15.0g | carbs: 51.0g | fiber: 13.0g | sodium: 1180mg

Turkish Canned Pinto Bean Salad

Prep time: 10 minutes | Cook time: 3 minutes | Serves 4 to 6

¼ cup extra-virgin olive oil,
divided
3 garlic cloves, lightly
crushed and peeled
2 (15-ounce / 425-g) cans
pinto beans, rinsed
2 cups plus
1 tablespoon water
Salt and pepper, to taste
¼ cup tahini
3 tablespoons lemon juice

1 tablespoon ground dried
Aleppo pepper, plus extra
for serving
8 ounces (227 g) cherry
tomatoes, halved
¼ red onion, sliced thinly
½ cup fresh parsley leaves
2 hard-boiled large eggs,
quartered
1 tablespoon toasted
sesame seeds

1. Add garlic and 1 tablespoon of the olive oil to a medium saucepan over medium heat. Cook for about 3 minutes, stirring constantly, or until the garlic turns golden but not brown.
2. Add the beans, 2 cups of the water and 1 teaspoon salt and bring to a simmer. Remove from the heat, cover and let it sit for 20 minutes. Drain the beans and discard the garlic.
3. In a large bowl, whisk together the remaining 3 tablespoons of the oil, tahini, lemon juice, Aleppo, the remaining 1 tablespoon of the water and ¼ teaspoon salt. Stir in the beans, tomatoes, onion and parsley. Season with salt and pepper to taste.
4. Transfer to a serving platter and top with the eggs. Sprinkle with the sesame seeds and extra Aleppo before serving.

Per Serving
calories: 402 | fat: 18.9g | protein: 16.2g | carbs: 44.4g | fiber: 11.2g | sodium: 4 56mg

Walnut and Ricotta Spaghetti

Prep time: 15 minutes | Cook time: 10 minutes | Serves 6

1 pound (454 g) cooked
whole-wheat spaghetti
2 tablespoons extra-virgin
olive oil
4 cloves garlic, minced
¾ cup walnuts, toasted and
finely chopped

2 tablespoons ricotta cheese
¼ cup flat-leaf parsley,
chopped
½ cup grated Parmesan
cheese
Sea salt and freshly ground
pepper, to taste

1. Reserve a cup of spaghetti water after cooking the spaghetti.
2. Heat the olive oil in a nonstick skillet over medium-low heat or until shimmering.
3. Add the garlic and sauté for a minute or until fragrant.
4. Pour the spaghetti water into the skillet and cook for 8 more minutes.
5. Turn off the heat and mix in the walnuts and ricotta cheese.
6. Put the cooked spaghetti on a large serving plate, then pour the walnut sauce over. Spread with parsley and Parmesan, then sprinkle with salt and ground pepper. Toss to serve.

Per Serving
calories: 264 | fat: 16.8g | protein: 8.6g | carbs: 22.8g | fiber: 4.0g | sodium: 336mg

Garlic and Parsley Chickpeas

Prep time: 10 minutes | Cook time: 18 to 20 minutes | Serves 4 to 6

¼ cup extra-virgin olive oil, divided
4 garlic cloves, sliced thinly
⅛ teaspoon red pepper flakes
1 onion, finely chopped
¼ teaspoon salt, plus more to taste
Black pepper, to taste
2 (15-ounce / 425-g) cans chickpeas, rinsed
1 cup vegetable broth
2 tablespoons minced fresh parsley
2 teaspoons lemon juice

1. Add 3 tablespoons of the olive oil, garlic, and pepper flakes to a skillet over medium heat. Cook for about 3 minutes, stirring constantly, or until the garlic turns golden but not brown. Stir in the onion and ¼ teaspoon salt and cook for 5 to 7 minutes, or until softened and lightly browned.
2. Add the chickpeas and broth to the skillet and bring to a simmer. Reduce the heat to medium-low, cover, and cook for about 7 minutes, or until the chickpeas are cooked through and flavors meld.
3. Uncover, increase the heat to high and continue to cook for about 3 minutes more, or until nearly all liquid has evaporated. Turn off the heat, stir in the parsley and lemon juice. Season to taste with salt and pepper and drizzle with remaining 1 tablespoon of the olive oil. Serve warm.

Per Serving
calories: 220 | fat: 11.4g | protein: 6.5g | carbs: 24.6g | fiber : 6.0g | sodium: 467mg

Mashed Beans with Cumin

Prep time: 10 minutes | Cook time: 10 to 12 minutes | Serves 4 to 6

1 tablespoon extra-virgin olive oil, plus extra for serving
4 garlic cloves, minced
1 teaspoon ground cumin
2 (15-ounce / 425-g) cans fava beans
3 tablespoons tahini
2 tablespoons lemon juice, plus lemon wedges for serving
Salt and pepper, to taste
1 tomato, cored and cut into ½-inch pieces
1 small onion, finely chopped
2 hard-boiled large eggs, chopped
2 tablespoons minced fresh parsley

1. Add the olive oil, garlic and cumin to a medium sauce-pan over medium heat. Cook for about 2 minutes, or until fragrant. Stir in the beans with their liquid and tahini. Bring to a simmer and cook for 8 to 10 minutes, or until the liquid thickens slightly.
2. Turn off the heat; mash the beans to a coarse consistency with a potato masher. Stir in the lemon juice and 1 teaspoon pepper.
3. Season with salt and pepper. Transfer the mashed beans to a serving dish. Top with the tomato, onion, eggs and parsley. Drizzle with the extra olive oil. Serve with the lemon wedges.

Per Serving
calories: 125 | fat: 8.6g | protein: 4.9g | carbs: 9.1g | fiber : 2.9g | sodium: 131mg

Butternut Squash, Spinach, and Cheeses Lasagna

Prep time: 30 minutes | Cook time: 3 hours 45 minutes | Serves 4 to 6

2 tablespoons extra-virgin olive oil, divided
1 butternut squash, halved lengthwise and deseeded
½ teaspoon sage
½ teaspoon sea salt
¼ teaspoon ground black pepper
¼ cup grated Parmesan cheese
2 cups ricotta cheese
½ cup unsweetened almond milk
5 layers whole-wheat lasagna noodles (about 12 ounces / 340 g in total)
4 ounces (113 g) fresh spinach leaves, divided
½ cup shredded part skim mozzarella, for garnish

1. Preheat the oven to 400ºF (205ºC). Line a baking sheet with parchment paper. Brush 1 tablespoon of olive oil on the cut side of the butternut squash, then place the squash on the baking sheet. Bake in the preheated oven for 45 minutes or until the squash is tender. Allow to cool until you can handle it, then scoop the flesh out and put the flesh in a food processor to purée. Combine the puréed butternut squash flesh with sage, salt, and ground black pepper in a large bowl. Stir to mix well.
2. Combine the cheeses and milk in a separate bowl, then sprinkle with salt and pepper, to taste.
3. Grease the slow cooker with 1 tablespoon of olive oil, then add a layer of lasagna noodles to coat the bottom of the slow cooker. Spread half of the squash mixture on top of the noodles, then top the squash mixture with another layer of lasagna noodles. Spread half of the spinach over the noodles, then top the spinach with half of the cheese mixture. Repeat with remaining 3 layers of lasagna noodles, squash mixture, spinach, and cheese mixture. Top the cheese mixture with mozzarella, then put the lid on and cook on low for 3 hours or until the lasagna noodles are al dente. Serve immediately.

Per Serving
calories: 657 | fat: 37.1g | protein: 30.9g | carbs: 57.2g | fiber : 8.3g | sodium: 918mg

Black-Eyed Peas Salad with Walnuts

Prep time: 10 minutes | Cook time: 0 minutes | Serves 4 to 6

3 tablespoons extra-virgin olive oil
3 tablespoons dukkah, divided
2 tablespoons lemon juice
2 tablespoons pomegran-ate molasses
¼ teaspoon salt, or more to taste
⅛ teaspoon pepper, or more to taste
2 (15-ounce / 425-g) cans black-eyed peas, rinsed
½ cup pomegranate seeds
½ cup minced fresh parsley
½ cup walnuts, toasted and chopped
4 scallions, thinly sliced

In a large bowl, whisk together the olive oil, 2 tablespoons of the dukkah, lemon juice, pomegranate molasses, salt and pepper. Stir in the remaining ingredients. Season with salt and pepper. Sprinkle with the remaining 1 tablespoon of the dukkah before serving.

Per Serving
calories: 155 | fat: 11.5g | protein: 2.0g | carbs: 12.5g | fiber : 2.1g | sodium: 105mg

Pasta Puttanesca

Prep time: 20 minutes | Cook time: 20 min | Serves: 4

3 eggplants	Parsley
32 oz (or more) tomato sauce	Extra virgin olive oil
	Basil
3 cloves of garlic	Salt
1 chopped onion	Red pepper flakes

1. Wash the eggplants, remove the seeds, cut them into cubes, add a little salt and let them drain for a few hours. After, rinse and dry them.
2. In the meanwhile, place the oil, garlic and chopped onion in a pan and let everything brown for a few minutes. Then add the tomato puree and the parsley and let it cook for 45 minutes, stirring occasionally.
3. Take the diced eggplants and place them in a pan with a drizzle of extra virgin olive oil for 5-10 minutes, then add them to the sauce and cook them for another 20 minutes. Cook the pasta.
4. Add the pepper and a fresh basil, now your sauce is ready for your pasta!

Per Serving
calories: 212 | fat: 9g | protein: 8g | carbs: 17g | fiber : 5g | sodium: 161mg

Freekeh Pilaf with Dates and Pistachios

Prep time: 10 minutes | Cook time: 10 minutes | Serves 4 to 6

2 tablespoons extra-virgin olive oil, plus extra for drizzling	1¾ cups water
	1½ cups cracked freekeh, rinsed
1 shallot, minced	3 ounces (85 g) pitted dates, chopped
1½ teaspoons grated fresh ginger	
¼ teaspoon ground coriander	¼ cup shelled pistachios, toasted and coarsely chopped
¼ teaspoon ground cumin	1½ tablespoons lemon juice
Salt and pepper, to taste	¼ cup chopped fresh mint

1. Set the Instant Pot to Sauté mode and heat the olive oil until shimmering. Add the shallot, ginger, coriander, cumin, salt, and pepper to the pot and cook for about 2 minutes, or until the shallot is softened. Stir in the water and freekeh. Secure the lid.
2. Select the Manual mode and set the cooking time for 4 minutes at High Pressure. Once cooking is complete, do a quick pressure release. Carefully open the lid. Add the dates, pistachios and lemon juice and gently fluff the freekeh with a fork to combine.
3. Season to taste with salt and pepper. Transfer to a serving dish and sprinkle with the mint. Serve drizzled with extra olive oil.

Per Serving
calories: 280 | fat: 8.0g | protein: 8.0g | carbs: 46.0g | fiber: 9.0g | sodium: 200mg

Quinoa with Baby Potatoes and Broccoli

Prep time: 5 minutes | Cook time: 10 minutes | Serves 4

2 tablespoons olive oil	2 cups cooked quinoa Zest of 1 lemon
1 cup baby potatoes, cut in half	
1 cup broccoli florets	Sea salt and freshly ground pepper, to taste

1. Heat the olive oil in a large skillet over medium heat until shimmering. Add the potatoes and cook for about 6 to 7 minutes, or until softened and golden brown. Add the broccoli and cook for about 3 minutes, or until tender.
2. Remove from the heat and add the quinoa and lemon zest. Season with salt and pepper to taste, then serve.

Per Serving
calories: 205 | fat: 8.6g | protein: 5.1g | carbs: 27.3g | fiber : 3.7g | sodium: 158mg

Black-Eyed Pea and Vegetable Stew

Prep time: 15 minutes | Cook time: 40 minutes | Serves 2

½ cup black-eyed peas, soaked in water overnight	¼ teaspoon turmeric
	¼ teaspoon cayenne pepper
3 cups water, plus more as needed	¼ teaspoon ground cumin seeds, toasted
1 large carrot, peeled and cut into ½-inch pieces (about ¾ cup)	¼ cup finely chopped parsley
	¼ teaspoon salt (optional)
1 large beet, peeled and cut into ½-inch pieces (about ¾ cup)	½ teaspoon fresh lime juice

1. Pour the black-eyed peas and water into a large pot, then cook over medium heat for 25 minutes. Add the carrot and beet to the pot and cook for 10 more minutes, adding more water as needed.
2. Add the turmeric, cayenne pepper, cumin, and parsley to the pot and cook for another 6 minutes, or until the vegetables are softened.
3. Stir the mixture periodically. Season with salt, if desired. Serve
4. drizzled with the fresh lime juice.

Per Serving
calories: 89 | fat: 0.7g | protein: 4.1g | carbs: 16.6g | fiber : 4.5g | sodium: 367mg

Bulgur Pilaf with Kale and Tomatoes

Prep time: 10 minutes | Cook time: 10 minutes | Serves 2

2 tablespoons olive oil,	Juice of 1 lemon
2 cloves garlic, minced	2 cups cooked bulgur wheat
1 bunch kale, trimmed and cut into bite-sized pieces	1 pint cherry tomatoes, halved
	Sea salt and freshly ground pepper, to taste

1. Heat the olive oil in a large skillet over medium heat. Add the garlic and sauté for 1 minute.
2. Add the kale leaves and stir to coat. Cook for 5 minutes until leaves are cooked through and thoroughly wilted.
3. Add the lemon juice, bulgur and tomatoes. Season with sea salt and freshly ground pepper to taste, then serve.

Per Serving
calories: 300 | fat: 14.0g | protein: 6.2g | carbs: 37.8g | fiber : 8.7g | sodium: 595mg

Brown Rice Pilaf with Pistachios and Raisins

Prep time: 5 minutes | Cook time: 15 minutes | Serves 6

1 tablespoon extra-virgin olive oil
1 cup chopped onion
½ cup shredded carrot
½ teaspoon ground cinnamon
1 teaspoon ground cumin
2 cups brown rice
1¾ cups pure orange juice
¼ cup water
½ cup shelled pistachios
1 cup golden raisins
½ cup chopped fresh chives

1. Heat the olive oil in a saucepan over medium-high heat until shimmering.
2. Add the onion and sauté for 5 minutes or until translucent.
3. Add the carrots, cinnamon, and cumin, then sauté for 1 minutes or until aromatic.
4. Pour in the brown rice, orange juice, and water. Bring to a boil. Reduce the heat to medium-low and simmer for 7 minutes or until the liquid is almost absorbed.
5. Transfer the rice mixture in a large serving bowl, then spread with pistachios, raisins, and chives. Serve immediately.

Per Serving
calories: 264 | fat: 7.1g | protein: 5.2g | carbs: 48.9g | fiber: 4.0g | sodium: 86mg

Lebanese Flavor Broken Thin Noodles

Prep time: 10 minutes | Cook time: 25 minutes | Serves 6

1 tablespoon extra-virgin olive oil
1 (3-ounce / 85-g) cup vermicelli, broken into 1- to 1½-inch pieces
3 cups shredded cabbage
1 cup brown rice
3 cups low-sodium vegetable broth
½ cup water
2 garlic cloves, mashed
¼ teaspoon sea salt
⅛ teaspoon crushed red pepper flakes
½ cup coarsely chopped cilantro
Fresh lemon slices, for serving

1. Heat the olive oil in a saucepan over medium-high heat until shimmering.
2. Add the vermicelli and sauté for 3 minutes or until toasted.
3. Add the cabbage and sauté for 4 minutes or until tender. Pour
4. in the brown rice, vegetable broth, and water. Add the garlic and sprinkle with salt and red pepper flakes. Bring to a boil over high heat. Reduce the heat to medium low.
5. Put the lid on and simmer for another 10 minutes.
6. Turn off the heat, then let sit for 5 minutes without opening the lid.
7. Pour onto a large serving platter and sprinkle with cilantro. Squeeze the lemon slices over and serve warm.

Per Serving
calories: 127 | fat: 3.1g | protein: 4.2g | carbs: 22.9g | fiber: 3.0g | sodium: 224mg

Israeli Style Eggplant and Chickpea Salad

Prep time: 5 minutes | Cook time: 20 minutes | Serves 6

2 tablespoons freshly squeezed lemon juice
1 teaspoon ground cumin
¼ teaspoon sea salt
2 tablespoons olive oil, divided
1 (1-pound / 454-g) medium globe eggplant, stem removed, cut into flat cubes (about ½ inch thick)
2 tablespoons balsamic vinegar
1 (15-ounce / 425-g) can chickpeas, drained and rinsed
¼ cup chopped mint leaves
1 cup sliced sweet onion
1 garlic clove, finely minced
1 tablespoon sesame seeds, toasted

1. Preheat the oven to 550ºF (288ºC) or the highest level of your oven or broiler. Grease a baking sheet with 1 tablespoon of olive oil.
2. Combine the balsamic vinegar, lemon juice, cumin, salt, and 1 tablespoon of olive oil in a small bowl. Stir to mix well.
3. Arrange the eggplant cubes on the baking sheet, then brush with 2 tablespoons of the balsamic vinegar mixture on both sides. Broil in the preheated oven for 8 minutes or until lightly browned.
4. Flip the cubes halfway through the cooking time.
5. Meanwhile, combine the chickpeas, mint, onion, garlic, and sesame seeds in a large serving bowl. Drizzle with remaining balsamic vinegar mixture.
6. Stir to mix well. Remove the eggplant from the oven. Allow to cool for 5 minutes, then slice them into ½-inch strips on a clean work surface.
7. Add the eggplant strips to the serving bowl, then toss to combine well before serving.

Per Serving
calories: 125 | fat: 2.9g | protein: 5.2g | carbs: 20.9g | fiber: 6.0g | sodium: 222mg

Broccoli and Carrot Pasta Salad

Prep time: 5 minutes | Cook time: 10 minutes | Serves 2

8 ounces (227 g) whole-wheat pasta
2 cups broccoli florets
1 cup peeled and shredded carrots
¼ cup plain Greek yogurt
Juice of 1 lemon
1 teaspoon red pepper flakes
Sea salt and freshly ground pepper, to taste

1. Bring a large pot of lightly salted water to a boil. Add the pasta to the boiling water and cook until al dente, about 8 to 10 minutes. Drain the pasta and let rest for a few minutes.
2. When cooled, combine the pasta with the veggies, yogurt, lemon juice, and red pepper flakes in a large bowl, and stir thoroughly to combine.
3. Taste and season to taste with salt and pepper. Serve immediately.

Per Serving
calories: 428 | fat: 2.9g | protein: 15.9g | carbs: 84.6g | fiber: 11.7g | sodium: 64 2mg

Papaya, Jicama, and Peas Rice Bowl

Prep time: 20 minutes | Cook time: 45 minutes | Serves 4

Sauce:
Juice of ¼ lemon
2 teaspoons chopped fresh basil
1 tablespoon raw honey
1 tablespoon extra-virgin olive oil
Sea salt, to taste

Rice:
1½ cups wild rice
2 papayas, peeled, seeded, and diced
1 jicama, peeled and shredded
1 cup snow peas, julienned 2 cups shredded cabbage 1 scallion, white and green parts, chopped

1. Combine the ingredients for the sauce in a bowl. Stir to mix well. Set aside until ready to use.
2. Pour the wild rice in a saucepan, then pour in enough water to cover. Bring to a boil.
3. Reduce the heat to low, then simmer for 45 minutes or until the wild rice is soft and plump. Drain and transfer to a large serving bowl.
4. Top the rice with papayas, jicama, peas, cabbage, and scallion. Pour the sauce over and stir to mix well before serving.

Per Serving
calories: 446 | fat: 7.9g | protein: 13.1g | carbs: 85.8g | fiber: 16.0g | sodium: 70mg

Lentil and Vegetable Curry Stew

Prep time: 20 minutes | Cook time: 4 hours 7 minutes | Serves 8

1 tablespoon coconut oil
1 yellow onion, diced
¼ cup yellow Thai curry paste
2 cups unsweetened coconut milk
2 cups dry red lentils, rinsed well and drained
3 cups bite-sized cauliflower florets
2 golden potatoes, cut into chunks

2 carrots, peeled and diced
8 cups low-sodium vegetable soup, divided
1 bunch kale, stems removed and roughly chopped
Sea salt, to taste
½ cup fresh cilantro, chopped
Pinch crushed red pepper flakes

1. Heat the coconut oil in a nonstick skillet over medium-high heat until melted. Add the onion and sauté for 5 minutes or until translucent. Pour in the curry paste and sauté for another 2 minutes, then fold in the coconut milk and stir to combine well.
2. Bring to a simmer and turn off the heat.
3. Put the lentils, cauliflower, potatoes, and carrot in the slow cooker. Pour in 6 cups of vegetable soup and the curry mixture. Stir to combine well.
4. Cover and cook on high for 4 hours or until the lentils and vegetables are soft. Stir periodically.
5. During the last 30 minutes, fold the kale into the slow cooker and pour in the remaining vegetable soup. Sprinkle with salt. Pour the stew into a large serving bowl and spread the cilantro and red pepper flakes on top before serving hot.

Per Serving
calories: 530 | fat: 19.2g | protein: 20.3g | carbs: 75.2g | fiber: 15.5g | sodium: 562mg

Chickpea, Vegetable, and Fruit Stew

Prep time: 20 minutes | Cook time: 6 hours 4 minutes | Serves 6

1 large bell pepper, any color, chopped
6 ounces (170 g) green beans, trimmed and cut into bite-size pieces
3 cups canned chickpeas, rinsed and drained
1 (15-ounce / 425-g) can diced tomatoes, with the juice
1 large carrot, cut into ¼-inch rounds
2 large potatoes, peeled and cubed
1 large yellow onion, chopped

1 teaspoon grated fresh ginger
2 garlic cloves, minced
1¾ cups low-sodium vegetable soup
1 teaspoon ground cumin
1 tablespoon ground coriander
¼ teaspoon ground red pepper flakes
Sea salt and ground black pepper, to taste
8 ounces (227 g) fresh baby spinach
¼ cup diced dried figs
¼ cup diced dried apricots
1 cup plain Greek yogurt

1. Place the bell peppers, green beans, chickpeas, tomatoes and juice, carrot, potatoes, onion, ginger, and garlic in the slow cooker. Pour in the vegetable soup and sprinkle with cumin, coriander, red pepper flakes, salt, and ground black pepper. Stir to mix well.
2. Put the slow cooker lid on and cook on high for 6 hours or until the vegetables are soft. Stir periodically.
3. Remove the lid and fold in the spinach, figs, apricots, and yogurt. Stir to mix well.
4. Cook for 4 minutes or until the spinach is wilted. Pour into a large serving bowl. Allow to cool for at least 20 minutes, then serve warm.

Per Serving
calories: 611 | fat: 9.0g | protein: 30.7g | carbs: 107.4g | fiber: 20.8g | sodium: 344m g

Quinoa and Chickpea Vegetable Bowls

Prep time: 20 minutes | Cook time: 15 minutes | Serves 4

1 cup red dry quinoa, rinsed and drained
2 cups low-sodium vegetable soup
2 cups fresh spinach
2 cups finely shredded red cabbage
1 (15-ounce / 425-g) can chickpeas, drained and rinsed
1 ripe avocado, thinly sliced
1 cup shredded carrots
1 red bell pepper, thinly sliced
4 tablespoons Mango Sauce

½ cup fresh cilantro, chopped
Mango Sauce:
1 mango, diced
¼ cup fresh lime juice
½ teaspoon ground turmeric
1 teaspoon finely minced fresh ginger
¼ teaspoon sea salt
Pinch of ground red pepper
1 teaspoon pure maple syrup
2 tablespoons extra-virgin olive oil

1. Pour the quinoa and vegetable soup in a saucepan. Bring to a boil.
2. Reduce the heat to low. Cover and cook for 15 minutes or until tender. Fluffy with a fork. Meanwhile, combine the ingredients for the mango sauce in a food processor. Pulse until smooth.
3. Divide the quinoa, spinach, and cabbage into 4 serving bowls, then top with chickpeas, avocado, carrots, and bell pepper. Dress them with the mango sauce and spread with cilantro. Serve immediately.

Per Serving
calories: 366 | fat: 11.1g | protein: 15.5g | carbs: 55.6g | fiber: 17.7g | sodium: 746mg

Italian Sautééd Cannellini Beans

Prep time: 10 minutes | Cook time: 15 minutes | Serves 6

2 teaspoons extra-virgin olive oil
½ cup minced onion
¼ cup red wine vinegar
1 (12-ounce / 340-g) can no-salt-added tomato paste

2 tablespoons raw honey ½ cup water
¼ teaspoon ground cinnamon
2 (15-ounce / 425-g) cans cannellni beans

1 Heat the olive oil in a saucepan over medium heat until shimmering.
2 Add the onion and sauté for 5 minutes or until translucent.
3 Pour in the red wine vinegar, tomato paste, honey, and water.
4 Sprinkle with cinnamon. Stir to mix well. Reduce the heat to low, then pour all the beans into the saucepan. Cook for 10 more minutes. Stir constantly.
5 Serve immediately.

Per Serving
calories: 435 | fat: 2.1g | protein: 26.2g | carbs: 80.3g | fiber: 24.0g | sodium: 72mg

Wild Rice, Celery, and Cauliflower Pilaf

Prep time: 10 minutes | Cook time: 45 minutes | Serves 4

1 tablespoon olive oil, plus more for greasing the baking dish
1 cup wild rice
2 cups low-sodium chicken broth
1 sweet onion, chopped
2 stalks celery, chopped

1 teaspoon minced garlic
2 carrots, peeled, halved lengthwise, and sliced
½ cauliflower head, cut into small florets
1 teaspoon chopped fresh thyme
Sea salt, to taste

1. Preheat the oven to 350ºF (180ºC). Line a baking sheet with parchment paper and grease with olive oil.
2. Put the wild rice in a saucepan, then pour in the chicken broth. Bring to a boil. Reduce the heat to low and simmer for 30 minutes or until the rice is plump.
3. Meanwhile, heat the remaining olive oil in an oven-proof skillet over medium-high heat until shimmering.
4. Add the onion, celery, and garlic to the skillet and sauté for 3 minutes or until the onion is translucent.
5. Add the carrots and cauliflower to the skillet and sauté for 5 minutes. Turn off the heat and set aside.
6. Pour the cooked rice into the skillet with the vegetables. Sprinkle with thyme and salt.
7. Set the skillet in the preheated oven and bake for 15 minutes or until the vegetables are soft. Serve immediately.

Per Serving
calories: 214 | fat: 3.9g | protein: 7.2g | carbs: 37.9g | fiber: 5.0g | sodium: 122mg

Minestrone Chickpeas and Macaroni Casserole

Prep time: 20 minutes | Cook time: 7 hours 20 minutes | Serves 5

1 (15-ounce / 425-g) can chickpeas, drained and rinsed
1 (28-ounce / 794-g) can diced tomatoes, with the juice
1 (6-ounce / 170-g) can no-salt-added tomato paste
3 medium carrots, sliced
3 cloves garlic, minced
1 medium yellow onion, chopped

1 cup low-sodium vegetable soup
½ teaspoon dried rosemary
1 teaspoon dried oregano
2 teaspoons maple syrup
½ teaspoon sea salt
¼ teaspoon ground black pepper
½ pound (227-g) fresh green beans, trimmed and cut into bite-size pieces
1 cup macaroni pasta
2 ounces (57 g) Parmesan cheese, grated

1. Except for the green beans, pasta, and Parmesan cheese, combine all the ingredients in the slow cooker and stir to mix well. Put the slow cooker lid on and cook on low for 7 hours.
2. Fold in the pasta and green beans. Put the lid on and cook on high for 20 minutes or until the vegetables are soft and the pasta is al dente. Pour into a large serving bowl and spread with Parmesan cheese before serving.

Per Serving
calories: 349 | fat: 6.7g | protein: 16.5g | carbs: 59.9g | fiber: 12.9g | sodium: 937mg

Fava and Garbanzo Bean Ful

Prep time: 10 minutes | Cook time: 10 minutes | Serves 6

1 (15-ounce / 425-g) can fava beans, rinsed and drained
1 (1-pound / 454-g) can garbanzo beans, rinsed and drained
3 cups water

½ cup lemon juice
3 cloves garlic, peeled and minced
1 teaspoon salt
3 tablespoons extra-virgin olive oil

1. In a pot over medium heat, cook the beans and water for 10 minutes.
2. Drain the beans and transfer to a bowl. Reserve 1 cup of the liquid from the cooked beans.
3. Add the reserved liquid, lemon juice, minced garlic and salt to the bowl with the beans. Mix to combine well. Using a potato masher, mash up about half the beans in the bowl.
4. Give the mixture one more stir to make sure the beans are evenly mixed.
5. Drizzle with the olive oil and serve.

Per Serving
calories: 199 | fat: 9.0g | protein: 10.0g | carbs: 25.0g | fiber: 9.0g | sodium: 395mg

Pork and Spinach Spaghetti

Prep time: 15 minutes | Cook time: 16 minutes | Serves 4

2 tablespoons olive oil
½ cup onion, chopped
1 garlic clove, minced
1 pound (454 g) ground pork
2 cups water
1 (14-ounce / 397-g) can diced tomatoes, drained
½ cup sun-dried tomatoes

1 tablespoon dried oregano
1 teaspoon Italian seasoning
1 fresh jalapeño chile, stemmed, seeded, and minced
1 teaspoon salt
8 ounces (227 g) dried spaghetti, halved
1 cup spinach

1. Warm oil on Sauté (low). Add onion and garlic and cook for 2 minutes until softened. Stir in pork and cook for 5 minutes. Stir in jalapeño, water, sun-dried tomatoes, Italian seasoning, oregano, diced tomatoes, and salt with the chicken; mix spaghetti and press to submerge into the sauce.
2. Seal the lid and cook on High Pressure for 9 minutes. Release the pressure quickly. Stir in spinach, close lid again, and simmer on Keep Warm for 5 minutes until spinach is wilted.

Per Serving
calories: 621 | fat: 32.2g | protein: 29.1g | carbs: 53.9g | fiber: 5.9g | sodium: 738mg

Gouda, Beef and Spinach Fettuccine

Prep time: 10 minutes | Cook time: 15 minutes | Serves 6

10 ounces (283 g) ground beef
1 pound (454 g) fettuccine pasta
1 cup gouda cheese, shredded
1 cup fresh spinach, torn
1 medium onion, chopped

2 cups tomatoes, diced
1 tablespoon olive oil
1 teaspoon salt
½ teaspoon ground black pepper

1. Heat the olive oil on Sauté mode in the Instant Pot. Stir-fry the beef and onion for 5 minutes. Add the pasta. Pour enough water to cover and season with salt and pepper. Cook on High Pressure for 5 minutes. Do a quick release. Press Sauté and stir in the tomato and spinach; cook for 5 minutes. Top with gouda to serve.

Per Serving
calories: 493 | fat: 17.7g | protein: 20.6g | carbs: 64.3g | fiber: 9.5g | sodium: 561mg

Cranberry and Almond Quinoa

Prep time: 5 minutes | Cook time: 10 minutes | Serves 2

2 cups water
1 cup quinoa, rinsed ¼ cup salted sunflower seeds

½ cup slivered almonds
1 cup dried cranberries

1. Combine water and quinoa in the Instant Pot. Secure the lid.
2. Select the Manual mode and set the cooking time for 10 minutes at High Pressure.
3. Once cooking is complete, do a quick pressure release.
4. Carefully open the lid.
5. Add sunflower seeds, almonds, and dried cranberries and gently mix until well combined. Serve hot.

Per Serving
calories: 445 | fat: 14.8g | protein: 15.1g | carbs: 64.1g | fiber: 10.2g | sodium: 113mg

Pasta with Gorgonzola, Walnuts, and Thyme

Prep time: 10 minutes | Cook time: 15 minutes | Serves: 4

11 oz (320g) pasta
12 oz(350g) gorgonzola
3.5 oz(100g) heavy whipped cream

3.5 oz (100g) walnuts, coarsely chopped
Thyme
Black pepper
Salt

1. Boil a large pot of water; once boiling, add salt. Slice the gorgonzola and cut it into cubes.
2. In a saucepan, heat the whipped cream for 3 minutes, then add the cubes of gorgonzola.
3. Add a pinch of ground black pepper and a few leaves of thyme. Cook over low heat for another 5 minutes.
4. When the pasta is ready, put it in the pan with the gorgonzola over low heat. Stir to mix and add the chopped walnuts. Serve immediately.

Per Serving
Calories: 83|Carbs: 70.9g|Protein: 30.5g|Fat: 47.5g|Fiber: 3.9g|Sodium: 1035mg

Chickpea Curry

Prep time: 10 minutes | Cook time: 24 minutes | Serves 4

½ cup raw chickpeas
1½ tablespoons cooking oil
½ cup chopped onions
1 bay leaf
½ tablespoon grated garlic
¼ tablespoon grated ginger
¾ cup water

1 cup fresh tomato purée
½ green chili, finely chopped
¼ teaspoon turmeric
½ teaspoon coriander powder
1 teaspoon chili powder
1 cup chopped baby spinach
Salt, to taste
Boiled white rice, for serving

1. Add the oil and onions to the Instant Pot. Sauté for 5 minutes.
2. Stir in ginger, garlic paste, green chili and bay leaf. Cook for 1 minute, then add all the spices.
3. Add the chickpeas, tomato purée and the water to the pot.
4. Cover and secure the lid. Turn its pressure release handle to the sealing position.
5. Cook on the Manual function with High Pressure for 15 minutes.
6. After the beep, do a Natural release for 20 minutes.
7. Stir in spinach and cook for 3 minutes on the Sauté setting.
8. Serve hot with boiled white rice.

Per Serving
calories: 176 | fat: 6.8g | protein: 6.7g | carbs: 24.1g | fiber: 5.1g | sodium: 185mg

Cumin Quinoa Pilaf

Prep time: 5 minutes | Cook time: 5 minutes | Serves 2

2 tablespoons extra virgin olive oil
2 cloves garlic, minced
3 cups water
2 cups quinoa, rinsed
2 teaspoons ground cumin
2 teaspoons turmeric Salt, to taste
1 handful parsley, chopped

1. Press the Sauté button to heat your Instant Pot. Once hot, add the oil and garlic to the pot, stir and cook for 1 minute.
2. Add water, quinoa, cumin, turmeric, and salt, stirring well. Lock the lid. Select the Manual mode and set the cooking time for 1 minute at High Pressure.
3. When the timer beeps, perform a natural pressure release for 10 minutes, then release any remaining pressure. Carefully remove the lid.
4. Fluff the quinoa with a fork. Season with more salt, if needed.
5. Sprinkle the chopped parsley on top and serve.

Per Serving
calories: 384 | fat: 12.3g | protein: 12.8g | carbs: 57.4g | fiber: 6.9g | sodium: 44 8mg

Mint Brown Rice

Prep time: 5 minutes | Cook time: 22 minutes | Serves 2

2 cloves garlic, minced
¼ cup chopped fresh mint, plus more for garnish
1 tablespoon chopped dried chives
1 cup short- or long-grain brown rice
1½ cups water or low-sodium vegetable broth
½ to 1 teaspoon sea salt

1. Place the garlic, mint, chives, rice, and water in the Instant Pot. Stir to combine.
2. Secure the lid. Select the Manual mode and set the cooking time for 22 minutes at High Pressure.
3. Once cooking is complete, do a natural pressure release for 10 minutes, then release any remaining pressure. Carefully open the lid.
4. Add salt to taste and serve garnished with more mint.

Per Serving
calories: 514 | fat: 6.6g | protein: 20.7g | carbs: 80.4g | fiber: 3.3g | sodium: 7 86mg

Pancetta with Garbanzo Beans

Prep time: 10 minutes | Cook time: 38 minutes | Serves 6

3 strips pancetta
1 onion, diced
15 ounces (425 g) canned garbanzo beans
2 cups water
1 cup apple cider
2 garlic cloves, minced
½ cup ketchup
¼ cup sugar
1 teaspoon ground mustard powder
1 teaspoon salt
1 teaspoon black pepper
Fresh parsley, for garnish

1. Cook pancetta in the instant pot for 5 minutes, until crispy, on Sauté mode. Add onion and garlic, and cook for 3 minutes until soft.
2. Mix in garbanzo beans, ketchup, sugar, salt, apple cider, mustard powder, water, and pepper. Seal the lid, press Bean/Chili and cook on High Pressure for 30 minutes. Release pressure naturally for 10 minutes. Serve in bowls garnished with parsley.

Per Serving
calories: 163 | fat: 5.7g | protein: 5.4g | carbs: 22.1g | fiber: 3.7g | sodium: 7 05mg

Spinach and Ricotta Stuffed Pasta Shells

Prep time: 15 minutes | Cook time: 35 minutes | Serves 6

2 cups onion, chopped
1 cup carrot, chopped
3 garlic cloves, minced
3½ tablespoons olive oil,
1 (28-ounce / 794-g) canned tomatoes, crushed
12 ounces (340 g) conchiglie pasta
1 tablespoon olive oil
2 cups ricotta cheese, crumbled
1½ cups feta cheese, crumbled
2 cups spinach, chopped
¾ cup grated pecorino Romano cheese
2 tablespoons chopped fresh chives
1 tablespoon chopped fresh dill
Salt and ground black pepper to taste
1 cup shredded cheddar cheese

1. Warm olive oil on Sauté. Add onion, carrot, and garlic, and cook for 5 minutes until tender. Stir in tomatoes and cook for another 10 minutes.
2. Remove to a bowl and set aside.
3. Wipe the pot with a damp cloth, add pasta and cover with enough water. Seal the lid and cook for 5 minutes on High Pressure. Do a quick release and drain the pasta. Lightly Grease olive oil to a baking sheet.
4. In a bowl, combine feta and ricotta cheese.
5. Add spinach, pecorino romano cheese, dill, and chives, and stir well. Adjust the seasonings. Using a spoon, fill the shells with the mixture. Spread 4 cups tomato sauce on the baking sheet.
6. Place the stuffed shells over with seam-sides down and sprinkle cheddar cheese atop. Use aluminum foil to the cover the baking dish. Pour 1 cup of water in the pot of the pressure cooker and insert the trivet.
7. Lower the baking dish onto the trivet. Seal the lid, and cook for 15 minutes on High Pressure.
8. Do a quick pressure release. Take away the foil. Place the stuffed shells on serving plates and top with tomato sauce before serving.

Per Serving
calories: 730 | fat: 41.5g | protein: 30.0g | carbs: 62.7g | fiber: 10.6g | sodium: 966mg

Chili Halloumi Cheese with Rice

Prep time: 10 minutes | Cook time: 8 minutes | Serves 6

2 cups water
2 tablespoons brown sugar
2 tablespoons rice vinegar
1 tablespoon sweet chili sauce
1 tablespoon olive oil
1 teaspoon fresh minced garlic
20 ounces (567 g) Halloumi cheese, cubed
1 cup rice
¼ cup chopped fresh chives, for garnish

1. Heat the oil on Sauté and fry the halloumi for 5 minutes until golden brown. Set aside.
2. To the pot, add water, garlic, olive oil, vinegar, sugar, soy sauce, and chili sauce and mix well until smooth. Stir in rice noodles. Seal the lid and cook on High Pressure for 3 minutes. Release the pressure quickly. Split the rice between bowls. Top with fried halloumi and sprinkle with fresh chives before serving.

Per Serving
calories: 534 | fat: 34.3g | protein: 24.9g | carbs: 30.1g | fiber: 1.0g | sodium: 652mg

Mediterranean Lentils

Prep time: 7 minutes | Cook time: 24 minutes | Serves 2

1 tablespoon olive oil
1 small sweet or yellow
onion, diced
1 garlic clove, diced
1 teaspoon dried oregano
½ teaspoon ground cumin
½ teaspoon dried parsley

½ teaspoon salt, plus more
as needed
¼ teaspoon freshly ground
black pepper, plus more as
needed
1 tomato, diced
1 cup brown or green lentils
2½ cups vegetable stock
1 bay leaf

1. Set your Instant Pot to Sauté and heat the olive oil until it shimmers. Add the onion and cook for 3 to 4 minutes until soft. Turn off the Instant Pot and add the garlic, oregano, cumin, parsley, salt, and pepper. Cook until fragrant, about 1 minute.
2. Stir in the tomato, lentils, stock, and bay leaf.
3. Lock the lid. Select the Manual mode and set the cooking time for 18 minutes at High Pressure.
4. When the timer beeps, perform a natural pressure release for 10 minutes, then release any remaining pressure. Carefully open the lid. Remove and discard the bay leaf. Taste and season with more salt and pepper, as needed. If there's too much liquid remaining, select Sauté and cook until it evaporates. Serve warm.

Per Serving
calories: 426 | fat: 8.1g | protein: 26.2g | carbs: 63.8g | fiber: 31.0g | sodium: 591mg

Cheesy Tomato Linguine

Prep time: 15 minutes | Cook time: 11 minutes | Serves 4

2 tablespoons olive oil
1 small onion, diced
2 garlic cloves, minced
1 cup cherry tomatoes,
halved
1½ cups vegetable stock
¼ cup julienned basil
leaves
1 teaspoon salt

½ teaspoon ground black
pepper
¼ teaspoon red chili flakes
1 pound (454 g) linguine
noodles, halved
Fresh basil leaves for garnish
½ cup Parmigiano-Reggiano
cheese, grated

1. Warm oil on Sauté. Add onion and Sauté for 2 minutes until soft. Mix garlic and tomatoes and sauté for 4 minutes. To the pot, add vegetable stock, salt, julienned basil, red chili flakes and pepper.
2. Add linguine to the tomato mixture until covered. Seal the lid and cook on High Pressure for 5 minutes.
3. Naturally release the pressure for 5 minutes. Stir the mixture to ensure it is broken down.
4. Divide into plates. Top with basil and Parmigiano-Reggiano cheese and serve.

Per Serving
calories: 311 | fat: 11.3g | protein: 10.3g | carbs: 42.1g | fiber: 1.9g | sodium: 1210mg

Beef and Bean Stuffed Pasta Shells

Prep time: 15 minutes | Cook time: 17 minutes | Serves 4

2 tablespoons olive oil
1 pound (454 g) ground beef
1 pound (454 g) pasta shells
2 cups water
15 ounces (425 g) tomato
sauce
1 (15-ounce / 425-g) can
black beans, drained and
rinsed
15 ounces (425 g) canned
corn, drained (or 2 cups
frozen corn)

10 ounces (283 g) red
enchilada sauce
4 ounces (113 g) diced green
chiles
1 cup shredded mozzarella
cheese
Salt and ground black
pepper to taste Additional
cheese for topping
Finely chopped parsley for
garnish

1. Heat the oil in an instant pot on Sauté (low). Add ground beef and cook for 7 minutes until it starts to brown.
2. Mix in pasta, tomato sauce, enchilada sauce, black beans, water, corn, and green chiles and stir to coat well. Add more water if desired.
3. Seal the lid and cook on High Pressure for 10 minutes. Do a quick Pressure release. Stir mozzarella cheese into the pasta mixture until melted; add black pepper and salt. Garnish with parsley to serve.

Per Serving
calories: 1006 | fat: 30.0g | protein: 53.3g | carbs: 138.9g | fiber: 24.4g | sodium: 1139mg

Roasted Butternut Squash and Rice

Prep time: 15 minutes | Cook time: 15 minutes | Serves 4

½ cup water
2 cups vegetable broth
1 small butternut squash,
peeled and sliced
2 tablespoons olive oil,
divided
1 teaspoon salt

1 teaspoon freshly ground
black pepper
1 cup feta cheese, cubed
1 tablespoon coconut
aminos
2 teaspoons arrowroot
starch
1 cup jasmine rice, cooked

1. Pour the rice and broth in the instant pot and stir to combine. In a bowl, toss butternut squash with 1 tablespoon of olive oil and season with salt and black pepper.
2. In another bowl, mix the remaining olive oil, water and coconut aminos. Toss feta in the mixture, add the arrowroot starch, and toss again to combine well. Transfer to a greased baking dish.
3. Lay a trivet over the rice and place the baking dish on the trivet. Seal the lid and cook on High for 15 minutes. Do a quick pressure release. Fluff the rice with a fork and serve with squash and feta.

Per Serving
calories: 258 | fat: 14.9g | protein: 7.8g | carbs: 23.2g | fiber: 1.2g | sodium: 1180mg

Pesto Pasta

Prep time: 10 minutes | Cook time: 8 minutes | Serves 4 to 6

1 pound (454 g) spaghetti
4 cups fresh basil leaves, stems removed
3 cloves garlic
1 teaspoon salt

½ teaspoon freshly ground black pepper
½ cup toasted pine nuts
¼ cup lemon juice
½ cup grated Parmesan cheese
1 cup extra-virgin olive oil

1. Bring a large pot of salted water to a boil.
2. Add the spaghetti to the pot and cook for 8 minutes.
3. In a food processor, place the remaining ingredients, except for the olive oil, and pulse.
4. While the processor is running, slowly drizzle the olive oil through the top opening. Process until all the olive oil has been added.
5. Reserve ½ cup of the cooking liquid. Drain the pasta and put it into a large bowl. Add the pesto and cooking liquid to the bowl of pasta and toss everything together. Serve immediately.

Per Serving
calories: 1067 | fat: 72.0g | protein: 23.0g | carbs: 91..0g | fiber: 6.0g | sodium: 817mg

Israeli Couscous with Asparagus

Prep time: 5 minutes | Cook time: 25 minutes | Serves 6

1½ pounds (680 g) asparagus spears, ends trimmed and stalks chopped into 1-inch pieces
1 garlic clove, minced
1 tablespoon extra-virgin olive oil
¼ teaspoon freshly ground black pepper

1¾ cups water
1 (8-ounce / 227-g) box uncooked whole-wheat or regular Israeli couscous (about 1⅓ cups)
¼ teaspoon kosher salt
1 cup garlic-and-herb goat cheese, at room temperature

1. Preheat the oven to 425ºF (220ºC).
2. In a large bowl, stir together the asparagus, garlic, oil, and pepper. Spread the asparagus on a large, rimmed baking sheet and roast for 10 minutes, stirring a few times.
3. Remove the pan from the oven, and spoon the asparagus into a large serving bowl. Set aside. While the asparagus is roasting, bring the water to a boil in a medium saucepan.
4. Add the couscous and season with salt, stirring well. Reduce the heat to medium-low. Cover and cook for 12 minutes, or until the water is absorbed.
5. Pour the hot couscous into the bowl with the asparagus. Add the goat cheese and mix thoroughly until completely melted. Serve immediately.

Per Serving
calories: 103 | fat: 2.0g | protein: 6.0g | carbs: 18.0g | fiber: 5.0g | sodium: 343mg

Lentil Risotto

Prep time: 10 minutes | Cook time: 20 minutes | Serves 2

½ tablespoon olive oil
½ medium onion, chopped
½ cup dry lentils, soaked overnight
½ celery stalk, chopped

1 sprig parsley, chopped
½ cup Arborio (short-grain Italian) rice
1 garlic clove, lightly mashed
2 cups vegetable stock

1. Press the Sauté button to heat your Instant Pot.
2. Add the oil and onion to the Instant Pot and sauté for 5 minutes.
3. Add the remaining ingredients to the Instant Pot, stirring well. Secure the lid.
4. Select the Manual mode and set the cooking time for 15 minutes at High Pressure.
5. Once cooking is complete, do a natural pressure release for 20 minutes, then release any remaining pressure. Carefully open the lid.
6. Stir and serve hot.

Per Serving
calories: 261 | fat: 3.6g | protein: 10.6g | carbs: 47.1g | fiber: 8.4g | sodium: 247mg

Orecchiette Broccoli Rabe

Prep time: 20 minutes | Cook time: 15 minutes | Serves: 4

14 oz (400g) orecchiette pasta
2 bunches of broccoli rabe
Lots of garlic
Extra virgin olive oil

Red pepper
Salt
Breadcrumbs (sautéed with olive oil until golden)

1. Wash the broccoli rabe and remove the hard parts of the stem.
2. Place garlic in a pan with olive oil and sauté on medium heat until golden. Add the broccoli rabe and let them cook until soft. Add salt and water as needed.
3. When the broccoli rabes are almost ready, add red pepper. Turn off the heat when the broccoli rabes are soft, remove the garlic, and cut the broccoli into smaller pieces.
4. Bring water to boiling, add salt, and cook the pasta. When the pasta is ready, add it to the pan with the broccoli rabe and quickly sauté, mixing them together. Place on a serving plate and add the golden breadcrumbs on top. Add red pepper to taste.

Per Serving
Calories: 691 | Carbs: 68.6g | Protein: 21g | Fat: 36.3g | Fiber: 4.1g | Sodium: 890mg

Super Cheesy Tagliatelle

Prep time: 10 minutes | Cook time: 20 minutes | Serves 6

¼ cup goat cheese, chevre
¼ cup grated Pecorino cheese
½ cup grated Parmesan
1 cup heavy cream
½ cup grated Gouda

2 tablespoons olive oil
1 tablespoon Italian seasoning mix
1 cup vegetable broth
1 pound (454 g) tagliatelle

1. In a bowl, mix goat cheese, pecorino, Parmesan, and heavy cream. Stir in Italian seasoning. Transfer to your instant pot. Stir in the broth and olive oil.
2. Seal the lid and cook on High Pressure for 4 minutes. Do a quick release.
3. Meanwhile, drop the tagliatelle in boiling water and cook for 6 minutes.
4. Remove the instant pot's lid and stir in the tagliatelle. Top with grated gouda and let simmer for about 10 minutes on Sauté mode.

Per Serving
calories: 511 | fat: 22.0g | protein: 14.5g | carbs: 65.7g | fiber: 9.0g | sodium: 548mg

Red Wine Risotto

Cook time: 25 minutes | Serves 8

1 cup finely shredded Parmigian-Reggiano cheese, divided
2 tsp tomato paste
1 ¾ cups dry red wine
¼ tsp salt

1 ½ cups Italian 'risotto' rice
2 cloves garlic, minced
1 medium onion, freshly chopped
2 tbsp extra-virgin olive oil
4 ½ cups reduced sodium beef broth

1. On medium high heat, bring broth to a simmer in a medium fry pan. Lower heat so broth is steaming but not simmering.
2. On medium-low heat, place a Dutch oven and heat oil. Sauté onions for 5 minutes. Add garlic and cook for 2 minutes. Add rice, mix well, and season with salt.
3. Into rice, add a generous splash of wine and ½ cup of broth. Lower heat to a gentle simmer and cook until liquid is fully absorbed while stirring rice every once in a while.
4. Add another splash of wine and ½ cup of broth. Stirring once in a while.
5. Add tomato paste and stir to mix well.
6. Continue cooking and adding wine and broth until broth is used up.
7. Once done cooking, turn off heat and stir in pepper and ¾ cup cheese.
8. To serve, sprinkle with remaining cheese and enjoy.

Per Serving
Calories : 231; Carbs: 33.9g; Protein: 7.9g; Fat: 5.7g

Mushroom Bolognese

Cook time: 65 minutes | Serves 6

¼ cup chopped fresh parsley
oz Parmigiano-Reggiano cheese, grated
1 tbsp kosher salt
10-oz whole wheat spaghetti, cooked and drained
¼ cup milk
14-oz can whole peeled tomatoes
½ cup white wine

1 tbsp tomato paste
1 tbsp minced garlic
8 cups finely chopped cremini mushrooms
½ lb. ground pork
½ tsp freshly ground black pepper, divided
¾ tsp kosher salt, divided
2 ½ cups chopped onion
1 tbsp olive oil
1 cup boiling water
½-oz dried porcini mushrooms

1. Let porcini stand in a boiling bowl of water for twenty minutes, drain (reserve liquid), rinse and chop. Set aside.
2. On medium high fire, place a Dutch oven with olive oil and cook for ten minutes cook pork, ¼ tsp pepper, ¼ tsp salt and onions. Constantly mix to break ground pork pieces.
3. Stir in ¼ tsp pepper, ¼ tsp salt, garlic and cremini mushrooms.
4. Continue cooking until liquid has evaporated, around fifteen minutes.
5. Stirring constantly, add porcini and sauté for a minute. Stir in wine, porcini liquid, tomatoes, and tomato paste. Let it simmer for forty minutes. Stir occasionally. Pour milk and cook for another two minutes before removing from fire.
6. Stir in pasta and transfer to a serving dish. Garnish with parsley and cheese before serving.

Per Serving
Calories : 358; Carbs: 32.8g; Protein: 21.1g; Fat: 15.4g

Spanish Rice

Prep time: 10 minutes | Cook time: 20 minutes | Serves 4

2 tablespoons extra-virgin olive oil
1 medium onion, finely chopped
1 large tomato, finely diced

2 tablespoons tomato paste
1 teaspoon smoked paprika
1 teaspoon salt
1½ cups basmati rice
3 cups water

1. In a medium pot over medium heat, cook the olive oil, onion, and tomato for 3 minutes.
2. Stir in the tomato paste, paprika, salt, and rice. Cook for 1 minute.
3. Add the water, cover the pot, and turn the heat to low. Cook for 12 minutes.
4. Gently toss the rice, cover, and cook for another 3 minutes.

Per Serving
calories: 328 | fat: 7g | protein: 6g | carbs: 60g | fiber : 2g | sodium: 651mg

Veggie Pasta with Shrimp

Cook time: 5 minutes | Serves 4

2 cups baby spinach
½ tsp salt
2 tbsp fresh lemon juice
2 tbsp extra virgin olive oil
3 tbsp drained capers

¼ cup chopped fresh basil
lb. peeled and deveined large shrimp 4
1 cups zucchini, spirals

1. Divide ingredients into 4 serving plates, top with ¼ cup of spinach, serve and enjoy.

Per Serving
Calories : 51; Carbs: 4.4g; Protein: 1.8g; Fat: 3.4g

Fried Rice

Cook time: 20 minutes | Serves 4

4 cups cold cooked rice
1/2 cup peas
1 medium yellow onion, diced
5 tbsp olive oil
4 oz frozen medium shrimp, thawed, shelled, deveined and chopped finely

6 oz roast pork
2 large eggs
Salt and freshly ground black pepper
1/2 tsp cornstarch

1. Combine the salt, ground black pepper and 1/2 tsp cornstarch, coat the shrimp with it. Chop the roasted pork. Beat the eggs
2. and set aside.
3. Stir-fry the shrimp in a wok on high fire with 1 tbsp heated oil until pink, around 3 minutes. Set the shrimp aside and stir fry the roasted pork briefly. Remove both from the pan.
4. In the same pan, stir-fry the onion until soft. Stir the peas and cook until bright green. Remove both from pan.
5. Add 2 tbsp oil in the same pan; add the cooked rice. Stir and separate the individual grains. Add the beaten eggs, toss the rice. Add the roasted pork, shrimp, vegetables and onion.
6. Toss everything together. Season with salt and pepper to taste.

Per Serving
Calories : 556; Carbs: 60.2g; Protein: 20.2g; Fat: 25.2g

Simple Penne Anti-Pasto

Cook time: 15 minutes | Serves 4

¼ cup pine nuts, toasted
½ cup grated Parmigiano-Reggiano cheese, divided
8oz penne pasta, cooked and drained
16oz jar artichoke hearts drained, sliced, marinated and quartered

17 oz jar drained and chopped sun-dried tomato halves packed in oil
3 oz chopped prosciutto
1/3 cup pesto
½ cup pitted and chopped Kalamata olives
1 medium red bell pepper

1. Slice bell pepper; discard membranes, seeds and stem.
2. On a foiled-lined baking sheet, place bell pepper halves; press down by hand and broil in oven for eight minutes. Remove from oven; put in a sealed bag for 5 minutes before peeling and chopping.
3. Place chopped bell pepper in a bowl and mix in artichokes, tomatoes, prosciutto, pesto and olives. Toss in ¼ cup cheese and pasta.
4. Transfer to a serving dish and garnish with ¼ cup cheese and pine nuts. Serve and enjoy!

Per Serving
Calories : 606; Carbs: 70.3g; Protein: 27.2g; Fat: 27.6g

Tortellini Salad

Cook time: 20 minutes | Serves 12

1 red onion, chopped finely
1 cup sunflower seeds
1 cup raisins
3 heads fresh broccoli, cut into florets

2 tsp cider vinegar
½ cup white sugar
½ cup mayonnaise 20-oz fresh cheese filled tortellini

1. In a large pot of boiling water, cook tortellini according to manufacturer's instructions. Drain and rinse with cold water and set aside.
2. Whisk vinegar, sugar and mayonnaise to create your salad dressing.
3. Mix together in a large bowl red onion, sunflower seeds, raisins, tortellini and broccoli. Pour dressing and toss to coat.
4. Serve and enjoy.

Per Serving
Calories : 272; Carbs: 38.7g; Protein: 5.0g; Fat: 8.1g

Spaghetti with Zucchini, Shrimp, and Saffron

Prep time: 15 minutes | Cook time: 20 minutes | Serves: 4

2 oz (350g) spaghetti
0 oz (300g) zucchini
0 oz (300g) clean shrimp
tails
.150g saffron

Scallions
Milk
White wine
Extra virgin olive oil
Black pepper and salt

- While bringing the water to boil for the pasta, place olive oil and scallions in a pan and let them sauté over medium-low heat.
- When the scallion is golden, add the freshly cut zucchini. Add salt and pepper and cook for a few minutes. Add the shrimp tails and cook, adding some white wine.
- In the meantime, take some boiling water and dissolve the saffron. Add it to the sauce when the wine has completely evaporated. Add a little bit of milk to create a creamy sauce.
- In the meantime, cook the spaghetti, and when ready, toss them in the pan. Mix and serve.

Per Serving
Calories: 794; Carbs: 65g; Protein: 21.9g; Fat: 49.5g

Pasta Salad with Chicken Club

Servings: 6

8 oz corkscrew pasta
3/4 cup Italian dressing
1/4 cup mayonnaise
2 cups roasted chicken, cooked and minced
12 slices of crispy cooked bacon, crumbled

1 cup diced Münster cheese
1 cup chopped celery
1 cup chopped green pepper
8 oz. cherry tomatoes halved
1 avocado, peeled, seeded, and chopped

1. Bring a pot of water to boil. Boil the pasta, occasionally stirring until well-cooked, but firm, 10 to 12 minutes. Drain and rinse with cold water.
2. Beat the Italian dressing and mayonnaise in a large bowl. Stir the pasta, chicken, bacon, Münster cheese, celery, green pepper, cherry tomatoes, and avocado through the vinaigrette until everything is well mixed.

Pomodoro Pasta

Servings: 4

1 pack of 16 angel hair pasta
1/4 cup of olive oil
1/2 onion, minced
4 cloves of chopped garlic
2 cups of Roma tomatoes, diced
2 tablespoons balsamic vinegar

1 low-sodium chicken broth
ground red pepper freshly to taste
ground black pepper to taste
1/4 cup grated Parmesan cheese
2 tablespoons chopped fresh basil

1. Boil water. Cook pasta for 9 minutes; drain.
2. Put the olive oil into a large deep pan over high heat. Fry onions and garlic until light brown. Lower the heat to medium and add tomatoes, vinegar, and chicken. Stir in the red pepper, black pepper, basil, and cooked pasta and mix well with the sauce.
3. Simmer for about 5 minutes and serve garnished with grated cheese.

Sausage Pasta

Servings: 6

3/4 pound of pasta
1 tablespoon of olive oil
1 pound spicy Italian sausage
1 onion, minced
4 cloves of chopped garlic

1 cup chicken broth
1 teaspoon dried basil
1 can diced tomatoes
1 pack (10 oz) of frozen chopped spinach
1/2 cup of grated Parmesan cheese

1. Boil lightly salted water in a large pot, then add pasta and cook until al dente, 8-10 minutes.
2. Drain and set aside.
3. Heat oil and sausage in a large skillet; cook until pink. Add onion and garlic to the skillet during the last 5 minutes of cooking. Add the stock, basil, and tomatoes with the liquid.
4. Simmer over medium heat for 5 minutes to reduce slightly. Add the chopped spinach; cover the pan and simmer over low heat until the spinach is soft.
5. Add pasta and mix. Sprinkle with cheese and serve immediately.

Milanese Chicken

Servings: 4

½ cup of sun-dried tomatoes, minced
1 cup of chicken broth, divided
1 cup thick cream
1 pound skinless and skinless chicken fillet
1 tablespoon butter
cloves of garlic, minced

2 tablespoons chopped fresh basil 8 grams of dry fettuccine
salt and pepper to taste
2 tablespoons vegetable oil

1. Season chicken fillet with garlic and allow to simmer for 30 seconds. Add tomatoes and 3/4 cup chicken broth, and keep heating on medium heat. Once the liquid starts to boil, reduce the heat and simmer for about 10 minutes without a lid or until the tomatoes are soft.
2. Add the cream and keep simmering until the sauce thickens. Season chicken with salt and pepper the chicken on both sides. Heat oil in a large frying pan over medium-high heat and fry the chicken. Press the chicken occasionally with a slotted spatula. Bake for about 4 minutes per side. Set aside, cover, and keep warm. Discard the fat from the pan.
3. In the same pan, bring to a boil 1/4 cup chicken broth over medium heat. Reduce slightly and add to the cream sauce; stir in the basil and adjust the seasonings to taste.
4. Meanwhile, boil a large pot with lightly salted water. Add fettuccine and cook for about 8 to 10 minutes or until al dente; drain, transfer to a bowl and mix with 3 to 4 tablespoons of sauce. Cut chicken fillet into 4 diagonal slices. Heat the sauce carefully if necessary. Transfer the pasta to plates; garnish with chicken and sprinkle with cream sauce to serve.

Shrimp Scampi with Pasta

Servings: 6

1 pack of linguine (16 oz)
2 tablespoons butter
2 tablespoons extra virgin olive oil
2 chopped shallots
2 cloves of chopped garlic
1 pinch of red pepper flakes
1 pound of shrimp, peeled and thawed

1 pinch of kosher salt and pepper
1/2 cup of dry white wine
1 lemon, juiced
2 tablespoons butter
2 tablespoons extra virgin olive oil
1/4 cup fresh parsley leaves
1 teaspoon extra virgin olive oil

1. Boil water; add linguine and cook in boiling water for 6 to 8 minutes until soft. Drain.
2. Melt 2 tbsp of butter in a large frying pan followed by 2 tablespoons of olive oil over medium-high heat. Lightly fry the shallots, garlic, and red pepper flakes in the hot butter and oil until the shallots are transparent, 3 to 4 minutes. Season the shrimp with kosher salt and black pepper; add to the pan and cook until pink, occasionally stirring, 2 to 3 minutes. Remove the shrimp from the skillet and keep them warm.
3. Pour the white wine and lemon juice into the pan and bring to a boil. Melt 2 tablespoons of butter in a pan, mix 2 tablespoons of olive oil and let it simmer. Mix the linguine, shrimp, and parsley in the butter mixture until everything is well covered; season with salt and black pepper. Drizzle with 1 teaspoon of olive oil to serve.

Bow Ties with Sausages, Tomatoes, & Cream

Servings: 6

1 package of bowtie pasta
2 tablespoons of olive oil
1 pound of sweet Italian sausages, crumbled
1/2 teaspoon of red pepper flakes
1/2 cup diced onion

3 finely chopped garlic cloves
1 can of Italian tomatoes, drained and roughly chopped
1 1/2 cups whipped cream
1/2 teaspoon salt
3 tablespoons fresh parsley

1. Bring a large pot of lightly salted water to a boil. Cook the pasta for 8 to 10 minutes in boiling water or until al dente; drain.
2. Heat the oil in a deep frying pan over medium heat.
3. Cook the sausages and chili flakes until the sausages are golden brown.
4. Cook the onion until soft. Stir in the tomatoes, cream, and salt. Simmer until thickened, 8 to 10 minutes. Add the pasta to the sauce and heat. Sprinkle with parsley.

Pasta Fazool (Pasta e Fagioli)

Servings: 2

1 tablespoon of olive oil
12 ounces of sweet Italian sausage
1 celery stem, diced
1/2 yellow onion, chopped
3/4 cup dry macaroni
1/4 cup tomato puree
3 cups chicken broth or more if necessary, divided

salt and freshly ground black pepper
1/4 teaspoon of ground red pepper flakes
1/4 teaspoon dried oregano
3 cups finely chopped chard
1 can cannellini (15 oz), drained
1/4 cup grated Parmigia-no-Reggiano cheese

1. Heat the oil in a frying pan over medium heat. Brown the sausage by cutting it into small pieces, about 5 minutes. Return the heat to medium. Add diced celery and chopped onion. Bake until the onions are transparent, 4 to 5 minutes. Add the dry pasta. Boil and stir for 2 minutes.
2. Stir the tomato puree until smooth, 2 to 3 minutes. Add 3 cups of broth.
3. Season with salt, black pepper, pepper flakes, and oregano.
4. Lower heat once soup comes to a boil, then let it simmer for about 5 minutes, often stirring. Check the consistency of the soup and add stock if necessary.
5. Place the chopped chard in a bowl and soak with cold water to rinse the leaves; some grains will fall to the bowl's bottom. Put the chard in a colander to drain briefly; add to the soup. Boil and stir until the leaves fade, 2 to 3 minutes.
6. Stir in the white beans; keep cooking, stir until the pasta is cooked, 4 or 5 minutes. Remove from heat and stir in the grated cheese. Serve garnished with grated cheese, if desired.

Chapter 5
Vegetable Mains

Stir-Fried Eggplant

Prep time: 25 minutes | Cook time: 15 minutes | Serves 2

1 cup water, plus more as needed
½ cup chopped red onion
1 tablespoon finely chopped garlic
1 tablespoon dried Italian herb seasoning
1 teaspoon ground cumin
1 small eggplant (about 8 ounces / 227 g), peeled and cut into ½-inch cubes

1 medium carrot, sliced
2 cups green beans, cut into 1-inch pieces
2 stalks celery, sliced
1 cup corn kernels
2 tablespoons almond butter
2 medium tomatoes, chopped

1. Heat 1 tablespoon of water in a large soup pot over medium-high heat until it sputters.
2. Cook the onion for 2 minutes, adding a little more water as needed.
3. Add the garlic, Italian seasoning, cumin, and eggplant and stir-fry for 2 to 3 minutes, adding a little more water as needed.
4. Add the carrot, green beans, celery, corn kernels, and ½ cup of water and stir well. Reduce the heat to medium, cover, and cook for 8 to 10 minutes, stirring occasionally, or until the vegetables are tender.
5. Meanwhile, in a bowl, stir together the almond butter and ½ cup of water.
6. Remove the vegetables from the heat and stir in the almond butter mixture and chopped tomatoes. Cool for a few minutes before serving.

Per Serving
calories: 176 | fat: 5.5g | protein: 5.8g | carbs: 25.4g | fiber: 8.6g | sodium: 198mg

Garlic-Butter Asparagus with Parmesan

Prep time: 5 minutes | Cook time: 8 minutes | Serves 2

1 cup water
1 pound (454 g) asparagus, trimmed
2 cloves garlic, chopped
3 tablespoons almond butter

Salt and ground black pepper, to taste
3 tablespoons grated Parmesan cheese

1. Pour the water into the Instant Pot and insert a trivet. Put
2. the asparagus on a tin foil and add the butter and garlic. Season to taste with salt and pepper.
3. Fold over the foil and seal the asparagus inside so the foil doesn't come open. Arrange the asparagus on the trivet.
4. Secure the lid. Select the Manual mode and set the cooking time for 8 minutes at High Pressure. Once cooking is complete, do a quick pressure release.
5. Carefully open the lid. Unwrap the foil packet and serve sprinkled with the Parmesan cheese.

Per Serving
calories: 243 | fat: 15.7g | protein: 12.3g | carbs: 15.3g | fiber: 7.3g | sodium: 435mg

Caponata

Prep time: 40 minutes | Cook time: 40 minutes | Serves: 4

3 eggplants (roughly 2 pounds)
4 large peppers (roughly 2 pounds)
2 pounds of ripe tomatoes
1 stalk celery
1 onion, diced

A jar of green olives
Basil
4 tablespoons of vinegar
1 tablespoon of sugar
Corn oil for frying
Extra virgin olive oil
3 tablespoons of capers

1. Cut the eggplants into cubes, salt them, and let them release water for a few hours.
2. Cut the peppers into cubes and fry them. Rinse the eggplant cubes, dry them, and fry them.
3. Cut the celery and quickly steam it.
4. Sauté the onion with extra virgin olive oil and add the celery. When golden, add the tomatoes, diced. Add the basil and let it cook on medium heat.
5. Add the vinegar and sugar. When the sauce is getting thick, add the olives and capers.
6. Finally, add the fried eggplants and peppers. Mix and let it flavor for a little bit.

Per Serving
Calories: 553 | Carbs: 31.7g | Protein: 10.3g | Fat: 42.7g | Fiber: 10.9g | Sodium: 702mg

Cauliflower with Sweet Potato

Prep time: 15 minutes | Cook time: 8 minutes | Serves 8

1 small onion
4 tomatoes
4 garlic cloves, chopped
2-inch ginger, chopped
2 teaspoons olive oil
1 teaspoon turmeric
2 teaspoons ground cumin
Salt, to taste

1 teaspoon paprika
2 medium sweet potatoes, cut into small cubes
2 small cauliflowers, diced
2 tablespoons fresh cilantro for topping, chopped

1. Blend the tomatoes, garlic, ginger and onion in a blender.
2. Add the oil and cumin in the instant pot and Sauté for 1 minute.
3. Stir in the blended mixture and the remaining spices.
4. Add the sweet potatoes and cook for 5 minutes on Sauté.
5. Add the cauliflower chunks and secure the lid.
6. Cook on Manual for 2 minutes at High Pressure.
7. Once done, Quick release the pressure and remove the lid.
8. Stir and serve with cilantro on top.

Per Serving
calories: 76 | fat: 1.6g | protein: 2.7g | carbs: 14.4g | fiber: 3.4g | sodium: 55mg

Lentils and Eggplant Curry

Prep time: 10 minutes | Cook time: 22 minutes | Serves 4

¾ cup lentils, soaked and rinsed
1 teaspoon olive oil
½ onion, chopped
4 garlic cloves, chopped
1 teaspoon ginger, chopped
1 hot green chili, chopped
¼ teaspoon turmeric
½ teaspoon ground cumin

2 tomatoes, chopped
1 cup eggplant, chopped
1 cup sweet potatoes, cubed
¾ teaspoon salt
2 cups water
1 cup baby spinach leaves
Cayenne and lemon/lime to taste
Pepper flakes (garnish)

1. Add the oil, garlic, ginger, chili and salt into the instant pot and Sauté for 3 minutes.
2. Stir in the tomatoes and all the spices. Cook for 5 minutes.
3. Add all the remaining ingredients, except the spinach leaves and garnish.
4. Secure the lid and cook on Manual function for 12 minutes at High Pressure.
5. After the beep, release the pressure naturally and remove the lid. Stir in the spinach leaves and let the pot simmer for 2 minutes on Sauté.
6. Garnish with the pepper flakes and serve warm.

Per Serving
calories: 88 | fat: 1.5g | protein: 3.4g | carbs: 17.4g | fiber : 3.3g | sodium: 470mg

Sweet Potato and Tomato Curry

Prep time: 5 minutes | Cook time: 8 minutes | Serves 8

2 large brown onions, finely diced
4 tablespoons olive oil
4 teaspoons salt
4 large garlic cloves, diced
1 red chili, sliced
4 tablespoons cilantro, chopped
4 teaspoons ground cumin

2 teaspoons ground coriander
2 teaspoons paprika
2 pounds (907 g) sweet potato, diced
4 cups chopped, tinned tomatoes
2 cups water
2 cups vegetable stock
Lemon juice and cilantro (garnish)

1. Put the oil and onions into the instant pot and Sauté for 5 minutes.
2. Stir in the remaining ingredients and secure the lid. Cook on
3. Manual function for 3 minutes at High Pressure. Once done,
4. Quick release the pressure and remove the lid.
5. Garnish with cilantro and lemon juice.
6. Serve.

Per Serving
calories: 224 | fat: 8.0g | protein: 4.6g | carbs: 35.9g | fiber: 7.5g | sodium: 1385mg

Cabbage Stuffed Acorn Squash

Prep time: 15 minutes | Cook time: 23 minutes | Serves 4

½ tablespoon olive oil
2 medium acorn squashes
¼ small yellow onion, chopped
1 jalapeño pepper, chopped
½ cup green onions, chopped
½ cup carrots, chopped
¼ cup cabbage, chopped
1 garlic clove, minced

½ (6-ounce / 170-g) can sugar-free tomato sauce
½ tablespoon chili powder
½ tablespoon ground cumin
Salt and freshly ground black pepper to taste
2 cups water
¼ cup cheddar cheese, shredded

1. Pour the water into the instant pot and place the trivet inside. Slice the squash into 2 halves and remove the seeds. Place over the trivet, skin side down, and sprinkle some salt and pepper over it.
2. Secure the lid and cook on Manual for 15 minutes at High Pressure.
3. Release the pressure naturally and remove the lid. Empty the pot into a bowl.
4. Now add the oil, onion, and garlic in the instant pot and Sauté for 5 minutes.
5. Stir in the remaining vegetables and stir-fry for 3 minutes.
6. Add the remaining ingredients and secure the lid. Cook on Manual function for 2 minutes at High Pressure.
7. After the beep, natural release the pressure and remove the lid.
8. Stuff the squashes with the prepared mixture and serve warm.

Per Serving
calories: 163 | fat: 5.1g | protein: 4.8g | carbs: 28.4g | fiber : 4.9g | sodium: 146m g

Quick Steamed Broccoli

Prep time: 5 minutes | Cook time: 10 minutes | Serves 2

¼ cup water
3 cups broccoli florets

Salt and ground black pepper, to taste

1. Pour the water into the Instant Pot and insert a steamer basket. Place the broccoli florets in the basket. Secure the lid.
2. Select the Manual mode and set the cooking time for 10 minutes at High Pressure.
3. Once cooking is complete, do a quick pressure release. Carefully open the lid.
4. Transfer the broccoli florets to a bowl with cold water to keep bright green color.
5. Season the broccoli with salt and pepper to taste, then serve.

Per Serving
calories: 16 | fat: 0.2g | protein: 1.9g | carbs: 1.7g | fiber : 1.6g | sodium: 292mg

Chickpea Lettuce Wraps with Celery

Prep time: 10 minutes | Cook time: 0 minutes | Serves 4

*1 (15-ounce / 425-g) can
low-sodium chickpeas,
drained and rinsed
1 celery stalk, thinly sliced
2 tablespoons finely
chopped red onion*

*2 tablespoons unsalted
tahini
3 tablespoons honey
mustard
1 tablespoon capers,
undrained
12 butter lettuce leaves*

1. In a bowl, mash the chickpeas with a potato masher or the back of a fork until mostly smooth.
2. Add the celery, red onion, tahini, honey mustard, and capers to the bowl and stir until well incorporated.
3. For each serving, place three overlapping lettuce leaves on a plate and top with ¼ of the mashed chickpea filling, then roll up. Repeat with the remaining lettuce leaves and chickpea mixture.

Per Serving
calories: 182 | fat: 7.1g | protein: 10.3g | carbs: 19.6g | fiber: 3.0g | sodium: 171mg

Honey-Glazed Baby Carrots

Prep time: 5 minutes | Cook time: 6 minutes | Serves 2

*⅔ cup water
1½ pounds (680 g) baby
carrots
4 tablespoons almond
butter*

*½ cup honey
1 teaspoon dried thyme
1½ teaspoons dried dill Salt,
to taste*

1. Pour the water into the Instant Pot and add a steamer basket.
2. Place the baby carrots in the basket.
3. Secure the lid. Select the Manual mode and set the cooking time for 4 minutes at High Pressure.
4. Once cooking is complete, do a quick pressure release. Carefully open the lid.
5. Transfer the carrots to a plate and set aside.
6. Pour the water out of the Instant Pot and dry it.
7. Press the Sauté button on the Instant Pot and heat the almond butter.
8. Stir in the honey, thyme, and dill.
9. Return the carrots to the Instant Pot and stir until well coated. Sauté for another 1 minute.
10. Taste and season with salt as needed. Serve warm.

Per Serving
calories: 575 | fat: 23.5g | protein: 2.8g | carbs: 90.6g | fiber: 10.3g | sodium: 547mg

Cauliflower Hash with Carrots

Prep time: 10 minutes | Cook time: 10 minutes | Serves 4

*3 tablespoons extra-virgin
olive oil
1 large onion, chopped
1 tablespoon minced garlic*

*2 cups diced carrots
4 cups cauliflower florets
½ teaspoon ground cumin
1 teaspoon salt*

1. In a large skillet, heat the olive oil over medium heat.
2. Add the onion and garlic and sauté for 1 minute. Stir in the carrots and stir-fry for 3 minutes.
3. Add the cauliflower florets, cumin, and salt and toss to combine.
4. Cover and cook for 3 minutes until lightly browned. Stir well and cook, uncovered, for 3 to 4 minutes, until softened. Remove from the heat and serve warm.

Per Serving
calories: 158 | fat: 10.8g | protein: 3.1g | carbs: 14.9g | fiber: 5.1g | sodium: 656mg

Butternut Noodles with Mushrooms

Prep time: 10 minutes | Cook time: 12 minutes | Serves 4

*¼ cup extra-virgin olive oil
1 pound (454 g) cremini
mushrooms, sliced
½ red onion, finely chopped
1 teaspoon dried thyme
½ teaspoon sea salt*

*3 garlic cloves, minced
½ cup dry white wine
Pinch of red pepper flakes
4 cups butternut noodles
4 ounces (113 g) grated
Parmesan cheese*

1. In a large skillet over medium-high heat, heat the olive oil until shimmering. Add the mushrooms, onion, thyme, and salt to the skillet. Cook for about 6 minutes, stirring occasionally, or until the mushrooms start to brown. Add the garlic and sauté for 30 seconds. Stir in the white wine and red pepper flakes.
2. Fold in the noodles. Cook for about 5 minutes, stirring occasionally, or until the noodles are tender. Serve topped with the grated Parmesan.

Per Serving
calories: 244 | fat: 14.0g | protein: 4.0g | carbs: 22.0g | fiber: 4.0g | sodium: 159mg

Roasted Veggies and Brown Rice Bowl

Prep time: 15 minutes | Cook time: 20 minutes | Serves 4

*2 cups cauliflower florets
2 cups broccoli florets
1 (15-ounce / 425-g) can
chickpeas, drained and rinsed
1 cup carrot slices (about 1
inch thick)
2 to 3 tablespoons extra-virgin olive oil, divided
Salt and freshly ground black
pepper, to taste
Nonstick cooking spray*

*2 cups cooked brown rice
2 to 3 tablespoons sesame
seeds, for garnish
Dressing: 3 to 4 tablespoons
tahini
2 tablespoons honey
1 lemon, juiced
1 garlic clove, minced
Salt and freshly ground
black pepper, to taste*

1. Preheat the oven to 400ºF (205ºC). Spritz two baking sheets with nonstick cooking spray.
2. Spread the cauliflower and broccoli on the first baking sheet and the second with the chickpeas and carrot slices. Drizzle
3. each sheet with half of the olive oil and sprinkle with salt and pepper. Toss to coat well.
4. Roast the chickpeas and carrot slices in the preheated oven for 10 minutes, leaving the carrots tender but crisp, and the cauliflower and broccoli for 20 minutes until fork-tender. Stir them once halfway through the cooking time.
5. Meanwhile, make the dressing: Whisk together the tahini, honey, lemon juice, garlic, salt, and pepper in a small bowl.
6. Divide the cooked brown rice among four bowls. Top each bowl evenly with roasted vegetables an d dressing. Sprinkle the sesame seeds on top for garnish before serving.

Per Serving
calories: 453 | fat: 17.8g | protein: 12.1g | carbs: 61.8g | fiber: 11.2g | sodium: 60mg

Zucchini Fritters

Prep time: 15 minutes | Cook time: 5 minutes | Makes 14 fritters

4 cups grated zucchini Salt, to taste
2 large eggs, lightly beaten
⅓ cup sliced scallions (green and white parts)
⅔ all-purpose flour
⅛ teaspoon black pepper
2 tablespoons olive oil

1. Put the grated zucchini in a colander and lightly season with salt. Set aside to rest for 10 minutes. Squeeze out as much liquid from the grated zucchini as possible.
2. Pour the grated zucchini into a bowl. Fold in the beaten eggs, scallions, flour, salt, and pepper and stir until everything is well combined.
3. Heat the olive oil in a large skillet over medium heat until hot.
4. Drop 3 tablespoons mounds of the zucchini mixture onto the hot skillet to make each fritter, pressing them lightly into rounds and spacing them about 2 inches apart.
5. Cook for 2 to 3 minutes. Flip the zucchini fritters and cook for 2 minutes more, or until they are golden brown and cooked through.
6. Remove from the heat to a plate lined with paper towels.
7. Repeat with the remaining zucchini mixture. Serve hot.

Per Serving
calories: 113 | fat: 6.1g | protein: 4.0g | carbs: 12.2g | fiber: 1.0g | sodium: 25mg

Moroccan Tagine with Vegetables

Prep time: 20 minutes | Cook time: 40 minutes | Serves 2

2 tablespoons olive oil
½ onion, diced
1 garlic clove, minced
2 cups cauliflower florets
1 medium carrot, cut into 1-inch pieces
1 cup diced eggplant
1 (28-ounce / 794-g) can whole tomatoes with their juices
1 (15-ounce / 425-g) can chickpeas, drained and rinsed
2 small red potatoes, cut into 1-inch pieces
1 cup water
1 teaspoon pure maple syrup
½ teaspoon cinnamon
½ teaspoon turmeric
1 teaspoon cumin
½ teaspoon salt
1 to 2 teaspoons harissa paste

1. In a Dutch oven, heat the olive oil over medium-high heat. Sauté the onion for 5 minutes, stirring occasionally, or until the onion is translucent.
2. Stir in the garlic, cauliflower florets, carrot, eggplant, tomatoes, and potatoes. Use a wooden spoon or spatula to break up the tomatoes into smaller pieces.
3. Add the chickpeas, water, maple syrup, cinnamon, turmeric, cumin, and salt and stir to incorporate. Bring the mixture to a boil.
4. Once it starts to boil, reduce the heat to medium-low. Stir in the harissa paste, cover, allow to simmer for about 40 minutes, or until the vegetables are softened. Taste and adjust seasoning as needed.
5. Let the mixture cool for 5 minutes before serving.

Per Serving
calories: 293 | fat: 9.9g | protein: 11.2g | carbs: 45.5g | fiber: 12.1g | sodium: 337mg

Vegan Lentil Bolognese

Prep time: 15 minutes | Cook time: 50 minutes | Serves 2

1 medium celery stalk
1 large carrot
½ large onion
1 garlic clove
2 tablespoons olive oil
1 (28-ounce / 794-g) can crushed tomatoes
1 cup red wine
½ teaspoon salt, plus more as needed
½ teaspoon pure maple syrup
1 cup cooked lentils (prepared from ½ cup dry)

1. Add the celery, carrot, onion, and garlic to a food processor and process until everything is finely chopped.
2. In a Dutch oven, heat the olive oil over medium-high heat. Add the chopped mixture and sauté for about 10 minutes, stirring occasionally, or until the vegetables are lightly browned.
3. Stir in the tomatoes, wine, salt, and maple syrup and bring to a boil.
4. Once the sauce starts to boil, cover, and reduce the heat to medium-low. Simmer for 30 minutes, stirring occasionally, or until the vegetables are softened.
5. Stir in the cooked lentils and cook for an additional 5 minutes until warmed through.
6. Taste and add additional salt, if needed. Serve warm.

Per Serving
calories: 367 | fat: 15.0g | protein: 13.7g | carbs: 44.5g | fiber: 17.6g | sodium: 1108mg

Stir-Fry Baby Bok Choy

Prep time: 12 minutes | Cook time: 10 to 13 minutes | Serves 6

2 tablespoons coconut oil
1 large onion, finely diced
2 teaspoons ground cumin
1-inch piece fresh ginger, grated
1 teaspoon ground turmeric
½ teaspoon salt
12 baby bok choy heads, ends trimmed and sliced lengthwise
Water, as needed
3 cups cooked brown rice

1. Heat the coconut oil in a large pan over medium heat. Sauté the onion for 5 minutes, stirring occasionally, or until the onion is translucent. Fold in the cumin, ginger, turmeric, and salt and stir to coat well.
2. Add the bok choy and cook for 5 to 8 minutes, stirring occasionally, or until the bok choy is tender but crisp. You can add 1 tablespoon of water at a time, if the skillet gets dry while sautéing.
3. Transfer the bok choy to a plate and serve over the cooked brown rice.

Per Serving
calories: 443 | fat: 8.8g | protein: 30.3g | carbs: 75.7g | fiber: 19.0g | sodium: 1289mg

Zoodles

Prep time: 10 minutes | Cook time: 5 minutes | Serves 2

2 tablespoons avocado oil
2 medium zucchini, spiralized
¼ teaspoon salt
Freshly ground black pepper, to taste

1. Heat the avocado oil in a large skillet over medium heat until it shimmers.
2. Add the zucchini noodles, salt, and black pepper to the skillet and toss to coat. Cook for 1 to 2 minutes, stirring constantly, until tender.
3. Serve warm.

Per Serving
calories: 128 | fat: 14.0g | protein: 0.3g | carbs: 0.3g | fiber: 0.1g | sodium: 291mg

Sweet Pepper Stew

Prep time: 20 minutes | Cook time: 50 minutes | Serves 2

2 tablespoons olive oil
2 sweet peppers, diced (about 2 cups)
½ large onion, minced
1 garlic clove, minced
1 tablespoon gluten-free Worcestershire sauce

1 teaspoon oregano
1 cup low-sodium tomato juice
1 cup low-sodium vegetable stock
¼ cup brown rice
¼ cup brown lentils
Salt, to taste

1. In a Dutch oven, heat the olive oil over medium-high heat.
2. Sauté the sweet peppers and onion for 10 minutes, stirring occasionally, or until the onion begins to turn golden and the peppers are wilted.
3. Stir in the garlic, Worcestershire sauce, and oregano and cook for 30 seconds more. Add the tomato juice, vegetable stock, rice, and lentils to the Dutch oven and stir to mix well. Bring the mixture to a boil and then reduce the heat to medium-low. Let it simmer covered for about 45 minutes, or until the rice is cooked through and the lentils are tender. Sprinkle with salt and serve warm.

Per Serving
calories: 378 | fat: 15.6g | protein: 11.4g | carbs: 52.8g | fiber: 7.0g | sodium: 391mg

Roasted Cauliflower and Carrots

Prep time: 10 minutes | Cook time: 30 minutes | Serves 2

4 cups cauliflower florets (about ½ small head)
2 medium carrots, peeled, halved, and then sliced into quarters lengthwise
2 tablespoons olive oil, divided
½ teaspoon salt, divided
½ teaspoon garlic powder, divided

2 teaspoons za'atar spice mix, divided
1 (15-ounce / 425-g) can chickpeas, drained, rinsed, and patted dry
¾ cup plain Greek yogurt
1 teaspoon harissa spice paste, plus additional as needed

1. Preheat the oven to 400ºF (205ºC). Line a sheet pan with foil or parchment paper.
2. Put the cauliflower and carrots in a large bowl. Drizzle with 1 tablespoon of olive oil and sprinkle with ¼ teaspoon of salt, ¼ teaspoon of garlic powder, and 1 teaspoon of za'atar. Toss to combine well.
3. Spread the vegetables onto one half of the prepared sheet pan in a single layer.
4. Put the chickpeas in the same bowl and season with the remaining 1 tablespoon of olive oil, ¼ teaspoon of salt, ¼ teaspoon of garlic powder, and the remaining 1 teaspoon of za'atar. Toss to combine well. Spread the chickpeas onto the other half of the sheet pan.
5. Roast in the preheated oven for 30 minutes, or until the vegetables are crisp-tender. Flip the vegetables halfway through and give the chickpeas a stir so they cook evenly.
6. Meanwhile, whisk the yogurt and harissa together in a small bowl. Taste and add additional harissa as needed. Serve the vegetables and chickpeas with the yogurt mixture on the side.

Per Serving
calories: 468 | fat: 23.0g | protein: 18.1g | carbs: 54.1g | fiber: 13.8g | sodium: 631mg

Zoodles with Beet Pesto

Prep time: 10 minutes | Cook time: 50 minutes | Serves 2

1 medium red beet, peeled, chopped
½ cup walnut pieces
½ cup crumbled goat cheese
3 garlic cloves
2 tablespoons freshly squeezed lemon juice

2 tablespoons plus 2 teaspoons extra-virgin olive oil, divided
¼ teaspoon salt
4 small zucchinis, spiralized

1. Preheat the oven to 375ºF (190ºC).
2. Wrap the chopped beet in a piece of aluminum foil and seal well.
3. Roast in the preheated oven for 30 to 40 minutes until tender.
4. Meanwhile, heat a skillet over medium-high heat until hot. Add the walnuts and toast for 5 to 7 minutes, or until fragrant and lightly browned.
5. Remove the cooked beets from the oven and place in a food processor.
6. Add the toasted walnuts, goat cheese, garlic, lemon juice, 2 tablespoons of olive oil, and salt. Pulse until smoothly blended. Set aside. Heat the remaining 2 teaspoons of olive oil in a large skillet over medium heat. Add the zucchini and toss to coat in the oil. Cook for 2 to 3 minutes, stirring gently, or until the zucchini is softened. Transfer the zucchini to a serving plate and toss with the beet pesto, then serve.

Per Serving
calories: 423 | fat: 38.8g | protein: 8.0g | carbs: 17.1g | fiber: 6.0g | sodium: 338mg

Fried Eggplant Rolls

Prep time: 20 minutes | Cook time: 10 minutes | Serves 4 to 6

1 large eggplants, trimmed and cut lengthwise into ¼-inch-thick slices
1 teaspoon salt
1 cup ricotta cheese

4 ounces (113 g) goat cheese, shredded
¼ cup finely chopped fresh basil
½ teaspoon freshly ground black pepper
Olive oil spray

1. Add the eggplant slices to a colander and season with salt. Set aside for 15 to 20 minutes.
2. Mix together the ricotta and goat cheese, basil, and black pepper in a large bowl and stir to combine. Set aside.
3. Dry the eggplant slices with paper towels and lightly mist them with olive oil spray.
4. Heat a large skillet over medium heat and lightly spray it with olive oil spray.
5. Arrange the eggplant slices in the skillet and fry each side for 3 minutes until golden brown.
6. Remove from the heat to a paper towel-lined plate and rest for 5 minutes.
7. Make the eggplant rolls: Lay the eggplant slices on a flat work surface and top each slice with a tablespoon of the prepared cheese mixture. Roll them up and serve immediately.

Per Serving
calories: 254 | fat: 14.9g | protein: 15.3g | carbs: 18.6g | fiber: 7.1g | sodium: 745mg

Mushroom and Spinach Stuffed Peppers

Prep time: 15 minutes | Cook time: 8 minutes | Serves 7

7 mini sweet peppers
1 cup button mushrooms, minced
5 ounces (142 g) organic baby spinach
½ teaspoon fresh garlic

½ teaspoon coarse sea salt
¼ teaspoon cracked mixed pepper
2 tablespoons water
1 tablespoon olive oil
1 cup organic mozzarella cheese, diced

1. Put the sweet peppers and water in the instant pot and Sauté for 2 minutes.
2. Remove the peppers and put the olive oil into the pot. Stir in the mushrooms, garlic, spices and spinach. Cook on Sauté until the mixture is dry.
3. Stuff each sweet pepper with the cheese and spinach mixture.
4. Bake the stuffed peppers in an oven for 6 minutes at 400ºF (205ºC).
5. Once done, serve hot.

Per Serving
calories: 81 | fat: 2.4g | protein: 4.1g | carbs: 13.2g | fiber: 2.4g | sodium: 217mg

Cheesy Sweet Potato Burgers

Prep time: 10 minutes | Cook time: 19 to 20 minutes | Serves 4

1 large sweet potato (about 8 ounces / 227 g)
2 tablespoons extra-virgin olive oil, divided
1 cup chopped onion
1 large egg

1 garlic clove
1 cup old-fashioned rolled oats
1 tablespoon dried oregano
1 tablespoon balsamic vinegar
¼ teaspoon kosher salt
½ cup crumbled Gorgonzola cheese

1. Using a fork, pierce the sweet potato all over and microwave on high for 4 to 5 minutes, until softened in the center. Cool slightly before slicing in half.
2. Meanwhile, in a large skillet over medium-high heat, heat 1 tablespoon of the olive oil. Add the onion and sauté for 5 minutes.
3. Spoon the sweet potato flesh out of the skin and put the flesh in a food processor. Add the cooked onion, egg, garlic, oats, oregano, vinegar and salt. Pulse until smooth. Add the cheese and pulse four times to barely combine.
4. Form the mixture into four burgers. Place the burgers on a plate, and press to flatten each to about ¾-inch thick.
5. Wipe out the skillet with a paper towel. Heat the remaining 1 tablespoon of the oil over medium-high heat for about 2 minutes. Add the burgers to the hot oil, then reduce the heat to medium. Cook the burgers for 5 minutes per side. Transfer the burgers to a plate and serve.

Per Serving
calories: 290 | fat: 12.0g | protein: 12.0g | carbs: 43.0g | fiber: 8.0g | sodium: 566mg

Black Bean and Corn Tortilla Bowls

Prep time: 10 minutes | Cook time: 8 minutes | Serves 4

1½ cups vegetable broth
½ cup diced tomatoes, undrained
1 small onion, diced
2 garlic cloves, finely minced
1 teaspoon chili powder
1 teaspoon cumin
½ teaspoon paprika
½ teaspoon ground coriander

2 small potatoes, cubed
½ cup bell pepper, chopped
½ can black beans, drained and rinsed
1 cup frozen corn kernels
½ tablespoon lime juice
2 tablespoons cilantro for topping, chopped
Whole-wheat tortilla chips
Salt and pepper to taste
½ cup carrots, diced

1. Add the oil and all the vegetables into the instant pot and Sauté for 3 minutes.
2. Add all the spices, corn, lime juice, and broth, along with the beans, to the pot.
3. Seal the lid and cook on Manual setting at High Pressure for 5 minutes.
4. Once done, natural release the pressure when the timer goes off. Remove the lid.
5. To serve, put the prepared mixture into a bowl.
6. Top with tortilla chips and fresh cilantro. Serve.

Per Serving
calories: 183 | fat: 0.9g | protein: 7.1g | carbs: 39.8g | fiber: 8.3g | sodium: 387mg

Mushroom Swoodles

Prep time: 5 minutes | Cook time: 3 minutes | Serves 4

2 tablespoons coconut aminos
1 tablespoon white vinegar
2 teaspoons olive oil
1 teaspoon sesame oil
1 tablespoon honey
¼ teaspoon red pepper flakes

3 cloves garlic, minced
1 large sweet potato, peeled and spiraled
1 pound (454 g) shiitake mushrooms, sliced
1 cup vegetable broth
¼ cup chopped fresh parsley

1. In a large bowl, whisk together coconut aminos, vinegar, olive oil, sesame oil, honey, red pepper flakes, and garlic.
2. Toss sweet potato and shiitake mushrooms in sauce. Refrigerate covered for 30 minutes.
3. Pour vegetable broth into Instant Pot. Add trivet. Lower steamer basket onto trivet and add the sweet potato mixture to the basket. Lock lid.
4. Press the Manual button and adjust time to 3 minutes. When timer beeps, let pressure release naturally for 5 minutes. Quick release any additional pressure until float valve drops and then unlock lid.
5. Remove basket from the Instant Pot and distribute sweet potatoes and mushrooms evenly among four bowls; pour liquid from the Instant Pot over bowls and garnish with chopped parsley.

Per Serving
calories: 127 | fat: 4.0g | protein: 4.2g | carbs: 20.9g | fiber: 4.1g | sodium: 671mg

Rice, Corn, and Bean Stuffed Peppers

Prep time: 15 minutes | Cook time: 15 minutes | Serves 4

4 large bell peppers
2 cups cooked white rice
1 medium onion, peeled and diced
3 small Roma tomatoes, diced
¼ cup marinara sauce
1 cup corn kernels (cut from the cob is preferred)
¼ cup sliced black olives
¼ cup canned cannellini beans, rinsed and drained
¼ cup canned black beans, rinsed and drained
1 teaspoon sea salt
1 teaspoon garlic powder
½ cup vegetable broth
2 tablespoons grated Parmesan cheese

1. Cut off the bell pepper tops as close to the tops as possible. Hollow out and discard seeds. Poke a few small holes in the bottom of the peppers to allow drippings to drain.
2. In a medium bowl, combine remaining ingredients except for broth and Parmesan cheese. Stuff equal amounts of mixture into each of the bell peppers.
3. Place trivet into the Instant Pot and pour in the broth. Set the peppers upright on the trivet. Lock lid.
4. Press the Manual button and adjust time to 15 minutes. When timer beeps, let pressure release naturally until float valve drops and then unlock lid.
5. Serve immediately and garnish with Parmesan cheese.

Per Serving
calories: 265 | fat: 3.0g | protein: 8.1g | carbs: 53.1g | fiber : 8.0g | sodium: 834m g

Brussels Sprouts Linguine

Prep time: 5 minutes | Cook time: 25 minutes | Serves 4

8 ounces (227 g) whole-wheat linguine
⅓ cup plus 2 tablespoons extra-virgin olive oil, divided
1 medium sweet onion, diced
2 to 3 garlic cloves, smashed
8 ounces (227 g) Brussels sprouts, chopped
½ cup chicken stock
⅓ cup dry white wine
½ cup shredded Parmesan cheese
1 lemon, quartered

1. Bring a large pot of water to a boil and cook the pasta for about 5 minutes, or until al dente. Drain the pasta and reserve 1 cup of the pasta water. Mix the cooked pasta with 2 tablespoons of the olive oil. Set aside.
2. In a large skillet, heat the remaining cup of the olive oil over medium heat. Add the onion to the skillet and sauté for about 4 minutes, or until tender. Add the smashed garlic cloves and sauté for 1 minute, or until fragrant.
3. Stir in the Brussels sprouts and cook covered for 10 minutes. Pour in the chicken stock to prevent burning. Once the Brussels sprouts have wilted and are fork-tender, add white wine and cook for about 5 minutes, or until reduced.
4. Add the pasta to the skillet and add the pasta water as needed.
5. Top with the Parmesan cheese and squeeze the lemon over the dish right before eating.

Per Serving
calories: 502 | fat: 31.0g | protein: 15.0g | carbs: 50.0g | fiber : 9.0g | sodium: 246mg

Beet and Watercress Salad

Prep time: 15 minutes | Cook time: 8 minutes | Serves 4

2 pounds (907 g) beets, scrubbed, trimmed and cut into ¾-inch pieces
½ cup water
1 teaspoon caraway seeds
½ teaspoon table salt, plus more for seasoning
1 cup plain Greek yogurt
1 small garlic clove, minced
5 ounces (142 g) watercress, torn into bite-size pieces
1 tablespoon extra-virgin olive oil, divided, plus more for drizzling
1 tablespoon white wine vinegar, divided
Black pepper, to taste
1 teaspoon grated orange zest
2 tablespoons orange juice
¼ cup coarsely chopped fresh dill
¼ cup hazelnuts, toasted, skinned and chopped Coarse sea salt, to taste

1. Combine the beets, water, caraway seeds and table salt in the Instant Pot. Set the lid in place. Select the Manual mode and set the cooking time for 8 minutes on High Pressure. When the timer goes off, do a quick pressure release.
2. Carefully open the lid. Using a slotted spoon, transfer the beets to a plate. Set aside to cool slightly.
3. In a small bowl, combine the yogurt, garlic and 3 tablespoons of the beet cooking liquid. In a large bowl, toss the watercress with 2 teaspoons of the oil and 1 teaspoon of the vinegar. Season with table salt and pepper.
4. Spread the yogurt mixture over a serving dish. Arrange the watercress on top of the yogurt mixture, leaving 1-inch border of the yogurt mixture. Add the beets to now-empty large bowl and toss with the orange zest and juice, the remaining 2 teaspoons of the vinegar and the remaining 1 teaspoon of the oil. Season with table salt and pepper.
5. Arrange the beets on top of the watercress mixture. Drizzle with the olive oil and sprinkle with the dill, hazelnuts and sea salt. Serve immediately.

Per Serving
calories: 240 | fat: 15.0g | protein: 9.0g | carbs: 19.0g | fiber : 5.0g | sodium: 440m g

Parmesan Stuffed Zucchini Boats

Prep time: 5 minutes | Cook time: 15 minutes | Serves 4

1 cup canned low-sodium chickpeas, drained and rinsed
1 cup no-sugar-added spaghetti sauce
2 zucchinis
¼ cup shredded Parmesan cheese

1. Preheat the oven to 425ºF (220ºC).
2. In a medium bowl, stir together the chickpeas and spaghetti sauce.
3. Cut the zucchini in half lengthwise and scrape a spoon gently down the length of each half to remove the seeds.
4. Fill each zucchini half with the chickpea sauce and top with one-quarter of the Parmesan cheese.
5. Place the zucchini halves on a baking sheet and roast in the oven for 15 minutes.
6. Transfer to a plate. Let rest for 5 minutes before serving.

Per Serving
calories: 139 | fat: 4.0g | protein: 8.0g | carbs: 20.0g | fiber : 5.0g | sodium: 344m g

Mushroom, Potato, and Green Bean Mix

Prep time: 10 minutes | Cook time: 18 minutes | Serves 3

1 tablespoon olive oil
½ carrot, peeled and minced
½ celery stalk, minced
½ small onion, minced
1 garlic clove, minced
½ teaspoon dried sage, crushed
½ teaspoon dried rosemary, crushed
4 ounces (113 g) fresh portabello mushrooms, sliced
4 ounces (113 g) fresh white mushrooms, sliced

¼ cup red wine
1 Yukon Gold potato, peeled and diced
¾ cup fresh green beans, trimmed and chopped
1 cup tomatoes, chopped
½ cup tomato paste
½ tablespoon balsamic vinegar
3 cups water
Salt and freshly ground black pepper to taste
2 ounces (57 g) frozen peas
½ lemon juice
2 tablespoons fresh cilantro for garnishing, chopped

1. Put the oil, onion, tomatoes and celery into the instant pot and Sauté for 5 minutes. Stir in the herbs and garlic and cook for 1 minute. Add the mushrooms and sauté for 5 minutes. Stir in the wine and cook for a further 2 minutes
2. Add the diced potatoes and mix. Cover the pot with a lid and let the potatoes cook for 2-3 minutes.
3. Now add the green beans, carrots, tomato paste, peas, salt, pepper, water and vinegar.
4. Secure the lid and cook on Manual function for 8 minutes at High Pressure with the pressure valve in the sealing position. Do a Quick release and open the pot, stir the veggies and then add lemon juice and cilantro, then serve with rice or any other of your choice.

Per Serving
calories: 238 | fat: 5.4g | protein: 8.3g | carbs: 42.7g | fiber: 8.5g | sodium: 113mg

Cauliflower and Broccoli Bowls

Prep time: 5 minutes | Cook time: 7 minutes | Serves 3

½ medium onion, diced
2 teaspoons olive oil
1 garlic clove, minced
½ cup tomato paste
½ pound (227 g) frozen cauliflower

½ pound (227 g) broccoli florets
½ cup vegetable broth
½ teaspoon paprika
¼ teaspoon dried thyme
2 pinches sea salt

1. Add the oil, onion and garlic into the instant pot and Sauté for 2 minutes.
2. Add the broth, tomato paste, cauliflower, broccoli, and all the spices, to the pot.
3. Secure the lid. Cook on the Manual setting at with pressure for 5 minutes.
4. After the beep, Quick release the pressure and remove the lid.
5. Stir well and serve hot.

Per Serving
calories: 109 | fat: 3.8g | protein: 6.1g | carbs: 16.7g | fiber: 6.1g | sodium: 265mg

Veggie Chili

Prep time: 15 minutes | Cook time: 10 minutes | Serves 3

½ tablespoon olive oil
1 small yellow onion, chopped
4 garlic cloves, minced
¾ (15-ounce / 425-g) can diced tomatoes
1 ounce (28 g) sugar-free tomato paste
½ (4-ounce / 113-g) can green chilies with liquid
1 tablespoon Worcestershire sauce

2 tablespoons red chili powder
½ cup carrots, diced
½ cup scallions, chopped
½ cup green bell pepper, chopped
¼ cup peas
1 tablespoon ground cumin
½ tablespoon dried oregano, crushed
Salt and freshly ground black pepper to taste

1. Add the oil, onion, and garlic into the instant pot and Sauté for 5 minutes.
2. Stir in the remaining vegetables and stir-fry for 3 minutes.
3. Add the remaining ingredients and secure the lid. Cook on
4. Manual function for 2 minutes at High Pressure.
5. After the beep, natural release the pressure and remove the lid.
6. Stir well and serve warm.

Per Serving
calories: 106 | fat: 3.9g | protein: 3.4g | carbs: 18.0g | fiber: 6.2g | sodium: 492mg

Potato, Corn, and Spinach Medley

Prep time: 10 minutes | Cook time: 10 minutes | Serves 6

1 tablespoon olive oil
3 scallions, chopped
½ cup onion, chopped
2 large white potatoes, peeled and diced
1 tablespoon ginger, grated
3 cups frozen corn kernels
1 cup vegetable stock

1 tablespoon fish sauce
2 tablespoons light soy sauce
2 large cloves garlic, diced
⅓ teaspoon white pepper
1 teaspoon salt
3-4 handfuls baby spinach leaves
Juice of ½ lemon

1. Put the oil, ginger, garlic and onions in the instant pot and
2. Sauté for 5 minutes. Add all the remaining ingredients except the spinach leaves and lime juice
3. Secure the lid and cook on the Manual setting for 5 minutes at High Pressure. After the beep, Quick release the pressure and remove the lid.
4. Add the spinach and cook for 3 minutes on Sauté Drizzle the lime juice over the dish and serve hot.

Per Serving
calories: 217 | fat: 3.4g | protein: 6.5g | carbs: 44.5g | fiber: 6.3g | sodium: 892mg

Italian Zucchini Pomodoro

Prep time: 10 minutes | Cook time: 12 minutes | Serves 4

1 tablespoon avocado oil
1 large onion, peeled and diced
3 cloves garlic, minced
1 (28-ounce / 794-g) can diced tomatoes, including juice

½ cup water
1 tablespoon Italian seasoning
1 teaspoon sea salt
½ teaspoon ground black pepper
2 medium zucchini, spiraled

1. Press Sauté button on the Instant Pot. Heat avocado oil. Add onions and stir-fry for 3 to 5 minutes until translucent. Add garlic and cook for an additional minute. Add tomatoes, water, Italian seasoning, salt, and pepper. Add zucchini and toss to combine. Lock lid.
2. Press the Manual button and adjust time to 1 minute. When timer beeps, let pressure release naturally for 5 minutes. Quick release any additional pressure until float valve drops and then unlock lid.
3. Transfer zucchini to four bowls. Press Sauté button, press Adjust button to change the temperature to Less, and simmer sauce in the Instant Pot unlidded for 5 minutes. Ladle over zucchini and serve immediately.

Per Serving
calories: 92 | fat: 4.1g | protein: 2.5g | carbs: 13.1g | fiber: 5.1g | sodium: 980mg

Radish and Cabbage Congee

Prep time: 5 minutes | Cook time: 20 minutes | Serves 3

1 cup carrots, diced
½ cup radish, diced
6 cups vegetable broth
Salt, to taste
1½ cups short grain rice, rinsed

1 tablespoon grated fresh ginger
4 cups cabbage, shredded
Green onions for garnishing, chopped

1. Add all the ingredients, except the cabbage and green onions, into the instant pot.
2. Select the Porridge function and cook on the default time and settings.
3. After the beep, Quick release the pressure and remove the lid Stir in the shredded cabbage and cover with the lid.
4. Serve after 10 minutes with chopped green onions on top.

Per Serving
calories: 438 | fat: 0.8g | protein: 8.7g | carbs: 98.4g | fiber: 6.7g | sodium: 1218mg

Farro Summer Salad

Prep time: 30 minutes | Cook time: 20 minutes | Serves 4

7 oz (200 grams) of farro
1 large red pepper
¼ red onion
3.5 oz (100 grams) of tuna in olive oil (drained)

1 can of kidney beans (washed and drained)
Lots of basil
Freshly squeezed lemon juice
Salt and pepper

1. Grill the pepper and remove the skin, or use it raw if you prefer. Cut it into thin strips.
2. Boil the farro for 20 minutes, drain it, and mix it with extra virgin olive oil. Let it cool.

3. Add all the ingredients to the farro and mix them up. Taste and adjust with salt, pepper, and lemon juice.

Per Serving
calories: 146 | fat: 10.6g | protein: 4.2g | carbs: 11.8g | fiber: 3.0g | sodium: 606mg

Stuffed Portobello Mushrooms with Tomatoes

Prep time: 10 minutes | Cook time: 15 minutes | Serves 4

4 large portobello mushroom caps
3 tablespoons extra-virgin olive oil
Salt and freshly ground black pepper, to taste

4 sun-dried tomatoes
1 cup shredded mozzarella cheese, divided
½ to ¾ cup low-sodium tomato sauce

1. Preheat the broiler to High.
2. Arrange the mushroom caps on a baking sheet and drizzle with olive oil.
3. Sprinkle with salt and pepper.
4. Broil for 10 minutes, flipping the mushroom caps halfway through, until browned on the top.
5. Remove from the broiler. Spoon 1 tomato, 2 tablespoons of cheese, and 2 to 3 tablespoons of sauce onto each mushroom
6. cap. Return the mushroom caps to the broiler and continue broiling for 2 to 3 minutes.
7. Cool for 5 minutes before serving.

Per Serving
calories: 217 | fat: 15.8g | protein: 11.2g | carbs: 11.7g | fiber: 2.0g | sodium: 243mg

Vegetable and Red Lentil Stew

Prep time: 10 minutes | Cook time: 35 minutes | Serves 6

1 tablespoon extra-virgin olive oil
2 onions, peeled and finely diced
6½ cups water
2 zucchini, finely diced

4 celery stalks, finely diced
3 cups red lentils
1 teaspoon dried oregano
1 teaspoon salt, plus more as needed

1. Heat the olive oil in a large pot over medium heat.
2. Add the onions and sauté for about 5 minutes, stirring constantly, or until the onions are softened.
3. Stir in the water, zucchini, celery, lentils, oregano, and salt and bring the mixture to a boil.
4. Reduce the heat to low and let simmer covered for 30 minutes, stirring occasionally, or until the lentils are tender.
5. Taste and adjust the seasoning as needed.

Per Serving
calories: 387 | fat: 4.4g | protein: 24.0g | carbs: 63.7g | fiber: 11.7g | sodium: 418mg

Potato and Broccoli Medley

Prep time: 10 minutes | Cook time: 20 minutes | Serves 3

1 tablespoon olive oil
½ white onion, diced
1½ cloves garlic, finely chopped
1 pound (454 g) potatoes, cut into chunks
1 pound (454 g) broccoli florets, diced

1 pound (454 g) baby carrots, cut in half
¼ cup vegetable broth
½ teaspoon Italian seasoning
½ teaspoon Spike original seasoning
Fresh parsley for garnishing

1. Put the oil and onion into the instant pot and Sauté for 5 minutes. Stir in the carrots, and garlic and stir-fry for 5 minutes. Add the remaining ingredients and secure the lid.
2. Cook on the Manual function for 10 minutes at High Pressure. After the beep, Quick release the pressure and remove the lid. Stir gently and garnish with fresh parsley, then serve.

Per Serving
calories: 256 | fat: 5.6g | protein: 9.1g | carbs: 46.1g | fiber: 12.2g | sodium: 274mg

Carrot and Turnip Purée

Prep time: 10 minutes | Cook time: 10 minutes | Serves 6

2 tablespoons olive oil, divided
3 large turnips, peeled and quartered
4 large carrots, peeled and cut into 2-inch pieces

2 cups vegetable broth
1 teaspoon salt
½ teaspoon ground nutmeg
2 tablespoons sour cream

1. Press the Sauté button on Instant Pot. Heat 1 tablespoon olive oil. Toss turnips and carrots in oil for 1 minute. Add broth. Lock lid. Press the Manual button and adjust time to 8 minutes. When timer beeps, quick release pressure until float valve drops and then unlock lid.
2. Drain vegetables and reserve liquid; set liquid aside. Add 2 tablespoons of reserved liquid plus remaining ingredients to vegetables in the Instant Pot.
3. Use an immersion blender to blend until desired smoothness. If too thick, add more liquid 1 tablespoon at a time. Serve warm.

Per Serving
calories: 95 | fat: 5.2g | protein: 1.4g | carbs: 11.8g | fiber: 3.0g | sodium: 669mg

Sautéed Spinach and Leeks

Prep time: 5 minutes | Cook time: 8 minutes | Serves 2

3 tablespoons olive oil
2 garlic cloves, crushed
2 leeks, chopped
2 red onions, chopped

9 ounces (255 g) fresh spinach
1 teaspoon kosher salt
½ cup crumbled goat cheese

1. Coat the bottom of the Instant Pot with the olive oil.
2. Add the garlic, leek, and onions and stir-fry for about 5 minutes, on Sauté mode.
3. Stir in the spinach. Sprinkle with the salt and sauté for an additional 3 minutes, stirring constantly.
4. Transfer to a plate and sprinkle with the goat cheese before serving.

Per Serving
calories: 447 | fat: 31.2g | protein: 14.6g | carbs: 28.7g | fiber: 6.3g | sodium: 937mg

Grilled Vegetable Skewers

Prep time: 15 minutes | Cook time: 10 minutes | Serves 4

4 medium red onions, peeled and sliced into 6 wedges
4 medium zucchinis, cut into 1-inch-thick slices
2 beefsteak tomatoes, cut into quarters
4 red bell peppers, cut into 2-inch squares

2 orange bell peppers, cut into 2-inch squares
2 yellow bell peppers, cut into 2-inch squares
2 tablespoons plus
1 teaspoon olive oil, divided
Special Equipment:
4 wooden skewers, soaked in water for at least 30 minutes

1. Preheat the grill to medium-high heat.
2. Skewer the vegetables by alternating between red onion, zucchini, tomatoes, and the different colored bell peppers. Brush them with 2 tablespoons of olive oil.
3. Oil the grill grates with 1 teaspoon of olive oil and grill the vegetable skewers for 5 minutes. Flip the skewers and grill for 5 minutes more, or until they are cooked to your liking.
4. Let the skewers cool for 5 minutes before serving.

Per Serving
calories: 115 | fat: 3.0g | protein: 3.5g | carbs: 18.7g | fiber: 4.7g | sodium: 12mg

Baked Tomatoes and Chickpeas

Prep time: 15 minutes | Cook time: 40 to 45 minutes | Serves 4

1 tablespoon extra-virgin olive oil
½ medium onion, chopped
3 garlic cloves, chopped
¼ teaspoon ground cumin
2 teaspoons smoked paprika

2 (15-ounce / 425-g) cans chickpeas, drained and rinsed
4 cups halved cherry tomatoes
½ cup plain Greek yogurt, for serving
1 cup crumbled feta cheese, for serving

1. Preheat the oven to 425ºF (220ºC).
2. Heat the olive oil in an ovenproof skillet over medium heat.
3. Add the onion and garlic and sauté for about 5 minutes, stirring occasionally, or until tender and fragrant.
4. Add the paprika and cumin and cook for 2 minutes. Stir in the chickpeas and tomatoes and allow to simmer for 5 to 10 minutes.
5. Transfer the skillet to the preheated oven and roast for 25 to 30 minutes, or until the mixture bubbles and thickens.
6. Remove from the oven and serve topped with yogurt and crumbled feta cheese.

Per Serving
calories: 411 | fat: 14.9g | protein: 20.2g | carbs: 50.7g | fiber: 13.3g | sodium: 44 3mg

Mushroom and Potato Oat Burgers

Prep time: 20 minutes | Cook time: 21 minutes | Serves 5

½ cup minced onion
1 teaspoon grated fresh ginger
½ cup minced mushrooms
½ cup red lentils, rinsed
¾ sweet potato, peeled and diced
1 cup vegetable stock
2 tablespoons hemp seeds
2 tablespoons chopped parsley

2 tablespoons chopped cilantro
1 tablespoon curry powder
1 cup quick oats
Brown rice flour, optional
5 tomato slices
Lettuce leaves
5 whole-wheat buns

1. Add the oil, ginger, mushrooms and onion into the instant pot and Sauté for 5 minutes.
2. Stir in the lentils, stock, and the sweet potatoes. Secure the lid and cook on the Manual function for 6 minutes at High Pressure. After the beep, natural release the pressure and remove the lid.
3. Meanwhile, heat the oven to 375ºF (190ºC) and line a baking tray with parchment paper. Mash the prepared lentil mixture with a potato masher.
4. Add the oats and the remaining spices. Put in some brown rice flour if the mixture is not thick enough. Wet your hands and prepare 5 patties, using the mixture, and place them on the baking tray.
5. Bake the patties for 10 minutes in the preheated oven. Slice the buns in half and stack each with a tomato slice, a vegetable patty and lettuce leaves. Serve and enjoy.

Per Serving
calories: 266 | fat: 5.3g | protein: 14.5g | carbs: 48.7g | fiber: 9.6g | sodium: 276mg

Sautéed Cabbage with Parsley

Prep time: 10 minutes | Cook time: 12 to 14 minutes | Serves 4 to 6

1 small head green cabbage (about 1¼ pounds / 567 g), cored and sliced thin
2 tablespoons extra-virgin olive oil, divided

1 onion, halved and sliced thin
¾ teaspoon salt, divided
¼ teaspoon black pepper
¼ cup chopped fresh parsley
1½ teaspoons lemon juice

1. Place the cabbage in a large bowl with cold water. Let sit for 3 minutes. Drain well. Heat 1 tablespoon of the oil in a skillet over medium-high heat until shimmering. Add the onion and ¼ teaspoon of the salt and cook for 5 to 7 minutes, or until softened and lightly browned. Transfer to a bowl. Heat the remaining 1 tablespoon of the oil in now-empty skillet over medium-high heat until shimmering. Add the cabbage and sprinkle with the remaining ½ teaspoon of the salt and black pepper. Cover and cook for about 3 minutes, without stirring, or until cabbage is wilted and lightly browned on bottom.
2. Stir and continue to cook for about 4 minutes, uncovered, or until the cabbage is crisp-tender and lightly browned in places, stirring once halfway through cooking. Off heat, stir in the cooked onion, parsley and lemon juice.
3. Transfer to a plate and serve.

Per Serving
calories: 117 | fat: 7.0g | protein: 2.7g | carbs: 13.4g | fiber: 5.1g | sodium: 472mg

Mini Crustless Spinach Quiches

Prep time: 10 minutes | Cook time: 20 minutes | Serves 6

2 tablespoons extra-virgin olive oil
1 onion, finely chopped
2 cups baby spinach
2 garlic cloves, minced
8 large eggs, beaten

¼ cup unsweetened almond milk
½ teaspoon sea salt
¼ teaspoon freshly ground black pepper
1 cup shredded Swiss cheese

Cooking spray

1. Preheat the oven to 375ºF (190ºC). Spritz a 6-cup muffin tin with cooking spray. Set aside.
2. In a large skillet over medium-high heat, heat the olive oil until shimmering. Add the onion and cook for about 4 minutes, or until soft. Add the spinach and cook for about 1 minute, stirring constantly, or until the spinach softens. Add the garlic and sauté for 30 seconds. Remove from the heat and let cool.
3. In a medium bowl, whisk together the eggs, milk, salt and pepper. Stir the cooled vegetables and the cheese into the egg mixture. Spoon the mixture into the prepared muffin tins. Bake for about 15 minutes, or until the eggs are set.
4. Let rest for 5 minutes before serving.

Per Serving
calories: 218 | fat: 17.0g | protein: 14.0g | carbs: 4.0g | fiber: 1.0g | sodium: 237mg

Potato Tortilla with Leeks and Mushrooms

Prep time: 30 minutes | Cook time: 50 minutes | Serves 2

1 tablespoon olive oil
1 cup thinly sliced leeks
4 ounces (113 g) baby bella (cremini) mushrooms, stemmed and sliced
1 small potato, peeled and sliced ¼-inch thick
½ cup unsweetened almond milk

5 large eggs, beaten
1 teaspoon Dijon mustard
½ teaspoon salt
½ teaspoon dried thyme
Pinch freshly ground black pepper
3 ounces (85 g) Gruyère cheese, shredded

1. Preheat the oven to 350ºF (180ºC).
2. In a large sauté pan over medium-high heat, heat the olive oil. Add the leeks, mushrooms, and potato and sauté for about 10 minutes, or until the potato starts to brown.
3. Reduce the heat to medium-low, cover, and cook for an additional 10 minutes, or until the potato begins to soften. Add 1 to 2 tablespoons of water to prevent sticking to the bottom of the pan, if needed.
4. Meanwhile, whisk together the milk, beaten eggs, mustard, salt, thyme, black pepper, and cheese in a medium bowl until combined. When the potatoes are fork-tender, turn off the heat. Transfer the cooked vegetables to a greased nonstick ovenproof pan and arrange them in a nice layer along the bottom and slightly up the sides of the pan. Pour the milk mixture evenly over the vegetables.
5. Bake in the preheated oven for 25 to 30 minutes, or until the eggs are completely set and the top is golden and puffed. Remove from the oven and cool for 5 minutes before cutting and serving.

Per Serving
calories: 541 | fat: 33.1g | protein: 32.8g | carbs: 31.0g | fiber: 4.0g | sodium: 912mg

Mushrooms Ragu with Cheesy Polenta

Prep time: 20 minutes | Cook time: 30 minutes | Serves 2

½ ounce (14 g) dried porcini mushrooms
1 pound (454 g) baby bella (cremini) mushrooms, quartered
2 tablespoons olive oil
1 garlic clove, minced
1 large shallot, minced
1 tablespoon flour
2 teaspoons tomato paste
½ cup red wine

1 cup mushroom stock (or reserved liquid from soaking the porcini mush-rooms, if using)
1 fresh rosemary sprig
½ teaspoon dried thyme
1½ cups water
½ teaspoon salt, plus more as needed
⅓ cup instant polenta
2 tablespoons grated Parmesan cheese

1. Soak the dried porcini mushrooms in 1 cup of hot water for about 15 minutes to soften them. When ready, scoop them out of the water, reserving the soaking liquid. Mince the porcini mushrooms. Heat the olive oil in a large sauté pan over medium-high heat. Add the mushrooms, garlic, and shallot and sauté for 10 minutes, or until the vegetables are beginning to caramelize.
2. Stir in the flour and tomato paste and cook for an additional 30 seconds. Add the red wine, mushroom stock, rosemary, and thyme. Bring the mixture to a boil, stirring constantly, or until it has thickened. Reduce the heat and allow to simmer for 10 minutes. Meanwhile, bring the water to a boil in a saucepan and sprinkle with the salt.
3. Add the instant polenta and stir quickly while it thickens. Scatter with the grated Parmesan cheese. Taste and season with more salt as needed. Serve warm.

Per Serving
calories: 450 | fat: 16.0g | protein: 14.1g | carbs: 57.8g | fiber: 5.0g | sodium: 165mg

Wilted Dandelion Greens with Sweet Onion

Prep time: 15 minutes | Cook time: 15 minutes | Serves 4

1 tablespoon extra-virgin olive oil
2 garlic cloves, minced
1 Vidalia onion, thinly sliced
½ cup low-sodium vegetable broth

2 bunches dandelion greens, roughly chopped
Freshly ground black pepper, to taste

1. Heat the olive oil in a large skillet over low heat.
2. Add the garlic and onion and cook for 2 to 3 minutes, stirring occasionally, or until the onion is translucent.
3. Fold in the vegetable broth and dandelion greens and cook for 5 to 7 minutes until wilted, stirring frequently. Sprinkle with the black pepper and serve on a plate while warm.

Per Serving
calories: 81 | fat: 3.9g | protein: 3.2g | carbs: 10.8g | fiber: 4.0g | sodium: 72mg

Vegetable and Tofu Scramble

Prep time: 5 minutes | Cook time: 10 minutes | Serves 2

2 tablespoons extra-virgin olive oil
½ red onion, finely chopped
1 cup chopped kale
8 ounces (227 g) mushrooms, sliced

8 ounces (227 g) tofu, cut into pieces
2 garlic cloves, minced
Pinch red pepper flakes
½ teaspoon sea salt
⅛ teaspoon freshly ground black pepper

1. Heat the olive oil in a medium nonstick skillet over medium-high heat until shimmering.
2. Add the onion, kale, and mushrooms to the skillet and cook for about 5 minutes, stirring occasionally, or until the vegetables start to brown.
3. Add the tofu and stir-fry for 3 to 4 minutes until softened.
4. Stir in the garlic, red pepper flakes, salt, and black pepper and cook for 30 seconds.
5. Let the mixture cool for 5 minutes before serving.

Per Serving
calories: 233 | fat: 15.9g | protein: 13.4g | carbs: 11.9g | fiber: 2.0g | sodium: 672mg

Lentil and Tomato Collard Wraps

Prep time: 15 minutes | Cook time: 0 minutes | Serves 4

2 cups cooked lentils
5 Roma tomatoes, diced
½ cup crumbled feta cheese
10 large fresh basil leaves, thinly sliced
¼ cup extra-virgin olive oil
1 tablespoon balsamic vinegar

2 garlic cloves, minced
½ teaspoon raw honey
½ teaspoon salt
¼ teaspoon freshly ground black pepper
4 large collard leaves, stems removed

1. Combine the lentils, tomatoes, cheese, basil leaves, olive oil, vinegar, garlic, honey, salt, and black pepper in a large bowl and stir until well blended.
2. Lay the collard leaves on a flat work surface. Spoon the equal-sized amounts of the lentil mixture onto the edges of the leaves. Roll them up and slice in half to serve.

Per Serving
calories: 318 | fat: 17.6g | protein: 13.2g | carbs: 27.5g | fiber: 9.9g | sodium: 475mg

Creamy Cauliflower Chickpea Curry

Prep time: 5 minutes | Cook time: 15 minutes | Serves 4

3 cups fresh or frozen cauliflower florets
2 cups unsweetened almond milk
1 (15-ounce / 425-g) can low-sodium chickpeas, drained and rinsed

1 tablespoon curry powder
¼ teaspoon garlic powder
¼ teaspoon ground ginger
⅛ teaspoon onion powder
¼ teaspoon salt
1 (15-ounce / 425-g) can coconut milk

1. Add the cauliflower florets, almond milk, chickpeas, coconut milk, curry powder, garlic powder, ginger, and onion powder to a large stockpot and stir to combine. Cover and cook over medium-high heat for 10 minutes, stirring occasionally.
2. Reduce the heat to low and continue cooking uncovered for 5 minutes, or until the cauliflower is tender.
3. Sprinkle with the salt and stir well. Serve warm.

Per Serving
calories: 409 | fat: 29.6g | protein: 10.0g | carbs: 29.8g | fiber: 9.1g | sodium: 117mg

Cauliflower Rice Risotto with Mushrooms

Prep time: 5 minutes | Cook time: 10 minutes | Serves 4

1 teaspoon extra-virgin olive oil
½ cup chopped portobello mushrooms
4 cups cauliflower rice

½ cup plain Greek yogurt
¼ cup low-sodium vegetable broth
1 cup shredded Parmesan cheese

1. In a medium skillet, heat the olive oil over medium-low heat until shimmering.
2. Add the mushrooms and stir-fry for 3 minutes.
3. Stir in the cauliflower rice, yogurt, and vegetable broth. Cover and bring to a boil over high heat for 5 minutes, stirring occasionally.
4. Add the Parmesan cheese and stir to combine. Continue cooking for an additional 3 minutes until the cheese is melted.
5. Divide the mixture into four bowls and serve warm.

Per Serving
calories: 167 | fat: 10.7g | protein: 12.1g | carbs: 8.1g | fiber: 3.0g | sodium: 326mg

Sautéed Green Beans with Tomatoes

Prep time: 10 minutes | Cook time: 20 minutes | Serves 4

¼ cup extra-virgin olive oil
1 large onion, chopped
4 cloves garlic, finely chopped
1 pound (454 g) green beans, fresh or frozen, cut into 2-inch pieces

1½ teaspoons salt, divided
1 (15-ounce / 425-g) can diced tomatoes
½ teaspoon freshly ground black pepper

1. Heat the olive oil in a large skillet over medium heat.
2. Add the onion and garlic and sauté for 1 minute until fragrant.
3. Stir in the green beans and sauté for 3 minutes. Sprinkle with ½ teaspoon of salt.
4. Add the tomatoes, remaining salt, and pepper and stir to mix well. Cook for an additional 12 minutes, stirring occasionally, or until the green beans are crisp and tender.
5. Remove from the heat and serve warm.

Per Serving
calories: 219 | fat: 13.9g | protein: 4.0g | carbs: 17.7g | fiber: 6.2g | sodium: 84 3mg

Celery and Mustard Greens

Prep time: 10 minutes | Cook time: 15 minutes | Serves 4

½ cup low-sodium vegetable broth
1 celery stalk, roughly chopped
½ sweet onion, chopped

½ large red bell pepper, thinly sliced
2 garlic cloves, minced
1 bunch mustard greens, roughly chopped

1. Pour the vegetable broth into a large cast iron pan and bring it to a simmer over medium heat.
2. Stir in the celery, onion, bell pepper, and garlic. Cook uncovered for about 3 to 5 minutes, or until the onion is softened.
3. Add the mustard greens to the pan and stir well. Cover, reduce the heat to low, and cook for an additional 10 minutes, or until the liquid is evaporated and the greens are wilted. Remove from the heat and serve warm.

Per Serving (1 cup)
calories: 39 | fat: 0g | protein: 3.1g | carbs: 6.8g | fiber: 3.0g | sodium: 120mg

Ratatouille

Prep time: 10 minutes | Cook time: 30 minutes | Serves 4

4 tablespoons extra-virgin olive oil, divided
1 cup diced zucchini
2 cups diced eggplant
1 cup diced onion
1 cup chopped green bell pepper

1 (15-ounce / 425-g) can no-salt-added diced tomatoes
½ teaspoon garlic powder
1 teaspoon ground thyme
Salt and freshly ground black pepper, to taste

1. Heat 2 tablespoons of olive oil in a large saucepan over medium heat until it shimmers.
2. Add the zucchini and eggplant and sauté for 10 minutes, stirring occasionally. If necessary, add the remaining olive oil.
3. Stir in the onion and bell pepper and sauté for 5 minutes until softened.
4. Add the diced tomatoes with their juice, garlic powder, and thyme and stir to combine. Continue cooking for 15 minutes until the vegetables are cooked through, stirring occasionally. Sprinkle with salt and black pepper.
   Remove from the heat and serve on a plate.

Per Serving
calories: 189 | fat: 13.7g | protein: 3.1g | carbs: 14.8g | fiber: 4.0g | sodium: 27mg

Zucchini Patties

Prep time: 15 minutes | Cook time: 5 minutes | Serves 2

2 medium zucchinis, shredded
1 teaspoon salt, divided
2 eggs
2 tablespoons chickpea flour

1 tablespoon chopped fresh mint
1 scallion, chopped
2 tablespoons extra-virgin olive oil

1. Put the shredded zucchini in a fine-mesh strainer and season with ½ teaspoon of salt. Set aside.
2. Beat together the eggs, chickpea flour, mint, scallion, and remaining ½ teaspoon of salt in a medium bowl. Squeeze the zucchini to drain as much liquid as possible. Add the zucchini to the egg mixture and stir until well incorporated.
3. Heat the olive oil in a large skillet over medium-high heat.
4. Drop the zucchini mixture by spoonfuls into the skillet. Gently flatten the zucchini with the back of a spatula. Cook for 2 to 3 minutes or until golden brown. Flip and cook for an additional 2 minutes.
5. Remove from the heat and serve on a plate.

Per Serving
calories: 264 | fat: 20.0g | protein: 9.8g | carbs: 16.1g | fiber: 4.0g | sodium: 1780mg

Zucchini Crisp

Prep time: 10 minutes | Cook time: 20 minutes | Serves 2

4 zucchinis, sliced into ½-inch rounds
½ cup unsweetened almond milk
1 teaspoon fresh lemon juice
1 teaspoon arrowroot powder
½ teaspoon salt, divided
½ cup whole wheat bread crumbs
¼ cup nutritional yeast
¼ cup hemp seeds
½ teaspoon garlic powder
¼ teaspoon crushed red pepper
¼ teaspoon black pepper

1. Preheat the oven to 375ºF (190ºC). Line two baking sheets with parchment paper and set aside.
2. Put the zucchini in a medium bowl with the almond milk, lemon juice, arrowroot powder, and ¼ teaspoon of salt. Stir to mix well.
3. In a large bowl with a lid, thoroughly combine the bread crumbs, nutritional yeast, hemp seeds, garlic powder, crushed red pepper and black pepper. Add the zucchini in batches and shake until the slices are evenly coated.
4. Arrange the zucchini on the prepared baking sheets in a single layer.
5. Bake in the preheated oven for about 20 minutes, or until the zucchini slices are golden brown.
6. Season with the remaining ¼ teaspoon of salt before serving.

Per Serving
calories: 255 | fat: 11.3g | protein: 8.6g | carbs: 31.9g | fiber: 3.8g | sodium: 826mg

Garlicky Broccoli Rabe

Prep time: 10 minutes | Cook time: 5 to 6 minutes | Serves 4

14 ounces (397 g) broccoli rabe, trimmed and cut into 1-inch pieces
2 teaspoons salt, plus more for seasoning
Black pepper, to taste
2 tablespoons extra-virgin olive oil
3 garlic cloves, minced
¼ teaspoon red pepper flakes

1. Bring 3 quarts water to a boil in a large saucepan. Add the broccoli rabe and 2 teaspoons of the salt to the boiling water and cook for 2 to 3 minutes, or until wilted and tender. Drain the broccoli rabe. Transfer to ice water and let it sit until chilled. Drain again and pat dry.
2. In a skillet over medium heat, heat the oil and add the garlic and red pepper flakes. Sauté for about 2 minutes, or until the garlic begins to sizzle. Increase the heat to medium-high. Stir in the broccoli rabe and cook for about 1 minute, or until heated through, stirring constantly. Season with salt and pepper. Serve immediately.

Per Serving
calories: 87 | fat: 7.3g | protein: 3.4g | carbs: 4.0g | fiber: 2.9g | sodium: 1196mg

Braised Cauliflower with White Wine

Prep time: 10 minutes | Cook time: 12 to 16 minutes | Serves 4 to 6

3 tablespoons plus 1 teaspoon extra-virgin olive oil, divided
3 garlic cloves, minced
⅛ teaspoon red pepper flakes
1 head cauliflower (2 pounds / 907 g), cored and cut into 1½-inch florets
¼ teaspoon salt, plus more for seasoning
Black pepper, to taste
⅓ cup vegetable broth
⅓ cup dry white wine
2 tablespoons minced fresh parsley

1. Combine 1 teaspoon of the oil, garlic and pepper flakes in small bowl.
2. Heat the remaining 3 tablespoons of the oil in a skillet over medium-high heat until shimmering. Add the cauliflower and ¼ teaspoon of the salt and cook for 7 to 9 minutes, stirring occasionally, or until florets are golden brown.
3. Push the cauliflower to sides of the skillet. Add the garlic mixture to the center of the skillet. Cook for about 30 seconds, or until fragrant. Stir the garlic mixture into the cauliflower.
4. Pour in the broth and wine and bring to simmer. Reduce the heat to medium-low. Cover and cook for 4 to 6 minutes, or until the cauliflower is crisp-tender. Off heat, stir in the parsley and season with salt and pepper.
5. Serve immediately.

Per Serving
calories: 143 | fat: 11.7g | protein: 3.1g | carbs: 8.7g | fiber: 3.1g | sodium: 263mg

Baby Kale and Cabbage Salad

Prep time: 10 minutes | Cook time: 0 minutes | Serves 6

2 bunches baby kale, thinly sliced
½ head green savoy cabbage, cored and thinly sliced
1 medium red bell pepper, thinly sliced
1 garlic clove, thinly sliced
1 cup roasted peanuts
Dressing:
Juice of 1 lemon
¼ cup apple cider vinegar
1 teaspoon ground cumin
¼ teaspoon smoked paprika

1. In a large mixing bowl, toss together the kale and cabbage.
2. Make the dressing: Whisk together the lemon juice, vinegar, cumin and paprika in a small bowl.
3. Pour the dressing over the greens and gently massage with your hands. Add the pepper, garlic and peanuts to the mixing bowl. Toss to combine. Serve immediately.

Per Serving
calories: 199 | fat: 12.0g | protein: 10.0g | carbs: 17.0g | fiber: 5.0g | sodium: 46mg

Veggie Rice Bowls with Pesto Sauce

Prep time: 15 minutes | Cook time: 1 minute | Serves 2

2 cups water
1 cup arborio rice, rinsed
Salt and ground black pepper, to taste
2 eggs
1 cup broccoli florets

½ pound (227 g) Brussels sprouts
1 carrot, peeled and chopped
1 small beet, peeled and cubed
¼ cup pesto sauce Lemon wedges, for serving

1. Combine the water, rice, salt, and pepper in the Instant Pot. Insert a trivet over rice and place a steamer basket on top. Add the eggs, broccoli, Brussels sprouts, carrots, beet cubes, salt, and pepper to the steamer basket.
2. Lock the lid. Select the Manual mode and set the cooking time for 1 minute at High Pressure.
3. When the timer beeps, perform a natural pressure release for 10 minutes, then release any remaining pressure. Carefully open the lid. Remove the steamer basket and trivet from the pot and transfer the eggs to a bowl of ice water. Peel and halve the eggs. Use a fork to fluff the rice.
4. Divide the rice, broccoli, Brussels sprouts, carrot, beet cubes, and eggs into two bowls. Top with a dollop of pesto sauce and serve with the lemon wedges.

Per Serving
calories: 590 | fat: 34.1g | protein: 21.9g | carbs: 50.0g | fiber: 19.6g | sodium: 670mg

Zucchini and Artichokes Bowl with Farro

Prep time: 15 minutes | Cook time: 10 minutes | Serves 4 to 6

⅓ cup extra-virgin olive oil
⅓ cup chopped red onions
½ cup chopped red bell pepper
2 garlic cloves, minced
1 cup zucchini, cut into ½-inch-thick slices
½ cup coarsely chopped artichokes
½ cup canned chickpeas, drained and rinsed
3 cups cooked farro

Salt and freshly ground black pepper, to taste
½ cup crumbled feta cheese, for serving (optional)
¼ cup sliced olives, for serving (optional)
2 tablespoons fresh basil, chiffonade, for serving (optional)
3 tablespoons balsamic vinegar, for serving (optional)

1. Heat the olive oil in a large skillet over medium heat until it shimmers. Add the onions, bell pepper, and garlic and sauté for 5 minutes, stirring occasionally, until softened.
2. Stir in the zucchini slices, artichokes, and chickpeas and sauté for about 5 minutes until slightly tender.
3. Add the cooked farro and toss to combine until heated through. Sprinkle the salt and pepper to season. Divide the mixture into bowls.
4. Top each bowl evenly with feta cheese, olive slices, and basil and drizzle with the balsamic vinegar, if desired.

Per Serving
calories: 366 | fat: 19.9g | protein: 9.3g | carbs: 50.7g | fiber: 9.0g | sodium: 86mg

Roasted Vegetables

Prep time: 20 minutes | Cook time: 35 minutes | Serves 2

6 teaspoons extra-virgin olive oil, divided
12 to 15 Brussels sprouts, halved
1 medium sweet potato, peeled and cut into 2-inch cubes

2 cups fresh cauliflower florets
1 medium zucchini, cut into 1-inch rounds
1 red bell pepper, cut into 1-inch slices
Salt, to taste

1. Preheat the oven to 425ºF (220ºC).
2. Add 2 teaspoons of olive oil, Brussels sprouts, sweet potato, and salt to a large bowl and toss until they are completely coated.
3. Transfer them to a large roasting pan and roast for 10 minutes, or until the Brussels sprouts are lightly browned.
4. Meantime, combine the cauliflower florets with 2 teaspoons of olive oil and salt in a separate bowl. Remove from the oven.
5. Add the cauliflower florets to the roasting pan and roast for 10 minutes more. Meanwhile, toss the zucchini and bell pepper with the remaining olive oil in a medium bowl until well coated. Season with salt.
6. Remove the roasting pan from the oven and stir in the zucchini and bell pepper. Continue roasting for 15 minutes, or until the vegetables are fork-tender. Divide the roasted vegetables between two plates and serve warm.

Per Serving
calories: 333 | fat: 16.8g | protein: 12.2g | carbs: 37.6g | fiber: 11.0g | sodium: 329mg

Creamy Sweet Potatoes and Collards

Prep time: 20 minutes | Cook time: 35 minutes | Serves 2

1 tablespoon avocado oil
3 garlic cloves, chopped
1 yellow onion, diced
½ teaspoon crushed red pepper flakes
1 large sweet potato, peeled and diced
2 bunches collard greens (about 2 pounds/907 g), stemmed, leaves chopped into 1-inch squares

1 (14.5-ounce / 411-g) can diced tomatoes with juice
1 (15-ounce / 425-g) can red kidney beans or chickpeas, drained and rinsed
1½ cups water
½ cup unsweetened coconut milk
Salt and black pepper, to taste

1. In a large, deep skillet over medium heat, heat the avocado oil.
2. Add the garlic, onion, and red pepper flakes and cook for 3 minutes.
3. Stir in the sweet potato and collards. Add the tomatoes with their juice, beans, water, and coconut milk and mix well. Bring the mixture just to a boil.
4. Reduce the heat to medium-low, cover, and simmer for about 30 minutes, or until softened.
5. Season to taste with salt and pepper and serve.

Per Serving
calories: 445 | fat: 9.6g | protein: 18.1g | carbs: 73.1g | fiber: 22.1g | sodium: 703mg

Potato and Kale Bowls

Prep time: 10 minutes | Cook time: 10 minutes | Serves 4

1 tablespoon olive oil
1 small onion, peeled and diced
1 stalk celery, diced
2 cloves garlic, minced
4 medium potatoes, peeled and diced
2 bunches kale, washed, deveined, and chopped

1½ cups vegetable broth
2 teaspoons salt
½ teaspoon ground black pepper
¼ teaspoon caraway seeds
1 tablespoon apple cider vinegar
4 tablespoons sour cream

1. Press the Sauté button on Instant Pot. Heat oil. Add onion and celery and stir-fry for 3 to 5 minutes until onions are translucent. Add garlic and cook for an additional minute. Add potatoes in an even layer. Add chopped kale in an even layer.
2. Add broth. Lock lid. Press the Manual button and adjust time to 5 minutes. Let the pressure release naturally for 10 minutes. Quick release any additional pressure until float valve drops and then unlock lid; then drain broth. Stir in salt, pepper, caraway seeds, and vinegar; slightly mash the potatoes in the Instant Pot. Garnish each serving with 1 tablespoon sour cream.

Per Serving
calories: 259 | fat: 5.5g | protein: 7.9g | carbs: 47.6g | fiber: 7.6g | sodium: 14 22mg

Eggplant and Millet Pilaf

Prep time: 5 minutes | Cook time: 17 minutes | Serves 4

1 tablespoon olive oil
¼ cup peeled and diced onion
1 cup peeled and diced eggplant
1 small Roma tomato, seeded and diced
1 cup millet

2 cups vegetable broth
1 teaspoon sea salt
¼ teaspoon ground black pepper
⅛ teaspoon saffron
⅛ teaspoon cayenne pepper
1 tablespoon chopped fresh chives

1. Press Sauté button on Instant Pot. Add the olive oil. Add onion and cook for 3 to 5 minutes until translucent. Toss in eggplant and stir-fry for 2 more minutes. Add diced tomato.
2. Add millet to Instant Pot in an even layer. Gently pour in broth. Lock lid.
3. Press the Rice button (the Instant Pot will determine the time, about 10 minutes pressurized cooking time). When timer beeps, let pressure release naturally for 5 minutes. Quick release any additional pressure until float valve drops and then unlock lid.
4. Transfer pot ingredients to a serving bowl. Season with salt, pepper, saffron, and cayenne pepper. Garnish with chives.

Per Serving
calories: 238 | fat: 5.6g | protein: 6.0g | carbs: 40.8g | fiber: 5.3g | sodium: 861mg

Grilled Romaine Lettuce

Prep time: 5 minutes | Cook time: 3 to 5 minutes | Serves 4

Romaine:
2 heads romaine lettuce, halved lengthwise
2 tablespoons extra-virgin olive oil
Dressing:
½ cup unsweetened almond milk

1 tablespoon extra-virgin olive oil
¼ bunch fresh chives, thinly chopped
1 garlic clove, pressed
1 pinch red pepper flakes

1. Heat a grill pan over medium heat.
2. Brush each lettuce half with the olive oil. Place the lettuce halves, flat-side down, on the grill. Grill for 3 to 5 minutes, or until the lettuce slightly wilts and develops light grill marks. Meanwhile, whisk together all the ingredients for the dressing in a small bowl. Drizzle 2 tablespoons of the dressing over each romaine half and serve.

Per Serving
calories: 126 | fat: 11.0g | protein: 2.0g | carbs: 7.0g | fiber: 1.0g | sodium: 41mg

Cauliflower Steaks with Arugula

Prep time: 5 minutes | Cook time: 20 minutes | Serves 4

Cauliflower:
1 head cauliflower Cooking spray
½ teaspoon garlic powder
4 cups arugula

Dressing:
1½ tablespoons extra-virgin olive oil
1½ tablespoons honey mustard
1 teaspoon freshly squeezed lemon juice

1. Preheat the oven to 425ºF (220ºC).
2. Remove the leaves from the cauliflower head, and cut it in half lengthwise. Cut 1½-inch-thick steaks from each half.
3. Spritz both sides of each steak with cooking spray and season both sides with the garlic powder.
4. Place the cauliflower steaks on a baking sheet, cover with foil, and roast in the oven for 10 minutes. Remove the baking sheet from the oven and gently pull back the foil to avoid the steam.
5. Flip the steaks, then roast uncovered for 10 minutes more.
6. Meanwhile, make the dressing: Whisk together the olive oil, honey mustard and lemon juice in a small bowl.
7. When the cauliflower steaks are done, divide into four equal portions. Top each portion with one-quarter of the arugula and dressing.
8. Serve immediately.

Per Serving
calories: 115 | fat: 6.0g | protein: 5.0g | carbs: 14.0g | fiber: 4.0g | sodium: 97mg

Savory Sweet Potatoes

Prep time: 10 minutes | Cook time: 18 minutes | Serves 4

2 large sweet potatoes,
peeled and cubed
¼ cup olive oil

1 teaspoon dried rosemary
½ teaspoon salt
2 tablespoons shredded
Parmesan

1. Preheat the air fryer to 360ºF (182ºC).
2. In a large bowl, toss the sweet potatoes with the olive oil, rosemary, and salt.
3. Pour the potatoes into the air fryer basket and roast for 10 minutes, then stir the potatoes and sprinkle the Parmesan over the top.
4. Continue roasting for 8 minutes more. Serve hot and enjoy.

Per Serving
calories: 186 | fat: 14g | protein: 2g | carbs: 13g | fiber: 2g | sodium: 369mg

Eggplant and Zucchini Gratin

Prep time: 10 minutes | Cook time: 19 minutes | Serves 6

2 large zucchini, finely
chopped
1 large eggplant, finely
chopped
¼ teaspoon kosher salt
¼ teaspoon freshly ground
black pepper
3 tablespoons extra-virgin
olive oil, divided

¾ cup unsweetened almond
milk
1 tablespoon all-purpose
flour
⅓ cup plus 2 tablespoons
grated Parmesan cheese,
divided
1 cup chopped tomato
1 cup diced fresh mozzarella
¼ cup fresh basil leaves

1. Preheat the oven to 425ºF (220ºC).
2. In a large bowl, toss together the zucchini, eggplant, salt and pepper.
3. In a large skillet over medium-high heat, heat 1 tablespoon of the oil. Add half of the veggie mixture to the skillet. Stir a few times, then cover and cook for about 4 minutes, stirring occasionally. Pour the cooked veggies into a baking dish.
4. Place the skillet back on the heat, add 1 tablespoon of the oil and repeat with the remaining veggies. Add the veggies to the baking dish. Meanwhile, heat the milk in the microwave for 1 minute. Set aside.
5. Place a medium saucepan over medium heat. Add the remaining 1 tablespoon of the oil and flour to the saucepan. Whisk together until well blended.
6. Slowly pour the warm milk into the saucepan, whisking the entire time. Continue to whisk frequently until the mixture thickens a bit. Add the cup of Parmesan cheese and whisk until melted. Pour the cheese sauce over the vegetables in the baking dish and mix well.
7. Fold in the tomatoes and mozzarella cheese. Roast in the oven for 10 minutes, or until the gratin is almost set and not
8. runny. Top with the fresh basil leaves and the remaining 2 tablespoons of the Parmesan cheese before serving.

Per Serving
calories: 122 | fat: 5g | protein: 10g | carbs: 11g | fiber: 4g | sodium: 364mg

Veggie-Stuffed Mushrooms

Prep time: 5 minutes | Cook time: 24 to 25 minutes | Serves 6

3 tablespoons extra-virgin
olive oil, divided
1 cup diced onion
2 garlic cloves, minced
1 large zucchini, diced
3 cups chopped mushrooms

1 cup chopped tomato
1 teaspoon dried oregano
¼ teaspoon kosher salt
¼ teaspoon crushed red
pepper
6 large portabello
mushrooms, stems and gills
removed
Cooking spray
4 ounces (113 g) fresh
mozzarella cheese, shredded

1. In a large skillet over medium heat, heat 2 tablespoons of the oil. Add the onion and sauté for 4 minutes. Stir in the garlic and sauté for 1 minute.
2. Stir in the zucchini, mushrooms, tomato, oregano, salt and red pepper.
3. Cook for 10 minutes, stirring constantly. Remove from the heat.
4. Meanwhile, heat a grill pan over medium-high heat. Brush the remaining 1 tablespoon of the oil over the portabello mushroom caps. Place the mushrooms, bottom-side down, on the grill pan.
5. Cover with a sheet of aluminum foil sprayed with nonstick cooking spray. Cook for 5 minutes.
6. Flip the mushroom caps over, and spoon about ½ cup of the cooked vegetable mixture into each cap. Top each with about 2½ tablespoons of the mozzarella. Cover and grill for 4 to 5 minutes, or until the cheese is melted.
7. Using a spatula, transfer the portabello mushrooms to a plate.
8. Let it cool for about 5 minutes before serving.

Per Serving
calories: 111 | fat: 4g | protein: 11g | carbs: 11g | fiber: 4g | sodium: 314mg

Easy Roasted Radishes

Prep time: 5 minutes | Cook time: 18 minutes | Serves 4

1 pound (454 g) radishes,
ends trimmed if needed

2 tablespoons olive oil
½ teaspoon sea salt

1. Preheat the air fryer to 360ºF (182ºC).
2. In a large bowl, combine the radishes with olive oil and sea salt.
3. Pour the radishes into the air fryer and cook for 10 minutes. Stir or turn the radishes over and cook for 8 minutes more, then serve.

Per Serving
calories: 78 | fat: 9g | protein: 1g | carbs: 4g | fiber: 2g | sodium: 335mg

Zucchini with Garlic and Red Pepper

Prep time: 5 minutes | Cook time: 15 minutes | Serves 6

2 medium zucchini, cubed
1 red bell pepper, diced

2 garlic cloves, sliced
2 tablespoons olive oil
½ teaspoon salt

1. Preheat the air fryer to 380ºF (193ºC).
2. In a large bowl, mix together the zucchini, bell pepper, and garlic with the olive oil and salt.
3. Pour the mixture into the air fryer basket, and roast for 7 minutes. Shake or stir, then roast for 7 to 8 minutes more.

Per Serving
calories: 60 | fat: 5g | protein: 1g | carbs: 4g | fiber : 1g | sodium: 195mg

Crispy Artichokes

Prep time: 10 minutes | Cook time: 15 minutes | Serves 2

1 (15-ounce / 425-g) can artichoke hearts in water, drained
1 egg
1 tablespoon water

¼ cup whole wheat bread crumbs
¼ teaspoon salt
¼ teaspoon paprika
½ lemon

1. Preheat the air fryer to 380ºF (193ºC).
2. In a medium shallow bowl, beat together the egg and water until frothy.
3. In a separate medium shallow bowl, mix together the bread crumbs, salt, and paprika.
4. Dip each artichoke heart into the egg mixture, then into the bread crumb mixture, coating the outside with the crumbs. Place the artichokes hearts in a single layer of the air fryer basket.
5. Fry the artichoke hearts for 15 minutes.
6. Remove the artichokes from the air fryer, and squeeze fresh lemon juice over the top before serving.

Per Serving
calories: 91 | fat: 2g | protein: 5g | carbs: 16g | fiber : 8g | sodium: 505mg

Lemon Green Beans

Prep time: 5 minutes | Cook time: 10 minutes | Serves 6

1 pound (454 g) fresh green beans, trimmed
½ red onion, sliced
2 tablespoons olive oil
½ teaspoon salt

¼ teaspoon black pepper
1 tablespoon lemon juice
Lemon wedges, for serving

1. Preheat the air fryer to 360ºF (182ºC). In a large bowl, toss the green beans, onion, olive oil, salt, pepper, and lemon juice until combined.
2. Pour the mixture into the air fryer and roast for 5 minutes.
3. Stir well and roast for 5 minutes more. Serve with lemon wedges.

Per Serving
calories: 67 | fat: 5g | protein: 1g | carbs: 6g | fiber : 2g | sodium: 199mg

Carrots with Honey Glaze

Prep time: 5 minutes | Cook time: 12 minutes | Serves 6

1 pound (454 g) baby carrots
2 tablespoons olive oil
¼ cup raw honey

¼ teaspoon ground cinnamon
¼ cup black walnuts, chopped

1. Preheat the air fryer to 360ºF (182ºC).
2. In a large bowl, toss the baby carrots with olive oil, honey, and cinnamon until well coated.
3. Pour into the air fryer and roast for 6 minutes. Shake the basket, sprinkle the walnuts on top, and roast for 6 more minutes.
4. Remove the carrots from the air fryer and serve.

Per Serving
calories: 146 | fat: 8g | protein: 1g | carbs: 20g | fiber : 3g | sodium: 60mg

Dill Beets

Prep time: 10 minutes | Cook time: 30 minutes | Serves 4

4 beets, cleaned, peeled, and sliced
1 garlic clove, minced
2 tablespoons chopped fresh dill

¼ teaspoon salt
¼ teaspoon black pepper
3 tablespoons olive oil

1. Preheat the air fryer to 380ºF (193ºC).
2. In a large bowl, mix together all of the ingredients so that the beets are well coated with the oil.
3. Pour the beet mixture into the air fryer basket, and roast for 15 minutes before stirring, then continue roasting for 15 minutes more.

Per Serving
calories: 126 | fat: 10g | protein: 1g | carbs: 8g | fiber : 2g | sodium: 210mg

Parmesan Butternut Squash

Prep time: 15 minutes | Cook time: 20 minutes | Serves 4

2 ½ cups butternut squash, cubed into 1-inch pieces (approximately 1 medium)
2 tablespoons olive oil
¼ teaspoon salt

¼ teaspoon garlic powder
¼ teaspoon black pepper
1 tablespoon fresh thyme
¼ cup grated Parmesan

1. Preheat the air fryer to 360ºF (182ºC).
2. In a large bowl, combine the cubed squash with the olive oil, salt, garlic powder, pepper, and thyme until the squash is well coated.
3. Pour this mixture into the air fryer basket, and roast for 10 minutes. Stir and roast another 8 to 10 minutes more.
4. Remove the squash from the air fryer and toss with freshly grated Parmesan before serving.

Per Serving
calories: 127 | fat: 9g | protein: 3g | carbs: 11g | fiber : 2g | sodium: 262mg

Roasted Brussels Sprouts

Prep time: 5 minutes | Cook time: 10 minutes | Serves 4

1 pound (454 g) Brussels sprouts, quartered
2 garlic cloves, minced
2 tablespoons olive oil
½ teaspoon salt
1 orange, cut into rings

1. Preheat the air fryer to 360ºF (182ºC).
2. In a large bowl, toss the quartered Brussels sprouts with the garlic, olive oil, and salt until well coated.
3. Pour the Brussels sprouts into the air fryer, lay the orange slices on top of them, and roast for 10 minutes.
4. Remove from the air fryer and set the orange slices aside. Toss the Brussels sprouts before serving.

Per Serving
calories: 111 | fat: 7g | protein: 4g | carbs: 11g | fiber: 4g | sodium: 319mg

Garlic Eggplant Slices

Prep time: 5 minutes | Cook time: 25 minutes | Serves 4

1 egg
1 tablespoon water
½ cup whole wheat bread crumbs
1 teaspoon garlic powder
½ teaspoon dried oregano
½ teaspoon salt
½ teaspoon paprika
1 medium eggplant, sliced into ¼-inch-thick rounds
1 tablespoon olive oil

1. Preheat the air fryer to 360ºF (182ºC).
2. In a medium shallow bowl, beat together the egg and water until frothy.
3. In a separate medium shallow bowl, mix together bread crumbs, garlic powder, oregano, salt, and paprika.
4. Dip each eggplant slice into the egg mixture, then into the bread crumb mixture, coating the outside with crumbs. Place the slices in a single layer in the bottom of the air fryer basket.
5. Drizzle the tops of the eggplant slices with the olive oil, then fry for 15 minutes. Turn each slice and cook for an additional 10 minutes.

Per Serving
calories: 137 | fat: 5g | protein: 5g | carbs: 19g | fiber: 5g | sodium: 409mg

Honey Roasted Broccoli

Prep time: 5 minutes | Cook time: 12 minutes | Serves 6

4 cups broccoli florets (approximately 1 large head)
2 tablespoons olive oil
½ teaspoon salt
½ cup orange juice
1 tablespoon raw honey
Orange wedges, for serving (optional)

1. Preheat the air fryer to 360ºF (182ºC).
2. In a large bowl, combine the broccoli, olive oil, salt, orange juice, and honey.
3. Toss the broccoli in the liquid until well coated.
4. Pour the broccoli mixture into the air fryer basket and cook for 6 minutes. Stir and cook for 6 minutes more. Serve alone or with orange wedges for additional citrus flavor, if desired.

Per Serving
calories: 80 | fat: 5g | protein: 2g | carbs: 9g | fiber: 2g | sodium: 203mg

Roasted Asparagus and Tomatoes

Prep time: 5 minutes | Cook time: 12 minutes | Serves 6

2 cups grape tomatoes
1 bunch asparagus, trimmed
2 tablespoons olive oil
3 garlic cloves, minced
½ teaspoon kosher salt

1. Preheat the air fryer to 380ºF (193ºC).
2. In a large bowl, combine all of the ingredients; tossing until the vegetables are well coated with oil.
3. Pour the vegetable mixture into the air fryer basket and spread into a single layer, then roast for 12 minutes.

Per Serving
calories: 57 | fat: 5g | protein: 1g | carbs: 4g | fiber: 1g | sodium: 197mg

Rosemary Roasted Red Potatoes

Prep time: 5 minutes | Cook time: 20 minutes | Serves 6

1 pound (454 g) red potatoes, quartered
¼ cup olive oil
½ teaspoon kosher salt
¼ teaspoon black pepper
1 garlic clove, minced
4 rosemary sprigs

1. Preheat the air fryer to 360ºF (182ºC).
2. In a large bowl, toss the potatoes with the olive oil, salt, pepper, and garlic until well coated.
3. Pour the potatoes into the air fryer basket and top with the sprigs of rosemary.
4. Roast for 10 minutes, then stir or toss the potatoes and roast for 10 minutes more.
5. Remove the rosemary sprigs and serve the potatoes.
6. Season with additional salt and pepper, if needed.

Per Serving
calories: 133 | fat: 9g | protein: 1g | carbs: 12g | fiber: 1g | sodium: 199mg

Vegetable Hummus Wraps

Prep time: 15 minutes | Cook time: 10 minutes | Serves 6

1 large eggplant
1 large onion
½ cup extra-virgin olive oil
1 teaspoon salt
6 lavash wraps or large pita bread
1 cup hummus

1. Preheat a grill, large grill pan, or lightly oiled large skillet on medium heat.
2. Slice the eggplant and onion into circles. Brush the vegetables with olive oil and sprinkle with salt.
3. Cook the vegetables on both sides, about 3 to 4 minutes each side.
4. To make the wrap, lay the lavash or pita flat. Spread about 2 tablespoons of hummus on the wrap.
5. Evenly divide the vegetables among the wraps, layering them along one side of the wrap. Gently fold over the side of the wrap with the vegetables, tucking them in and making a tight wrap.
6. Lay the wrap seam side-down and cut in half or thirds.
7. You can also wrap each sandwich with plastic wrap to help it hold its shape and eat it later.

Per Serving
calories: 362 | fat: 26g | protein: 15g | carbs: 28g | fiber: 11g | sodium: 1069mg

Easy Lentil & Rice Bowl

Serves: 4

¼ cup parsley, curly leaf, fresh & chopped
1 ½ tablespoons olive oil
sea salt & black pepper to taste
1 clove garlic, minced
tablespoon lemon juice, fresh
¼ cup red onion, diced

1 ounce can sliced onion, drained
½ cup celery, diced
½ cup carrots, diced
½ cup instant brown rice, uncooked
½ cup green lentils, uncooked
¼ vegetable broth, low sodium

1. Put a saucepan over high heat, and then bring your lentils to a boil with the broth. Cover once it begins to boil, and then lower the heat to medium-low. Cook for eight minutes.
2. Raise the heat to medium, and add in your rice. Stir well, and cover. Cook for fifteen more minutes. The liquid should be absorbed.
3. Allow it to set off the heat and cover for one minute before stirring.
4. Mix your celery, olives, onion, carrot, and parsley in a bowl while the rice and lentils are cooking.
5. Get out a bowl and whisk your oil, lemon juice, salt, pepper, and garlic together.
6. Set this to the side. When your rice and lentils are cooked, add them to a serving bowl and top with the dressing. Serve immediately.

Per Serving
calories: 124 | fat: 6g | protein: 2g | carbs: 35g | fiber : 2g |

Bean Lettuce Wraps

Servings: 4

15 Ounces Cannellini Beans, Canned, Drained & Rinsed Sea Salt & Black Pepper to Taste
¾ Cup Tomatoes, Fresh & Chopped
½ Cup Red Onion, Diced

1 Tbsp Olive Oil
¼ Cup Parsley, Fresh & Chopped Fine
8 Romaine Lettuce Leaves
½ Cup Hummus

1. Get out a skillet and place it over medium heat. Heat your oil. Once your oil is hot, adding in your onion, and cook for three minutes. Stir occasionally.
2. Add in your tomatoes and season with salt and pepper. Cook for another three minutes. Add in your beans and heat all the way through. Stir it, so it doesn't burn. Remove it from heat, and then mix in your parsley.
3. Spread a tablespoon of hummus on each lettuce leaf and then top with your bean mixture. Fold, and then wrap before serving.

Per Serving
calories: 178 | fat: 10g | protein: 17g | carbs: 10g | fiber : 7g

Chickpea Pita Patties

Serves: 4

Egg, large
2 teaspoons oregano
½ Cup panko bread crumbs,
Sea salt & black pepper to taste
1 tablespoon olive oil
1 cucumber, halved
6 ounces greek yogurt, 2%

Clove garlic, minced
Whole wheat peta bread, halved
1 tomato, cut into 4 thick slices
½ cup hummus
15 ounces chickpeas, drained & rinsed

1. Get out a large bowl, mash your chickpeas with a potato masher, and then add in your bread crumbs, eggs, hummus, oregano, and pepper. Stir well. Form four patties, and then press them flat on a plate. They should be ¾ inch thick.
2. Get out a skillet, placing it over medium-high heat. Heat the oil until hot, which should take three minutes. Cook the patties for five minutes per side.
3. While your patties are cooking, shred half of your cucumber with a grader, and then stir your shredded cucumber, garlic, and yogurt together to make a tzatziki sauce. Slice the remaining cucumber into slices that are a quarter of an inch thick before placing them to the side.
4. Toast your pita bread, and then assemble your sandwiches with each one having a tomato slice, a few slices of cucumber, chickpea patty, and drizzle each one with your sauce to serve.

Per Serving
calories: 103 | fat: 5g | protein: 3g | carbs: 17g | fiber : 4g

California Grilled Vegetable Sandwich

Servings: 4

1/4 cup mayonnaise
3 garlic cloves, minced
1 tablespoon lemon juice
1/8 cup olive oil
1 cup sliced red peppers

1 small zucchini, sliced
1 red onion, sliced
1 small yellow pumpkin, sliced
2 pieces of focaccia bread (4 x 6 inch), split horizontally
1/2 cup of crumbled feta cheese

1. Combine the mayonnaise, chopped garlic, and lemon juice in a bowl. Chill in the fridge.
2. Preheat the grill on high heat.
3. Brush the vegetables with olive oil on each side. Brush the grill with oil. Place the pepper and zucchini closest to the grill center and add the onions and squash pieces. Bake for about 3 minutes, turn around and cook for another 3 minutes.
4. Peppers can take a little longer. Remove from the grill and set aside.
5. Spread a little mayonnaise mixture on the sliced sides of the bread and sprinkle with feta cheese. Place the cheese on the grill and cover with the lid for 2 to 3 minutes.
Get away from the grill and brush with the vegetables. Enjoy open face grilled sandwiches.

Per Serving
calories: 143 | fat: 7g | protein: 9g | carbs: 14g | fiber : 3g

Barley & Mushroom Soup

Serves: 6

¼ cup red wine
2 tablespoons olive oil
1 cup carrots, chopped
1 cup onion, chopped
½ cups mushrooms, chopped

2 cups vegetable broth, low sodium
1 cup pearled barley, uncooked
2 tablespoons tomato paste
1 bay leaf
6 tablespoons parmesan cheese, grated
4 sprigs thyme, fresh

1. Get out a stockpot and place it over medium heat. Heat the oil and add in your carrots and onion. Cook for five minutes and frequently stir during this time. Turn your heat up to medium-high before throwing in your mushrooms. Cook for another three minutes. Make sure to stir frequently.
2. Add in your barley, tomato paste, thyme, wine, broth, and bay leaf. Stir and cover.
3. Bring to boil, and stir a few more times. Reduce to medium-low heat. Cover, and cook for another twelve to fifteen minutes. The barley should be cooked all the way through.
4. Remove your bay leaf and serve topped with cheese.

Per Serving
calories: 224 | fat: 8g | protein: 8g | carbs: 11g | fiber : 6g

Delicious Sweet Potato Casserole

Servings: 12

4 cups sweet potatoes, diced
1/2 cup white sugar
2 beaten eggs
1/2 teaspoon of salt
4 tablespoons of soft butter
1/2 cup milk

1/2 teaspoon vanilla extract
1/2 cup packed brown sugar
1/3 cup all-purpose flour
3 tablespoons butter
1/2 cup soft chopped pecans

1. Preheat the oven to 325° F (165 °C). Put the sweet potatoes in a medium-sized pan with water to cover.
2. Cook over medium heat until soft; drain and mash. Combine sweet potatoes, white sugar, eggs, salt, butter, milk, and vanilla extract in a large bowl. Mix until smooth. Transfer to a baking dish.
3. Put sugar and flour in a bowl. Cut the butter until the mixture is coarse. Stir in the pecans. Now sprinkle the mixture over the sweet potato mixture.
4. Bake in the preheated oven for 30 minutes or until light brown.

Per Serving
calories: 243 | fat: 13g | protein: 11g | carbs: 16g | fiber : 3g

Hot Artichoke and Spinach Dip

Serves: 12

1/4 cup mayonnaise
1 (8-oz) package cream cheese, softened
1/4 cup grated Parmesan cheese
1/4 cup grated Romano cheese
1 clove garlic, peeled and minced

1/2 teaspoon dried basil
1/4 teaspoon garlic
salt and pepper to taste
1 (14-oz) artichoke hearts, drained
1/2 cup frozen spinach
1/4 cup shredded mozzarella cheese

1. Preheat oven to 350ºF (175ºC). Lightly grease a small baking dish.
2. In a medium bowl, mix cream cheese, mayonnaise, Parmesan cheese, Romano cheese, garlic, basil, garlic salt, salt, and pepper. Gently stir in artichoke hearts and spinach.
3. Transfer the mixture to the baking dish. Top with mozzarella cheese. Bake in the preheated oven for 25 min, until bubbly and lightly browned.

Per Serving
calories: 215 | fat: 14g | protein: 11g | carbs: 12g | fiber : 1g |

Harvest Salad

Servings: 6

1/2 cup chopped nuts
1 bunch of spinach, rinsed and torn into bite-sized pieces
1/2 cup dried cranberries
1/2 cup of crumbled blue cheese
2 tomatoes, minced
1 avocado - peeled, seeded, and diced

1/2 red onion, thinly sliced
2 tablespoons red raspberry jam (with seeds)
2 tablespoons red wine vinegar
1/3 cup walnut oil
freshly ground black pepper
salt

1. Preheat the oven to 200 ºC. Put the nuts on a baking sheet. Grill in the oven for 5 minutes, or until the nuts start to turn brown. Combine spinach, walnuts, cranberries, blue cheese, tomatoes,
2. avocado, and red onion in a large bowl. Mix jam, vinegar, walnut oil, pepper, and salt in a small bowl. Add the salad dressing just before serving and mix well.

Per Serving
calories: 122 | fat: 7g | protein: 12g | carbs: 15g | fiber : 2g |

Spicy Bean Salsa

Servings: 12

1 (15 oz) can black-eyed peas
1 (15 oz) can black beans, rinsed and drained
1 can of whole-grain corn, drained
1/2 cup chopped onion

1/2 cup chopped green pepper
1 can diced jalapeño pepper
1 can of diced tomato, drained
1 cup of Italian dressing
1/2 teaspoon of garlic salt

Mix black-eyed peas, black beans, corn, onion, green pepper, jalapeño peppers, and tomatoes. Season with Italian dressing and salt with garlic; mix well. Put in the fridge overnight to mix the flavors.

Per Serving
calories: 192 | fat: 8g | protein: 18g | carbs: 11g | fiber : 2g |

Sheet-Pan Roasted Vegetables

Time: 20 minutes | Serves:6

3 tablespoons olive oil
1 tablespoon maple syrup
1 tablespoon fresh orange juice
2 teaspoons chopped fresh tarragon
3 cups butternut squash, peeled and cubed
2¼ cups parsnips, peeled and chopped into 1" pieces
1lbs of Brussels sprouts, trimmed and halved

8oz of small potatoes, halved (Preferably Yukon Gold)
1 teaspoon kosher salt
½ teaspoon freshly ground black pepper
1 teaspoon orange zest strips for seasoning
1 tablespoon orange juice for seasoning
1 teaspoon chopped fresh tarragon for seasoning
Cooking spray

1. Preheat your oven to 450°F / 232°C.
2. In a bowl, combine the olive oil, maple syrup, orange juice, 2 teaspoons of tarragon, salt and pepper using a whisk.
3. In a large bowl, combine butternut squash, parsnips, Brussels sprouts and potatoes.
4. Add the liquid mixture to the vegetables, and toss to coat everything evenly.
5. Line a baking sheet with some foil and coat with cooking spray.
6. Spread the coated veggies in a single layer onto the baking sheet.
7. Bake for 35 minutes, stirring gently after 25 minutes to ensure even baking.
8. Sprinkle the bake with the seasonings of orange zest strips, orange juice and tarragon.
9. Toss and serve.

Per Serving
Net Carbs: 38.09g | Fiber: 8.6 g | Protein: 4.97 g
Fat: 7.35 g | Kcal (per serving): 221

Brown Rice and Parsley Pilaf

Time: 40 minutes | Serves:2

½ cup uncooked brown rice
2 teaspoons olive oil
⅓ cup chopped yellow onion
¼ cup chopped carrot
2 teaspoons minced garlic

2 tablespoons chopped fresh flat leafed parsley
2 teaspoons grated lemon rind
½ teaspoon kosher salt
¼ teaspoon black pepper

1. Using the package directions, cook the rice, but do not add salt or any fats.
2. While your rice is cooking, heat olive oil over a medium heat, in a non-stick skillet.
3. Add the onion and the carrot. Cook for about 5 minutes or until tender, stirring occasionally.
4. Add garlic and cook for a further 1 minute.
5. Remove from heat and mix in the parsley, salt and pepper.
6. Put the cooked rice into a large bowl and fluff it with a fork.
7. Add the onion-carrot mixture to the rice and stir to combine.

Per Serving
Net Carbs: 40.37 g | Fiber: 2.5 g | Protein: 4.17 g
Fat: 7.42 g | Kcal (per serving): 244

Braised Fingerling Potatoes

Time: 20 minutes | Serves:3

1 tablespoon olive oil
2 teaspoons unsalted butter
½ cup white onion, thinly sliced
1 lb of fingerling potatoes. Halved length-wise.
½ cup of unsalted chicken stock

3 sprigs of oregano
2 sprigs of thyme
1 teaspoon of chopped oregano
1 teaspoon of chopped thyme
¼ teaspoon of kosher salt
¼ teaspoon of black pepper

1. Preheat oven to 375°F/190°C
2. In a large, oven-proof skillet, heat olive oil and unsalted butter together, over a medium to high heat.
3. Add the white onion and fingerling potatoes to the skillet, cook for 8 minutes.
4. Add the unsalted chicken stock, oregano and thyme sprigs.
5. Cover the skillet and bake in the oven for 10 minutes.
6. Remove from oven and discard the oregano and thyme sprigs.
7. Sprinkle the dish with the chopped oregano, chopped thyme, salt and pepper.

Per Serving
Net Carbs: 40.37 g | Fiber: 2.5 g | Protein: 4.17 g
Fat: 7.42 g | Kcal (per serving): 244

Honey Glazed Eggplant

Time: 40 minutes | Serves:2

2 large, thinly sliced, eggplants
½ teaspoon of salt
¼ cup of olive oil
5 tablespoons of honey
1 juiced large lemon
2 minced cloves of garlic

2 tablespoons of minced ginger
2 teaspoons of cumin
1 teaspoon of harissa (or 1/2 teaspoon of hot sauce if harissa is unavailable)
½ cup of chopped fresh cilantro
½ cup of hot water

1. Place your eggplant slices onto a towel and sprinkle all sides with salt. Allow the eggplants to sweat for about 15 minutes and wipe them dry with a paper towel.
2. Preheat a large-sized skillet over a medium high heat. Brush all sides of the eggplants with olive oil and cook until all sides are browned. Try not to crowd the eggplants in the pan, so perhaps do two slices at a time. Remove from pan once done.
3. In a small mixing bowl, combine the honey, lemon juice and hot water until the honey is dissolved.
4. Add the ginger and garlic to the skillet, stir for 30 seconds, and then add the cumin and harissa (or hot sauce).
5. Add the honey mixture to the skillet and stir until boiling.
6. Now add all the eggplant back in the skillet and cook over a medium heat for 10 minutes. After 5 minutes, turn the eggplants to make sure they are fully coated with the sauce.
7. Continue to cook until sauce becomes a thick glaze and eggplant is tender.
8. Garnish with the cilantro (or parsley of you prefer), and serve warm.

Per Serving
Net Carbs: 80.29 g | Fiber: 17.1 g | Protein: 6.4 g
Fat: 28.61 g | Kcal (per serving): 559

Chapter 6
Poultry and Meats

Almond-Crusted Chicken Tenders with Honey

Prep time: 10 minutes | Cook time: 20 minutes | Serves 4

1 tablespoon honey
1 tablespoon whole-grain or Dijon mustard
¼ teaspoon freshly ground black pepper
¼ teaspoon kosher or sea salt
1 pound (454 g) boneless, skinless chicken breast tenders or tenderloins
1 cup almonds, roughly chopped
Nonstick cooking spray

1. Preheat the oven to 425ºF (220ºC). Line a large, rimmed baking sheet with parchment paper. Place a wire cooling rack on the parchment-lined baking sheet, and spray the rack well with nonstick cooking spray.
2. In a large bowl, combine the honey, mustard, pepper, and salt.
3. Add the chicken and toss gently to coat. Set aside.
4. Spread the almonds over a large sheet of parchment paper and spread them out. Press the coated chicken tenders into the nuts until evenly coated on all sides. Place the chicken on the prepared wire rack.
5. Bake in the preheated oven for 15 to 20 minutes, or until the internal temperature of the chicken measures 165ºF (74ºC) on a meat thermometer and any juices run clear.
Cool for 5 minutes before serving.

Per Serving
calories: 222 | fat: 7.0g | protein: 11.0g | carbs: 29.0g | fiber: 2.0g | sodium: 44 8mg

Herbed-Mustard-Coated Pork Tenderloin

Prep time: 10 minutes | Cook time: 15 minutes | Serves 4

3 tablespoons fresh rosemary leaves
¼ cup Dijon mustard
½ cup fresh parsley leaves
6 garlic cloves
½ teaspoon sea salt
¼ teaspoon freshly ground black pepper
1 tablespoon extra-virgin olive oil
1 (1½-pound / 680-g) pork tenderloin

1. Preheat the oven to 400ºF (205ºC).
2. Put all the ingredients, except for the pork tenderloin, in a food processor. Pulse until it has a thick consistency.
3. Put the pork tenderloin on a baking sheet, then rub with the mixture to coat well.
4. Put the sheet in the preheated oven and bake for 15 minutes or until the internal temperature of the pork reaches at least 165ºF (74ºC). Flip the tenderloin halfway through the cooking time.
5. Transfer the cooked pork tenderloin to a large plate and allow to cool for 5 minutes before serving.

Per Serving
calories: 363 | fat: 18.1g | protein: 2.2g | carbs: 4.9g | fiber: 2.0g | sodium: 514mg

Macadamia Pork

Prep time: 10 minutes | Cook time: 10 minutes | Serves 4

1 (1-pound / 454-g) pork tenderloin, cut into ½-inch slices and pounded thin
1 teaspoon sea salt, divided
¼ teaspoon freshly ground black pepper, divided
½ cup macadamia nuts
1 cup unsweetened coconut milk
1 tablespoon extra-virgin olive oil

1. Preheat the oven to 400ºF (205ºC).
2. On a clean work surface, rub the pork with ½ teaspoon of the salt and teaspoon of the ground black pepper. Set aside. Ground the macadamia nuts in a food processor, then combine with remaining salt and black pepper in a bowl.
3. Stir to mix well and set aside. Combine the coconut milk and olive oil in a separate bowl. Stir to mix well.
4. Dredge the pork chops into the bowl of coconut milk mixture, then dunk into the bowl of macadamia nut mixture to coat well. Shake the excess off.
5. Put the well-coated pork chops on a baking sheet, then bake for 10 minutes or until the internal temperature of the pork reaches at least 165ºF (74ºC).
6. Transfer the pork chops to a serving plate and serve immediately.

Per Serving
calories: 436 | fat: 32.8g | protein: 33.1g | carbs: 5.9g | fiber: 3.0g | sodium: 310mg

Beef Kebabs with Onion and Pepper

Prep time: 15 minutes | Cook time: 10 minutes | Serves 6

2 pounds (907 g) beef fillet
1½ teaspoons salt
1 teaspoon freshly ground black pepper
½ teaspoon ground nutmeg
½ teaspoon ground allspice
⅓ cup extra-virgin olive oil
1 large onion, cut into 8 quarters
1 large red bell pepper, cut into 1-inch cubes

1. Preheat the grill to high heat.
2. Cut the beef into 1-inch cubes and put them in a large bowl.
3. In a small bowl, mix together the salt, black pepper, allspice, and nutmeg.
4. Pour the olive oil over the beef and toss to coat. Evenly sprinkle the seasoning over the beef and toss to coat all pieces. Skewer
5. the beef, alternating every 1 or 2 pieces with a piece of onion or bell pepper.
6. To cook, place the skewers on the preheated grill, and flip every 2 to 3 minutes until all sides have cooked to desired doneness, 6 minutes for medium-rare, 8 minutes for well done. Serve hot.

Per Serving
calories: 485 | fat: 36.0g | protein: 35.0g | carbs: 4.0g | fiber: 1.0g | sodium: 14 53mg

Slow-Cooked Lamb Shanks with Cannellini Beans Stew

Prep time: 20 minutes | Cook time: 10 hours 15 minutes | Serves 12

1 (19-ounce / 539-g) can cannellini beans, rinsed and drained	4 (1½-pound / 680-g) lamb shanks, fat trimmed
1 large yellow onion, chopped	2 teaspoons tarragon
2 medium-sized carrots, diced	½ teaspoon sea salt
1 large stalk celery, chopped	¼ teaspoon ground black pepper
2 cloves garlic, thinly sliced	1 (28-ounce / 794-g) can diced tomatoes, with the juice

1. Combine the beans, onion, carrots, celery, and garlic in the slow cooker. Stir to mix well.
2. Add the lamb shanks and sprinkle with tarragon, salt, and ground black pepper.
3. Pour in the tomatoes with juice, then cover the lid and cook on high for an hour.
4. Reduce the heat to low and cook for 9 hours or until the lamb is super tender.
5. Transfer the lamb to a plate, then pour the bean mixture in a colander over a separate bowl to reserve the liquid.
6. Let the liquid sit for 5 minutes until set, then skim the fat from the surface of the liquid. Pour the bean mixture back to the liquid.
7. Remove the bones from the lamb heat and discard the bones. Put the lamb meat and bean mixture back to the slow cooker. Cover and cook to reheat for 15 minutes or until heated through.
8. Place them on a large serving plate and serve immediately.

Per Serving
calories: 317 | fat: 9.7g | protein: 52.1g | carbs: 7.0g | fiber: 2.1g | sodium: 375mg

Grilled Pork Chops

Prep time: 20 minutes | Cook time: 10 minutes | Serves 4

¼ cup extra-virgin olive oil	1 teaspoon salt
2 tablespoons fresh thyme leaves	4 pork loin chops, ½-inch-thick
1 teaspoon smoked paprika	

1. In a small bowl, mix together the olive oil, thyme, paprika, and salt. Put the pork chops in a plastic zip-top bag or a bowl and coat them with the spice mix. Let them marinate for 15 minutes.
2. Preheat the grill to high heat. Cook the pork chops for 4 minutes on each side until cooked through. Serve warm.

Per Serving
calories: 282 | fat: 23.0g | protein: 21.0g | carbs: 1.0g | fiber: 0g | sodium: 832mg

Chicken Bruschetta Burgers

Prep time: 10 minutes | Cook time: 16 minutes | Serves 2

1 tablespoon olive oil	8 ounces (227 g) ground chicken breast
2 garlic cloves, minced	¼ teaspoon salt
3 tablespoons finely minced onion	3 pieces small Mozzarella balls, minced
1 teaspoon dried basil	
3 tablespoons minced sun-dried tomatoes packed in olive oil	

1. Heat the olive oil in a nonstick skillet over medium-high heat. Add the garlic and onion and sauté for 5 minutes until tender. Stir in the basil. Remove from the skillet to a medium bowl. Add the tomatoes, ground chicken, and salt and stir until incorporated. Mix in the Mozzarella balls.
2. Divide the chicken mixture in half and form into two burgers, each about ¾-inch thick.
3. Heat the same skillet over medium-high heat and add the burgers. Cook each side for 5 to 6 minutes, or until they reach an internal temperature of 165ºF (74ºC). Serve warm.

Per Serving
calories: 300 | fat: 17.0g | protein: 32.2g | carbs: 6.0g | fiber: 1.1g | sodium: 724mg

Potato, Lamb and Olive Stew

Prep time: 20 minutes | Cook time: 3 hours 42 minutes | Serves 10

4 tablespoons almond flour	Coarse sea salt and black pepper, to taste
¾ cup low-sodium chicken stock	3½ pounds (1.6 kg) lamb shanks, fat trimmed and cut crosswise into 1½- inch pieces
1¼ pounds (567 g) small potatoes, halved	
3 cloves garlic, minced	2 tablespoons extra-virgin olive oil
4 large shallots, cut into ½-inch wedges	
3 sprigs fresh rosemary	½ cup dry white wine
1 tablespoon lemon zest	1 cup pitted green olives, halved
	2 tablespoons lemon juice

1. Combine 1 tablespoon of almond flour with chicken stock in a bowl. Stir to mix well. Put the flour mixture, potatoes, garlic, shallots, rosemary, and lemon zest in the slow cooker. Sprinkle with salt and black pepper. Stir to mix well. Set aside.
2. Combine the remaining almond flour with salt and black pepper in a large bowl, then dunk the lamb shanks in the flour and toss to coat.
3. Heat the olive oil in a nonstick skillet over medium-high heat until shimmering.
4. Add the well-coated lamb and cook for 10 minutes or until golden brown. Flip the lamb pieces halfway through the cooking time. Transfer the cooked lamb to the slow cooker.
5. Pour the wine in the same skillet, then cook for 2 minutes or until it reduces in half. Pour the wine in the slow cooker.
6. Put the slow cooker lid on and cook on high for 3 hours and 30 minutes or until the lamb is very tender.
7. In the last 20 minutes of the cooking, open the lid and fold in the olive halves to cook.
8. Pour the stew on a large plate, let them sit for 5 minutes, then skim any fat remains over the face of the liquid.
9. Drizzle with lemon juice and sprinkle with salt and pepper. Serve warm.

Per Serving
calories: 309 | fat: 10.3g | protein: 36.9g | carbs: 16.1g | fiber: 2.2g | sodium: 239mg

Greek-Style Lamb Burgers

Prep time: 10 minutes | Cook time: 10 minutes | Serves 4

1 pound (454 g) ground lamb
½ teaspoon salt
½ teaspoon freshly ground black pepper

4 tablespoons crumbled feta cheese
Buns, toppings, and tzatziki, for serving (optional)

1. Preheat the grill to high heat. In a large bowl, using your hands, combine the lamb with the salt and pepper.
2. Divide the meat into 4 portions. Divide each portion in half to make a top and a bottom. Flatten each half into a 3-inch circle. Make a dent in the center of one of the halves and place 1 tablespoon of the feta cheese in the center. Place the second half of the patty on top of the feta cheese and press down to close the 2 halves together, making it resemble a round burger. Grill each side for 3 minutes, for medium-well. Serve on a bun with your favorite toppings and tzatziki sauce, if desired.

Per Serving
calories: 345 | fat: 29.0g | protein: 20.0g | carbs: 1.0g | fiber: 0g | sodium: 462mg

Parsley-Dijon Chicken and Potatoes

Prep time: 5 minutes | Cook time: 22 minutes | Serves 6

1 tablespoon extra-virgin olive oil
1½ pounds (680 g) boneless, skinless chicken thighs, cut into 1-inch cubes, patted dry
1½ pounds (680 g) Yukon Gold potatoes, unpeeled, cut into ½-inch cubes
2 garlic cloves, minced
¼ cup dry white wine

1 cup low-sodium or no-salt-added chicken broth
1 tablespoon Dijon mustard
¼ teaspoon freshly ground black pepper
¼ teaspoon kosher or sea salt
1 cup chopped fresh flat-leaf (Italian) parsley, including stems
1 tablespoon freshly squeezed lemon juice

1. In a large skillet over medium-high heat, heat the oil. Add the chicken and cook for 5 minutes, stirring only after the chicken has browned on one side. Remove the chicken and reserve on a plate.
2. Add the potatoes to the skillet and cook for 5 minutes, stirring only after the potatoes have become golden and crispy on one side. Push the potatoes to the side of the skillet, add the garlic, and cook, stirring constantly, for 1 minute. Add the wine and cook for 1 minute, until nearly evaporated. Add the chicken broth, mustard, salt, pepper, and reserved chicken. Turn the heat to high and bring to a boil. Once boiling, cover, reduce the heat to medium-low, and cook for 10 to 12 minutes, until the potatoes are tender and the internal temperature of the chicken measures 165ºF (74ºC) on a meat thermometer and any juices run clear. During the last minute of cooking, stir in the parsley. Remove from the heat, stir in the lemon juice, and serve.

Per Serving
calories: 324 | fat: 9.0g | protein: 16.0g | carbs: 45.0g | fiber: 5.0g | sodium: 560mg

Chicken Cacciatore

Prep time: 15 minutes | Cook time: 1 hour and 30 minutes | Serves 2

1½ pounds (680 g) bone-in chicken thighs, skin removed and patted dry Salt, to taste
2 tablespoons olive oil
½ large onion, thinly sliced
4 ounces (113 g) baby bella mushrooms, sliced
1 red sweet pepper, cut into 1-inch pieces

1 (15-ounce / 425-g) can crushed fire-roasted tomatoes
1 fresh rosemary sprig
½ cup dry red wine
1 teaspoon Italian herb seasoning
½ teaspoon garlic powder
3 tablespoons flour

1. Season the chicken thighs with a generous pinch of salt. Heat the olive oil in a Dutch oven over medium-high heat. Add the chicken and brown for 5 minutes per side.
2. Add the onion, mushrooms, and sweet pepper to the Dutch oven and sauté for another 5 minutes.
3. Add the tomatoes, rosemary, wine, Italian seasoning, garlic powder, and salt, stirring well.
4. Bring the mixture to a boil, then reduce the heat to low. Allow to simmer slowly for at least 1 hour, stirring occasionally, or until the chicken is tender and easily pulls away from the bone.
5. Measure out 1 cup of the sauce from the pot and put it into a bowl. Add the flour and whisk well to make a slurry.
6. Increase the heat to medium-high and slowly whisk the slurry into the pot. Stir until it comes to a boil and cook until the sauce is thickened.
7. Remove the chicken from the bones and shred it, and add it back to the sauce before serving, if desired.

Per Serving
calories: 520 | fat: 23.1g | protein: 31.8g | carbs: 37.0g | fiber: 6.0g | sodium: 484mg

Grilled Lemon Chicken

Prep time: 10 minutes | Cook time: 12 to 14 minutes | Serves 2

1 (4-ounce / 113-g) boneless, skinless chicken breasts Marinade:
4 tablespoons freshly squeezed lemon juice
2 tablespoons olive oil, plus more for greasing the grill grates

1 teaspoon dried basil
1 teaspoon paprika
½ teaspoon dried thyme
¼ teaspoon salt
¼ teaspoon garlic powder

1. Make the marinade: Whisk together the lemon juice, olive oil, basil, paprika, thyme, salt, and garlic powder in a large bowl until well combined.
2. Add the chicken breasts to the bowl and let marinate for at least 30 minutes.
3. When ready to cook, preheat the grill to medium-high heat. Lightly grease the grill grates with the olive oil. Discard the marinade and arrange the chicken breasts on the grill grates.
4. Grill for 12 to 14 minutes, flipping the chicken halfway through, or until a meat thermometer inserted in the center of the chicken reaches 165ºF (74ºC).
5. Let the chicken cool for 5 minutes and serve warm.

Per Serving
calories: 251 | fat: 15.5g | protein: 27.3g | carbs: 1.9g | fiber: 1.0g | sodium: 371mg

Baked Teriyaki Turkey Meatballs

Prep time: 20 minutes | Cook time: 20 minutes | Serves 6

1 pound (454 g) lean ground turkey
1 egg, whisked
¼ cup finely chopped scallions, both white and green parts
2 garlic cloves, minced

2 tablespoons reduced-sodium tamari or gluten-free soy sauce
1 teaspoon grated fresh ginger
1 tablespoon honey
2 teaspoons mirin
1 teaspoon olive oil

1. Preheat the oven to 400ºF (205ºC). Line a baking sheet with parchment paper and set aside.
2. Mix together the ground turkey, whisked egg, scallions, garlic, tamari, ginger, honey, mirin, and olive oil in a large bowl, and stir until well blended.
3. Use a tablespoon to scoop out rounded heaps of the turkey mixture, and then roll them into balls with your hands. Transfer the balls to the prepared baking sheet.
4. Bake in the preheated oven for 20 minutes, flipping the meatballs with a spatula halfway through, or until the meatballs are browned and cooked through. Serve warm.

Per Serving
calories: 158 | fat: 8.6g | protein: 16.2g | carbs: 4.0g | fiber: 0.2g | sodium: 269mg

Greek Beef Kebabs

Prep time: 15 minutes | Cook time: 20 minutes | Serves 2

6 ounces (170 g) beef sirloin tip, trimmed of fat and cut into 2-inch pieces
3 cups of any mixture of vegetables: mushrooms, summer squash, zucchini, onions, red peppers, cherry tomatoes
½ cup olive oil

¼ cup freshly squeezed lemon juice
2 tablespoons balsamic vinegar
2 teaspoons dried oregano
1 teaspoon garlic powder
1 teaspoon salt
1 teaspoon minced fresh rosemary
Cooking spray

1. Put the beef in a plastic freezer bag.
2. Slice the vegetables into similar-size pieces and put them in a second freezer bag.
3. Make the marinade: Mix the olive oil, lemon juice, balsamic vinegar, oregano, garlic powder, salt, and rosemary in a measuring cup. Whisk well to combine. Pour half of the marinade over the beef, and the other half over the vegetables.
4. Put the beef and vegetables in the refrigerator to marinate for 4 hours.
5. When ready, preheat the grill to medium-high heat and spray the grill grates with cooking spray.
6. Thread the meat onto skewers and the vegetables onto separate skewers.
7. Grill the meat for 3 minutes per side. They should only take 10 to 12 minutes to cook, depending on the thickness of the meat.
8. Grill the vegetables for about 3 minutes per side, or until they have grill marks and are softened. Serve hot.

Per Serving
calories: 284 | fat: 18.2g | protein: 21.0g | carbs: 9.0g | fiber: 3.9g | sodium: 122mg

Beef Stew with Beans and Zucchini

Prep time: 20 minutes | Cook time: 6 to 8 hours | Serves 2

1 (15-ounce / 425-g) can diced or crushed tomatoes with basil
1 teaspoon beef base
2 tablespoons olive oil, divided
8 ounces (227 g) baby bella (cremini) mushrooms, quartered
2 garlic cloves, minced
½ large onion, diced
1 pound (454 g) cubed beef stew meat
3 tablespoons flour

¼ teaspoon salt
Pinch freshly ground black pepper
¾ cup dry red wine
¼ cup minced brined olives
1 fresh rosemary sprig
1 (15-ounce / 425-g) can white cannellini beans, drained and rinsed
1 medium zucchini, cut in half lengthwise and then cut into 1-inch pieces.

1. Place the tomatoes into a slow cooker and set it to low heat. Add the beef base and stir to incorporate.
2. Heat 1 tablespoon of olive oil in a large sauté pan over medium heat. Add the mushrooms and onion and sauté for 10 minutes, stirring occasionally, or until they're golden. Add the garlic and cook for 30 seconds more. Transfer the vegetables to the slow cooker.
3. In a plastic food storage bag, combine the stew meat with the flour, salt, and pepper. Seal the bag and shake well to combine. Heat the remaining 1 tablespoon of olive oil in the sauté pan over high heat.
4. Add the floured meat and sear to get a crust on the outside edges. Deglaze the pan by adding about half of the red wine and scraping up any browned bits on the bottom.
5. Stir so the wine thickens a bit and transfer to the slow cooker along with any remaining wine. Stir the stew to incorporate the ingredients. Stir in the olives and rosemary, cover, and cook for 6 to 8 hours on Low. About 30 minutes before the stew is finished, add the beans and zucchini to let them warm through. Serve warm.

Per Serving
calories: 389 | fat: 15.1g | protein: 30.8g | carbs: 25.0g | fiber: 8.0g | sodium: 582mg

Beef, Tomato, and Lentils Stew

Prep time: 10 minutes | Cook time: 10 minutes | Serves 4

1 tablespoon extra-virgin olive oil
1 onion, chopped
1 (14-ounce / 397-g) can chopped tomatoes with garlic and basil, drained

1 (14-ounce / 397-g) can lentils, drained
½ teaspoon sea salt
⅛ teaspoon freshly ground black pepper
1 pound (454 g) extra-lean ground beef

1. Heat the olive oil in a pot over medium-high heat until shimmering.
2. Add the beef and onion to the pot and sauté for 5 minutes or until the beef is lightly browned.
3. Add the remaining ingredients. Bring to a boil. Reduce the heat to medium and cook for 4 more minutes or until the lentils are tender. Keep stirring during the cooking.
4. Pour them in a large serving bowl and serve immediately.

Per Serving
calories: 460 | fat: 14.8g | protein: 44.2g | carbs: 36.9g | fiber: 17.0g | sodium: 320mg

Ground Beef, Tomato, and Kidney Bean Chili

Prep time: 10 minutes | Cook time: 15 minutes | Serves 4

1 tablespoon extra-virgin olive oil
1 pound (454 g) extra-lean ground beef
1 onion, chopped
2 (14-ounce / 397-g) cans kidney beans
2 (28-ounce / 794-g) cans chopped tomatoes, juice reserved
Chili Spice:
1 teaspoon garlic powder
1 tablespoon chili powder
½ teaspoon sea salt

1. Heat the olive oil in a pot over medium-high heat until shimmering.
2. Add the beef and onion to the pot and sauté for 5 minutes or until the beef is lightly browned and the onion is translucent.
3. Add the remaining ingredients. Bring to a boil. Reduce the heat to medium and cook for 10 more minutes. Keep stirring during the cooking.
4. Pour them in a large serving bowl and serve immediately.

Per Serving
calories: 891 | fat: 20.1g | protein: 116.3g | carbs: 62.9g | fiber: 17.0g | sodium: 561mg

Chermoula Roasted Pork Tenderloin

Prep time: 15 minutes | Cook time: 20 minutes | Serves 2

½ cup fresh cilantro
½ cup fresh parsley
6 small garlic cloves
3 tablespoons olive oil, divided
3 tablespoons freshly squeezed lemon juice
2 teaspoons cumin
1 teaspoon smoked paprika
½ teaspoon salt, divided
Pinch freshly ground black pepper
1 (8-ounce / 227-g) pork tenderloin

1. Preheat the oven to 425ºF (220ºC).
2. In a food processor, combine the cilantro, parsley, garlic, 2 tablespoons of olive oil, lemon juice, cumin, paprika, and ¼ teaspoon of salt. Pulse 15 to 20 times, or until the mixture is fairly smooth. Scrape the sides down as needed to incorporate all the ingredients. Transfer the sauce to a small bowl and set aside.
3. Season the pork tenderloin on all sides with the remaining ¼ teaspoon of salt and a generous pinch of black pepper.
4. Heat the remaining 1 tablespoon of olive oil in a sauté pan.
5. Sear the pork for 3 minutes, turning often, until golden brown on all sides.
6. Transfer the pork to a baking dish and roast in the preheated oven for 15 minutes, or until the internal temperature registers 145ºF (63ºC).
7. Cool for 5 minutes before serving.

Per Serving
calories: 169 | fat: 13.1g | protein: 11.0g | carbs: 2.9g | fiber: 1.0g | sodium: 332mg

Lamb Kofta (Spiced Meatballs)

Prep time: 15 minutes | Cook time: 30 minutes | Serves 2

¼ cup walnuts
1 garlic clove
½ small onion
1 roasted piquillo pepper
2 tablespoons fresh mint
2 tablespoons fresh parsley
¼ teaspoon cumin
¼ teaspoon allspice
¼ teaspoon salt Pinch cayenne pepper
8 ounces (227 g) lean ground lamb

1. Preheat the oven to 350ºF (180ºC). Line a baking sheet with aluminum foil.
2. In a food processor, combine the walnuts, garlic, onion, roasted pepper, mint, parsley, cumin, allspice, salt, and cayenne pepper. Pulse about 10 times to combine everything.
3. Transfer the spice mixture to a large bowl and add the ground lamb. With your hands or a spatula, mix the spices into the lamb.
4. Roll the lamb into 1½-inch balls (about the size of golf balls).
5. Arrange the meatballs on the prepared baking sheet and bake for 30 minutes, or until cooked to an internal temperature of 165ºF (74ºC).
6. Serve warm.

Per Serving
calories: 409 | fat: 22.9g | protein: 22.0g | carbs: 7.1g | fiber: 3.0g | sodium: 428mg

Chicken Gyros with Tzatziki Sauce

Prep time: 15 minutes | Cook time: 10 minutes | Serves 2

2 tablespoons freshly squeezed lemon juice
2 tablespoons olive oil, divided, plus more for oiling the grill
1 teaspoon minced fresh oregano
½ teaspoon garlic powder
Salt, to taste
8 ounces (227 g) chicken tenders
1 small eggplant, cut into 1-inch strips lengthwise
1 small zucchini, cut into ½-inch strips lengthwise
½ red pepper, seeded and cut in half lengthwise
½ English cucumber, peeled and minced
¾ cup plain Greek yogurt
1 tablespoon minced fresh dill
2 (8-inch) pita breads

1. Combine the lemon juice, 1 tablespoon of olive oil, oregano, garlic powder, and salt in a medium bowl. Add the chicken and let marinate for 30 minutes.
2. Place the eggplant, zucchini, and red pepper in a large mixing bowl and sprinkle with salt and the remaining 1 tablespoon of olive oil. Toss well to coat. Let the vegetables rest while the chicken is marinating.
3. Make the tzatziki sauce: Combine the cucumber, yogurt, salt, and dill in a medium bowl. Stir well to incorporate and set aside in the refrigerator. When ready, preheat the grill to medium-high heat and oil the grill grates.
4. Drain any liquid from the vegetables and put them on the grill. Remove the chicken tenders from the marinade and put them on the grill.
5. Grill the chicken and vegetables for 3 minutes per side, or until the chicken is no longer pink inside. Remove the chicken and vegetables from the grill and set aside. On the grill, heat the pitas for about 30 seconds, flipping them frequently.
6. Divide the chicken tenders and vegetables between the pitas and top each with ¼ cup of the prepared sauce. Roll the pitas up like a cone and serve.

Per Serving
calories: 586 | fat: 21.9g | protein: 39.0g | carbs: 62.0g | fiber: 11.8g | sodium: 955mg

Pesto Chicken Mix

Prep time: 10 minutes | Cook time: 40 minutes | Serves 4

4 halves of chicken breast, skinless and boneless
3 tomatoes, diced
1 cup mozzarella, shredded
½ cup of basil pesto
A pinch of salt and black pepper Cooking spray

1. Grease a baking sheet lined with baking paper with cooking spray.
2. In a bowl, mix chicken with salt, pepper and pesto and rub in well.
3. Place the chicken on the baking sheet, top with the tomatoes and shredded mozzarella and bake at 400 ºF for 40 minutes.
4. Divide the mix among plates and serve with a side salad.

Per Serving
calories 341 | fat 20 | fiber 1 | carbohydrates 4 | protein 32

Paprika Chicken Mix

Prep time: 10 minutes | Cook time: 15 minutes | Serves 2

2 cups of pineapple, peeled and diced
2 tablespoons of olive oil
1 tablespoon of smoked paprika
2 pounds of chicken breasts, skinless, boned and diced
A pinch of salt and black pepper
1 tablespoon chives, chopped

1. Heat a skillet with oil over medium-high heat, add chicken, salt and pepper and brown for 4 minutes on each side.
2. Add the rest of the ingredients; stir, cook for another 7 minutes, divide among plates and serve with a side salad.

Per Serving
calories 264, fat 13.2, fiber 8.3, carbohydrates 25.1, protein 15.4

Duck and tomato sauce

Prep time: 10 minutes | Cook time: 2 hours | Serves 4

4 duck legs
2 yellow onions, sliced
4 cloves of garlic, minced
¼ cup parsley, chopped
A pinch of salt and black pepper
1 teaspoon of Herbes de Provence
1 cup of tomato sauce
2 cups of black olives, pitted and sliced

1. In a baking dish, combine the duck legs with the onions, garlic and the rest of the ingredients; place in the oven and bake at 370 ºF for 2 hours.
2. Divide the mix among the plates and serve.

Per Serving
calories 300, fat 13.5, fiber 9.2, carbohydrates 16.7, protein 15.2

Chicken and Olives

Prep time: 10 minutes | Cook time: 15 minutes | Serves 4

4 chicken breasts, skinless and boneless
2 tablespoons minced garlic
1 tablespoon of dried oregano
Salt and black pepper to taste
2 tablespoons olive oil
½ cup chicken broth Juice of 1 lemon
1 cup red onion, chopped
1 ½ cups tomatoes, diced
¼ cup green olives, pitted and sliced
A handful of parsley, chopped

1. Heat a skillet with the oil over medium-high heat, add the chicken, garlic, salt and pepper and brown for 2 minutes on each side.
2. Add the rest of the ingredients; stir, bring the mixture to a simmer and cook over medium heat for 13 minutes. Divide
3. the mix among the plates and serve.

Per Serving
calories 135, fat 5.8, fiber 3.4, carbohydrates 12.1, protein 9.6

Turkey with Walnuts

Prep time: 10 minutes | Cook time: 1 hour | Serves 4

1 turkey breast, skinless, boned and cut into slices
¼ cup of chicken broth
1 tablespoon walnuts, chopped
1 red onion, chopped
Salt and black pepper to taste
2 tablespoons olive oil
4 peaches, pitted and cut into quarters
1 tablespoon coriander, chopped

1. In a pan greased with oil, combine the turkey and onion and the rest of the ingredients; except the cilantro, place in the oven and bake at 390 ºF for 1 hour.
2. Divide mixture among plates, sprinkle cilantro on top and serve.

Per Serving
calories 500, fat 14, fiber 3, carbohydrates 15, protein 10

Chicken with Feta

Prep time: 10 minutes | Cook time: 25 minutes | Serves 4

1 chicken breast, skinless, boned and cut into strips
1 red cabbage, shredded
2 tablespoons of olive oil
Salt and black pepper to taste
2 tablespoons of balsamic vinegar
1 ½ cups tomatoes, diced
1 tablespoon chives, chopped
¼ cup feta cheese, crumbled

1. Heat a skillet with the oil over medium-high heat, add the chicken and sauté for 5 minutes.
2. Add the rest of the ingredients except the cheese, and cook over medium heat for 20 minutes, stirring often.
3. Add cheese, stir, divide between plates and serve.

Per Serving
calories 277, fat 15, fiber 8.6, carbohydrates 14.9, protein 14.2

Baked Chicken

Prep time: 10 minutes | Cook time: 30 minutes | Serves 4

1 1/2 pounds of skinless chicken thighs, boned and diced
2 cloves of garlic, minced
1 tablespoon oregano, chopped
2 tablespoons olive oil
1 tablespoon of red wine vinegar
½ cup canned artichokes, drained and chopped
1 red onion, sliced

1 pound of whole wheat fusili pasta, cooked
½ cup canned white beans, drained and rinsed
½ cup parsley, chopped
1 cup mozzarella, shredded
Salt and black pepper to taste

1. Heat a skillet with half of the oil over medium-high heat, add the meat and brown it for 5 minutes.
2. Grease a baking dish with the rest of the oil, add the browned chicken and the rest of the ingredients except the pasta and mozzarella.
3. Spread the dough over the entire surface and toss gently.
4. Sprinkle mozzarella cheese on top and bake at 425 ºF for 25 minutes.
5. Divide the cake among the plates and serve.

Per Serving
calories 195, fat 5.8, fiber 3.4, carbohydrates 12.1, protein 11.6

Chicken with chives

Prep time: 10 minutes | Cook time: 30 minutes | Serves 4

1 chicken breast, skinless, boned and cut into cubes
Salt and black pepper to taste
2 tablespoons olive oil
1 cup chicken broth

½ cup of tomato sauce
½ pound red radishes, diced
2 tablespoons chives, chopped

1. Heat a Dutch oven with the oil over medium-high heat, add the chicken and brown for 4 minutes on each side.
2. Add the rest of the ingredients except the chives, bring to a boil and cook over medium heat for 20 minutes.
3. Divide the mixture among plates, sprinkle with chives and serve.

Per Serving
calories 277, fat 15, fiber 9.3, carbohydrates 20.9, protein 33.2

Chicken and Caper Mix

Prep time: 5 minutes | Cook time: 7 hours | Serves 4

2 chicken breasts, skinless, boned and halved
2 cups canned tomatoes, crushed
2 cloves garlic, minced
1 yellow onion, minced

2 cups chicken broth
2 tablespoons capers, drained
¼ cup rosemary, chopped
Salt and black pepper to taste

1. In your slow cooker, combine the chicken with the tomatoes, capers and the rest of the ingredients; put the lid on and cook on Low for 7 hours.
2. Divide the mix among the plates and serve.

Per Serving
calories 292, fat 9.4, fiber 11.8, carbohydrates 25.1, protein 36.4

Chicken and Quinoa Mix

Prep time: 10 minutes | Cook time: 50 minutes | Serves 4

4 chicken things, skinless and boneless
1 tablespoon olive oil
Salt and black pepper to taste
2 stalks of celery, chopped

2 spring onions, chopped
2 cups chicken broth
½ cup cilantro, chopped
½ cup of quinoa
2 tablespoons lime zest, grated

1. Heat a saucepan with the oil over medium-high heat, add the chicken and brown for 4 minutes on each side.
2. Add the onion and celery, stir and sauté for another 5 minutes.
3. Add the rest of the ingredients; stir, bring to a boil and cook over medium-low heat for 35 minutes.
4. Divide everything among plates and serve.

Per Serving
calories 241, fat 12.6, fiber 9.5, carbohydrates 15.6, protein 34.1

Chicken Soup

Cooking Time: 45 Minutes | Serves 4

1 pound whole chicken, boneless and chopped into small chunks
1/2 cup onions, chopped
1/2 cup rutabaga, cubed
2 carrots, peeled
celery stalks
Salt and black pepper, to taste
1 cup chicken bone broth

1/2 teaspoon ginger-garlic paste
1/2 cup taro leaves, roughly chopped
1 tablespoon fresh coriander, chopped
3 cups water
1 teaspoon paprika

1. Place all ingredients in a heavy-bottomed pot. Bring to a boil over the highest heat.
2. Turn the heat to simmer. Continue to cook, partially covered, an additional 40 minutes.
3. Store.
4. Spoon the soup into four airtight containers or Ziploc bags; keep in your refrigerator for up to 3 to days. For freezing, place the soup in airtight containers. It will maintain the best quality for about to 6 months. Defrost in the refrigerator. Bon appétit!

Per Serving
calories 25; Fat 12.9g; Carbs 3.2g; Protein 35.1g; Fiber 2.2g

Turkey Bacon Bites

Cooking Time: 5 Minutes | Serves 4

4 ounces turkey bacon, chopped
4 ounces Neufchatel cheese
1 tablespoon butter, cold

jalapeno pepper, deveined and minced
1 teaspoon Mexican oregano
2 tablespoons scallions, finely chopped

1. Thoroughly combine all ingredients in a mixing bowl.
2. Roll the mixture into 8 balls.
   Store
3. Divide the turkey bacon bites between two airtight containers or Ziploc bags; keep in your refrigerator for up 3 to days.

Per Serving
Calories 195; Fat 16.7g; Carbs 2.2g; Protein 8.8g; Fiber 0.3g

Simple/Aromatic Meatballs

Servings: 4

2 cups ground beef
1 egg, beaten
1 teaspoon garlic, minced
½ teaspoon salt

1 teaspoon taco seasoning
1 tablespoon sugar-free
marinara sauce

1. Take a mixing bowl and put all the ingredients into the bowl
2. Add all the ingredients into the bowl. Mix all the ingredients with a spoon or fingertips. Then make the small size meatballs and put them in a layer in the air fryer rack. Lower the air fryer lid.
3. Cook the meatballs for 11 minutes at 350° F. Serve immediately and enjoy!

Per Serving
calories: 223 | fat: 9g | protein: 16g | carbs: 11g | fiber : 3g

Tantalizing Beef Jerky

Servings: 4

½ pound beef, sliced into
1/8 inch thick strips
½ cup of soy sauce
2 tablespoons
Worcestershire sauce

1 teaspoon onion powder
½ teaspoon garlic powder
1 teaspoon salt
2 teaspoons ground black
pepper

1. Place all ingredient in a large-sized Ziploc bag, seal it shut.
2. Shake and leave it in the fridge overnight.
3. Lay strips on dehydrator trays, making sure not to overlap them.
4. Lock Air Crisping Lid and set the temperature to 135°F, cook for 7 hours.
5. Store in an airtight container, enjoy!

Per Serving
calories: 241 | fat: 11g | protein: 18g | carbs: 14g | fiber : 4g

Salsa Pulled Pork

Servings: 4

Ingredients:
2 lbs pork shoulder, boneless
and cut into chunks
1/4 cup fresh cilantro chopped
1/2 cup beef stock
1 tbsp honey

15 oz can tomato, drained
and diced 15 oz salsa
1 tsp dried oregano,
1 tsp ground cumin
Salt and Pepper

1. Season meat with pepper and salt.
2. Add meat, stock, oregano, cumin, honey, tomatoes, and salsa to the instant pot.
3. Seal the instant pot with lid and cook on high for 15 minutes. Release pressure naturally, then open the lid.
4. Shred the meat using a fork. Add cilantro and stir everything well.
5. Serve and enjoy.

Per Serving
calories: 416 | fat: 9g | protein: 29g | carbs: 21g | fiber : 5g

Pork with Vegetables

Servings: 3

1 lb pork, cut into pieces
1 tbsp tomato paste
tbsp Dijon mustard
1 chili pepper chopped
spring onions chopped cup
broccoli chopped
1/4 cup celery stalk chopped
2 tbsp apple cider vinegar

1 tbsp olive oil
1/2 tsp garlic powder,
1 tsp dried celery
1/2 tsp pepper
4 cup beef stock
1 tsp sea salt

1. Add oil into the instant pot and set to sauté mode.
2. Season meat with pepper and salt and add in the pot.
3. Add vegetables, garlic powder, celery, tomato paste, and stock and stir well.
4. Seal skillet with lid and cook on high for 20 minutes.
5. Release pressure naturally, then open the lid.
6. Serve hot and enjoy.

Per Serving
calories: 373 | fat: 10g | protein: 22g | carbs: 25g | fiber : 4g

Beef Kofta

Servings: 4

Olive oil cooking spray
½ onion, roughly chopped
1-inch piece ginger, peeled
2 garlic cloves, peeled
⅓ cup fresh parsley
⅓ cup fresh mint
1 pound ground beef

1 tbsp ground cumin
1 tbsp ground coriander
1 teaspoon ground cinnamon
¾ teaspoon kosher salt
½ teaspoon ground sumac
¼ teaspoon ground cloves
¼ teaspoon freshly ground
black pepper

1. Preheat the oven to 400° F. Grease a 12-cup muffin tin.
2. In a food processor, add the onion, ginger, garlic, parsley, and mint; process until minced.
3. Place the mixture in a bowl. Add the beef, cumin, coriander, cinnamon, salt, sumac, cloves, and black pepper, and mix thoroughly with your hands.
4. Split the beef mixture into 12 balls and place each one in a prepared muffin tin cup. Bake for 20 minutes.

Per Serving
calories: 221 | fat: 8g | protein: 21g | carbs: 14g | fiber : 2g

Rosemary Broccoli Pork

Servings: 4

1 lb pork loin, chopped
2 cups cherry tomatoes,
chopped
1 cup broccoli, chopped
1 onion, chopped

1/2 tsp chili powder
1 fresh rosemary sprig
1/4 cup olive oil
1/2 tsp pepper
1 tsp salt

1. Season meat with pepper and salt.
2. Add oil to the instant pot and set to sauté mode.
3. Place meat into the pot.
4. Add tomatoes, broccoli, onion, and sauté for a minute.
5. Season with rosemary and chili powder.
6. Seal the instant pot with lid and cook on stew mode.
7. Release pressure naturally, then open the lid.
8. Serve and enjoy!

Per Serving
calories: 364 | fat: 8g | protein: 27g | carbs: 19g | fiber : 6g

Lamb Meatballs

Servings: 4

Olive oil cooking spray
1 pound ground lamb
¼ cup fresh mint, chopped
¼ cup shallot, chopped
1 large egg, beaten
1 garlic clove, chopped

1 teaspoon ground coriander
1 teaspoon ground cumin
¼ teaspoon ground cinnamon
¼ teaspoon red pepper flakes

1. Preheat the oven to 400° F. Grease a 12-cup muffin tin with olive oil cooking spray.
2. In a large bowl, combine the lamb, mint, shallot, egg, garlic, coriander, cumin, salt, cinnamon, and red pepper flakes; mix well. Form the mixture into 12 balls and place one in each cup of the prepared muffin tin. Bake for 20 minutes, or until golden brown.

Per Serving
calories: 287 | fat: 11g | protein: 23g | carbs: 15g | fiber: 3g

Herb Roasted Lamb Chops

Servings: 4

3 tbsp. extra virgin olive oil
8 lamb chops
2 garlic cloves, cut into small slices

Kosher salt, to taste
2 tbsp. freshly rosemary leaves

1. Preheat oven to 375°F .
2. Place chops on rack in a baking sheet. Brush chops with olive oil.
3. Cut 1 small, shallow slit in the top of each lamb chop. Place a sliver of garlic in each cut.
4. Season lamb with salt and sprinkle with rosemary. Roast chops for 20 minutes or until an instant-read thermometer inserted in the thickest part of the chop registers 160° F for medium.
5. Serve warm. Enjoy!

Per Serving
calories: 244 | fat: 13g | protein: 17g | carbs: 13g | fiber: 2g

Pork Souvlaki

Servings: 4

For the Marinade:
1/4 cup olive oil
1/4 cup red wine
2 tbsp. lemon juice
1 tbsp. dried mint
1 tbsp. oregano
4 garlic cloves, minced

1 bay leaf, crumbled into tiny pieces
For the Kabobs:
1 pound pork shoulder, trimmed and cubed
1/2 tsp. salt
1 tsp. pepper
1 lemon, cut into wedges

1. Combine all the ingredients for the marinade and mix well.
2. Add the cubed pork to the mixing bowl and stir well.
3. Cover tightly and refrigerate. Let sit until you are ready to grill.
4. To assemble the kabobs, attach 6 pieces of pork per skewer.
5. Sprinkle each kabob with salt and pepper and then transfer to the hot grill. Cook kabobs for 12 minutes, turning throughout the process to ensure they cook evenly.
6. Remove from the grill and serve with lemon wedges. Enjoy!

Per Serving
calories: 436 | fat: 8g | protein: 17g | carbs: 11g | fiber: 3g |

Blue Cheese Topped Pork Chops

Servings: 4

1 pinch cayenne pepper
2 tbsp. fat-free Italian salad dressing
4 (6 oz.) bone-in pork loin chops

1 tbsp. fresh rosemary snipped
1/4 cup reduced-fat blue cheese, crumbled

1. Preheat the oven at broiler settings and line a broiler tray with a foil sheet.
2. Mix the Italian salad dressing with cayenne pepper.
3. Cover the 2 sides of the pork chops with this dressing mixture.
4. Place the pork chops on the broiler tray, and broil the pork chops for about 10 minutes, flipping in between.
5. Top the chops with cheese and rosemary. Serve and enjoy!

Per Serving
calories: 426 | fat: 9g | protein: 31g | carbs: 17g | fiber: 4g

Flank Steak and Blue Cheese Wraps

Servings: 6

1 cup leftover flank steak, cut into 1-inch slices
1/4 cup red onion, thinly sliced
1/4 cup cherry tomatoes, chopped
1/4 cup low-salt olives, pitted

1/4 cup roasted peppers, drained and coarsely chopped
1/4 cup blue cheese crumbles
6 whole-wheat or spinach wraps
Sea salt and pepper, to taste

1. Combine the flank steak, onion, tomatoes, olives, bell pepper, and blue cheese in a small bowl.
2. Spread 1/2 cup of this mixture on each wrap and roll halfway.
3. Fold the end in, and finish rolling like a burrito. Cut on a diagonal if you'd like, season to taste, and serve.

Per Serving
calories: 222 | fat: 10g | protein: 18g | carbs: 16g | fiber: 4g

Pork and Cannellini Bean Stew

Servings: 6

1 cup dried cannellini beans
1/4 cup olive oil
1 medium onion, diced
2 pounds pork roast, cut into 1-inch chunks
3 cups of water

1 (8-ounce) can tomato paste
1/4 cup flat-leaf parsley, chopped
1/2 teaspoon dried thyme
Sea salt and pepper, to taste

1. Rinse and sort the beans.
2. Cover beans with water and leave overnight. Heat the olive oil in a large stew skillet.
3. Add the onion, occasionally stirring, until golden brown.
4. Add the pork chunks and cook for 5–8 minutes, frequently stirring, until the pork is browned.
5. Add the water and bring to a boil.
6. Add the tomato paste, parsley, and thyme, simmer an additional 15 minutes, or until the sauce is slightly thickened. Season to taste.

Per Serving
calories: 397 | fat: 14g | protein: 34g | carbs: 22g | fiber: 4g

Steak Pinwheels

Prep time: 15 minutes | Serves 5

1 lb./ 450 g beef steak
⅓ cup of lemon juice
2 tablespoons of olive oil
2 tablespoons of dried oregano leaves

⅓ cup of olive tapenade
¼ cup of crumbled feta cheese
1 cup of frozen spinach
4 cups of cherry tomatoes
Salt to taste

1. Cover the beef in plastic wrap and pound it up to around ½ inches of thickness. Remove from plastic.
2. Mix olive oil, dried oregano leaves and lemon juice as marinade ingredients, and coat both sides of the flank. Leave it in a bag to refrigerate for around 4 hours. Preheat the oven to 425° F/220°C Placing baking paper over a baking sheet.
3. Take out the steak and place it on a cutting board. Spread the tapenade and top it off with spinach and feta. Roll the steak into a log and tie it up using kitchen strings.
4. Slice it into six even pieces, and pour the remains of the marinade over it. Arrange tomatoes around the beef pinwheels. Roast for around 30 minutes or until tender.
5. Allow to cool for 5 minutes.

Per Serving
Net Carbs: 8 g | Fiber: 2 g | Protein: 27 g | Fat: 13 g | Kcal (per serving): 117

Quick Chicken Marsala

Prep time: 20 minutes | Serves 4

2 tablespoons of olive oil, divided between 2 separate tablespoons
4 skinless, boneless chicken breast cutlets
¾ teaspoon of black pepper, divided into ¼ and ½ teaspoons
½ teaspoon of kosher salt, divided into ¼'s
10 oz./280 g. pre-sliced button mushrooms

4 thyme sprigs
1 tablespoon of all-purpose flour
2/3 cup of unsalted chicken stock
2/3 cup of Marsala wine
2 ½ tablespoons of unsalted butter
1 tablespoon of chopped fresh thyme
Peta bread

1. Heat one of your tablespoons of olive oil in a non-stick pan.
2. Season the chicken breast cutlets with the ¼ teaspoon of salt and ½ teaspoon of pepper.
3. Cook for 4 minutes per side, until the chicken is golden brown.
4. Once the chicken is done, remove it from the pan leaving the oils and the juice that chicken has released.
5. To the same pan, add another tablespoon of olive oil, mushrooms, and thyme sprigs. Cook for around 6 minutes until browned.
6. Add flour and continue stirring for a minute more. Add the wine and stock to the pan, bringing everything to boiling. Add the remaining spices, and bring the chicken back to the pan.
7. Cook for a few more minutes, and remove the sprigs just before the end. Serve with pita bread as a side.

Per Serving
Net Carbs: 9 g | Fiber: 1 g | Protein: 28 g | Fat: 17 g | Kcal (per serving): 344

Gyro-Inspired Turkey Burgers

Prep time: 20 minutes | Serves 4

1 lb./453 g 93% of lean ground turkey
¼ cup of canola mayonnaise
2 teaspoons of dried oregano
1 teaspoon of ground cumin
¼ teaspoon of kosher salt
¼ teaspoon black pepper, divided into two
⅛ teaspoons
Cooking spray

⅓ cup plain of whole-milk Greek yogurt
⅓ cup of chopped kalama-ta olives
1 tablespoon of fresh lemon juice
4 whole-wheat hamburger buns
2 cups of arugula
½ cup of sliced cucumber
½ cup of thinly sliced red onion

1. Combine turkey, cumin, mayo, oregano, 1/8 teaspoon pepper, and salt and make 4 medium patties.
2. Place a non-stick skillet on a medium-high temperature and coat with a tablespoon of olive oil. Cook each burger for around 5 minutes per side, until they are golden brown.
3. Combine yogurt, olives, lemon juice, salt and 1/8 teaspoon of pepper in a bowl to make a dressing. Spread it over both the top and bottom of the bun. Follow up by placing arugula, the cooked burger, red onion, and cucumber.

Per Serving
Net Carbs: 28 g | Fiber: 4 g | Protein: 22 g| Fat: 17 g | Kcal (per serving): 375

Mediterranean Chicken Cucumber Salad

Prep time: 15 minutes | Serves 6

2 cups of packed fresh flat-leaf parsley leaves (from 1 bunch)
1 cup of fresh baby spinach
2 tablespoons of fresh lemon juice
1 tablespoon of toasted pine nuts
1 tablespoon of grated Parmesan cheese
1 medium garlic clove, smashed
1 teaspoon of kosher salt

¼ teaspoon of black pepper
½ cup of extra-virgin olive oil
4 cups of shredded rotisserie chicken
2 cups of cooked, shelled edamame
15 oz./420 g can of unsalted chickpeas, drained and rinsed
1 cup of chopped English cucumber
4 cups of arugula

1. Put the pine nuts, lemon juice, spinach, parsley, cheese, garlic, salt and pepper in a blender for about a minute.
2. Add a bit of olive oil and blend for another minute.
3. Take a large bowl and combine chickpeas, edamame, cucumber, and chicken together. Toss around and add an amount of pesto sauce.
4. Separate into six bowls, and top each off with a 2/3 cup of arugula and one cup of the dressing.

Per Serving
Net Carbs: 26 g | Fiber: 7 g | Protein: 40 g | Fat: 26 g | Kcal (per serving): 482

Chapter 7
Fish and Seafood

Lemon Grilled Shrimp

Prep time: 20 minutes | Cook time: 4 to 6 minutes | Serves 4

2 tablespoons garlic, minced
3 tablespoons fresh Italian parsley, finely chopped
¼ cup extra-virgin olive oil
½ cup lemon juice

1 teaspoon salt
2 pounds (907 g) jumbo shrimp (21 to 25), peeled and deveined
Special Equipment:
4 wooden skewers, soaked in water for at least 30 minutes

1. Whisk together the garlic, parsley, olive oil, lemon juice, and salt in a large bowl.
2. Add the shrimp to the bowl and toss well, making sure the shrimp are coated in the marinade. Set aside to sit for 15 minutes.
3. When ready, skewer the shrimps by piercing through the center. You can place about 5 to 6 shrimps on each skewer.
4. Preheat the grill to high heat.
5. Grill the shrimp for 4 to 6 minutes, flipping the shrimp halfway through, or until the shrimp are pink on the outside and opaque in the center. Serve hot.

Per Serving
calories: 401 | fat: 17.8g | protein: 56.9g | carbs: 3.9g | fiber: 0g | sodium: 1223mg

Lemony Shrimp with Orzo Salad

Prep time: 10 minutes | Cook time: 22 minutes | Serves 4

1 cup orzo
1 hothouse cucumber, deseeded and chopped
½ cup finely diced red onion
2 tablespoons extra-virgin olive oil
2 pounds (907 g) shrimp, peeled and deveined

3 lemons, juiced
Salt and freshly ground black pepper, to taste
¾ cup crumbled feta cheese
2 tablespoons dried dill
1 cup chopped fresh flat-leaf parsley

1. Bring a large pot of water to a boil. Add the orzo and cook covered for 15 to 18 minutes, or until the orzo is tender. Transfer to a colander to drain and set aside to cool.
2. Mix the cucumber and red onion in a bowl. Set aside. Heat the olive oil in a medium skillet over medium heat until it shimmers.
3. Reduce the heat, add the shrimp, and cook each side for 2 minutes until cooked through.
4. Add the cooked shrimp to the bowl of cucumber and red onion. Mix in the cooked orzo and lemon juice and toss to combine.
5. Sprinkle with salt and pepper. Scatter the top with the feta cheese and dill. Garnish with the parsley and serve immediately.

Per Serving
calories: 565 | fat: 17.8g | protein: 63.3g | carbs: 43.9g | fiber: 4.1g | sodium: 2225mg

Spicy Grilled Shrimp with Lemon Wedges

Prep time: 15 minutes | Cook time: 6 minutes | Serves 6

1 large clove garlic, crushed
1 teaspoon coarse salt
1 teaspoon paprika
½ teaspoon cayenne pepper
2 teaspoons lemon juice

2 tablespoons plus 1 teaspoon olive oil, divided
2 pounds (907 g) large shrimp, peeled and deveined
8 lemon wedges, for garnish

1. Preheat the grill to medium heat.
2. Stir together the garlic, salt, paprika, cayenne pepper, lemon juice, and 2 tablespoons of olive oil in a small bowl until a paste forms. Add the shrimp and toss until well coated.
3. Grease the grill grates lightly with remaining 1 teaspoon of olive oil.
4. Grill the shrimp for 4 to 6 minutes, flipping the shrimp halfway through, or until the shrimp is totally pink and opaque.
5. Garnish the shrimp with lemon wedges and serve hot.

Per Serving
calories: 163 | fat: 5.8g | protein: 25.2g | carbs: 2.8g | fiber: 0.4g | sodium: 585mg

Cod with Parsley Pistou

Prep time: 15 minutes | Cook time: 10 minutes | Serves 4

1 cup packed roughly chopped fresh flat-leaf Italian parsley
Zest and juice of 1 lemon
1 to 2 small garlic cloves, minced
1 teaspoon salt

½ teaspoon freshly ground black pepper
1 cup extra-virgin olive oil, divided
1 pound (454 g) cod fillets, cut into 4 equal-sized pieces

1. Make the pistou: Place the parsley, lemon zest and juice, garlic, salt, and pepper in a food processor until finely chopped. With the food processor running, slowly drizzle in ¾ cup of olive oil until a thick sauce forms. Set aside.
2. Heat the remaining ¼ cup of olive oil in a large skillet over medium-high heat.
3. Add the cod fillets, cover, and cook each side for 4 to 5 minutes, until browned and cooked through.
4. Remove the cod fillets from the heat to a plate and top each with generous spoonfuls of the prepared pistou. Serve immediately.

Per Serving
calories: 580 | fat: 54.6g | protein: 21.1g | carbs: 2.8g | fiber: 1.0g | sodium: 651mg

Lemon-Parsley Swordfish

Prep time: 10 minutes | Cook time: 17 to 20 minutes | Serves 4

1 cup fresh Italian parsley
¼ cup lemon juice
¼ cup extra-virgin olive oil
¼ cup fresh thyme

2 cloves garlic
½ teaspoon salt
4 swordfish steaks
Olive oil spray

1. Preheat the oven to 450ºF (235ºC). Grease a large baking dish generously with olive oil spray.
2. Place the parsley, lemon juice, olive oil, thyme, garlic, and salt in a food processor and pulse until smoothly blended.
3. Arrange the swordfish steaks in the greased baking dish and spoon the parsley mixture over the top.
4. Bake in the preheated oven for 17 to 20 minutes until flaky.
5. Divide the fish among four plates and serve hot.

Per Serving
calories: 396 | fat: 21.7g | protein: 44.2g | carbs: 2.9g | fiber: 1.0g | sodium: 494mg

Fried Cod Fillets

Prep time: 5 minutes | Cook time: 10 minutes | Serves 4

½ cup all-purpose flour
1 teaspoon garlic powder
1 teaspoon salt

4 (4- to 5-ounce / 113- to 142-g) cod fillets
1 tablespoon extra-virgin olive oil

1. Mix together the flour, garlic powder, and salt in a shallow dish. Dredge each piece of fish in the seasoned flour until they are evenly coated.
2. Heat the olive oil in a medium skillet over medium-high heat. Once hot, add the cod fillets and fry for 6 to 8 minutes, flipping the fish half way through, or until the fish is opaque and flakes easily.
3. Remove from the heat and serve on plates.

Per Serving
calories: 333 | fat: 18.8g | protein: 21.2g | carbs: 20.0g | fiber: 5.7g | sodium: 870mg

Baked Lemon Salmon

Prep time: 5 minutes | Cook time: 20 minutes | Serves 4

¼ teaspoon dried thyme
Zest and juice of ½ lemon
¼ teaspoon salt

½ teaspoon freshly ground black pepper
1 pound (454 g) salmon fillet
Nonstick cooking spray

1. Preheat the oven to 425ºF (220ºC). Coat a baking sheet with nonstick cooking spray.
2. Mix together the thyme, lemon zest and juice, salt, and pepper in a small bowl and stir to incorporate.
3. Arrange the salmon, skin-side down, on the coated baking sheet. Spoon the thyme mixture over the salmon and spread it all over.
4. Bake in the preheated oven for about 15 to 20 minutes, or until the fish flakes apart easily. Serve warm.

Per Serving
calories: 162 | fat: 7.0g | protein: 23.1g | carbs: 1.0g | fiber: 0g | sodium: 166mg

Glazed Broiled Salmon

Prep time: 5 minutes | Cook time: 5 to 10 minutes | Serves 4

4 (4-ounce / 113-g) salmon fillets
3 tablespoons miso paste
2 tablespoons raw honey

1 teaspoon coconut aminos
1 teaspoon rice vinegar

1. Preheat the broiler to High. Line a baking dish with aluminum foil and add the salmon fillets.
2. Whisk together the miso paste, honey, coconut aminos, and vinegar in a small bowl. Pour the glaze over the fillets and spread it evenly with a brush.
3. Broil for about 5 minutes, or until the salmon is browned on top and opaque. Brush any remaining glaze over the salmon and broil for an additional 5 minutes if needed. The cooking time depends on the thickness of the salmon.
4. Let the salmon cool for 5 minutes before serving.

Per Serving
calories: 263 | fat: 8.9g | protein: 30.2g | carbs: 12.8g | fiber: 0.7g | sodium: 716mg

Honey-Mustard Roasted Salmon

Prep time: 5 minutes | Cook time: 15 to 20 minutes | Serves 4

2 tablespoons whole-grain mustard
2 garlic cloves, minced
1 tablespoon honey
¼ teaspoon salt

¼ teaspoon freshly ground black pepper
1 pound (454 g) salmon fillet
Nonstick cooking spray

1. Preheat the oven to 425ºF (220ºC). Coat a baking sheet with nonstick cooking spray.
2. Stir together the mustard, garlic, honey, salt, and pepper in a small bowl.
3. Arrange the salmon fillet, skin-side down, on the coated baking sheet. Spread the mustard mixture evenly over the salmon fillet.
4. Roast in the preheated oven for 15 to 20 minutes, or until it flakes apart easily and reaches an internal temperature of 145ºF (63ºC). Serve hot.

Per Serving
calories: 185 | fat: 7.0g | protein: 23.2g | carbs: 5.8g | fiber: 0g | sodium: 311mg

Dill Baked Sea Bass

Prep time: 10 minutes | Cook time: 10 to 15 minutes | Serves 6

¼ cup olive oil
2 pounds (907 g) sea bass
Sea salt and freshly ground pepper, to taste

1 garlic clove, minced
¼ cup dry white wine
3 teaspoons fresh dill
2 teaspoons fresh thyme

1. Preheat the oven to 425ºF (220ºC).
2. Brush the bottom of a roasting pan with the olive oil.
3. Place the fish in the pan and brush the fish with oil. Season the fish with sea salt and freshly ground pepper. Combine the remaining ingredients and pour over the fish.
4. Bake in the preheated oven for 10 to 15 minutes, depending on the size of the fish. Serve hot.

Per Serving
calories: 224 | fat: 12.1g | protein: 28.1g | carbs: 0.9g | fiber: 0.3g | sodium: 104mg

Breaded Shrimp

Prep time: 10 minutes | Cook time: 4 to 6 minutes | Serves 4

2 large eggs
1 tablespoon water
2 cups seasoned Italian bread crumbs
1 teaspoon salt
1 cup flour
1 pound (454 g) large shrimp (21 to 25), peeled and deveined
Extra-virgin olive oil, as needed

1. In a small bowl, beat the eggs with the water, then transfer to a shallow dish. Add the bread crumbs and salt to a separate shallow dish, then mix well.
2. Place the flour into a third shallow dish.
3. Coat the shrimp in the flour, then the beaten egg, and finally the bread crumbs. Place on a plate and repeat with all of the shrimp. Heat a skillet over high heat. Pour in enough olive oil to coat the bottom of the skillet. Cook the shrimp in the hot skillet for 2 to 3 minutes on each side. Remove and drain on a paper towel. Serve warm.

Per Serving
calories: 714 | fat: 34.0g | protein: 37.0g | carbs: 63.0g | fiber: 3.0g | sodium: 1727mg

Slow Cooker Salmon in Foil

Prep time: 5 minutes | Cook time: 2 hours | Serves 2

2 (6-ounce / 170-g) salmon fillets
1 tablespoon olive oil
2 cloves garlic, minced
½ tablespoon lime juice
1 teaspoon finely chopped fresh parsley
¼ teaspoon black pepper

1. Spread aluminum foil onto a work surface and place the salmon fillets in the middle. Mix together the olive oil, garlic, lime juice, parsley, and black pepper in a small bowl. Brush the mixture over the fillets. Fold the foil over and crimp the sides to make a packet.
2. Place the packet into the slow cooker, cover, and cook on High for 2 hours, or until the fish flakes easily with a fork.
3. Serve hot.

Per Serving
calories: 446 | fat: 20.7g | protein: 65.4g | carbs: 1.5g | fiber: 0.2g | sodium: 240mg

Grilled Lemon Pesto Salmon

Prep time: 5 minutes | Cook time: 6 to 10 minutes | Serves 2

10 ounces (283 g) salmon fillet (1 large piece or 2 smaller ones)
Salt and freshly ground black pepper, to taste
2 tablespoons prepared pesto sauce
1 large fresh lemon, sliced
Cooking spray

1. Preheat the grill to medium-high heat. Spray the grill grates with cooking spray. Season the salmon with salt and black pepper.
2. Spread the pesto sauce on top. Make a bed of fresh lemon slices about the same size as the salmon fillet on the hot grill, and place the salmon on top of the lemon slices. Put any additional lemon slices on top of the salmon. Grill the salmon for 6 to 10 minutes, or until the fish is opaque and flakes apart easily. Serve hot.

Per Serving
calories: 316 | fat: 21.1g | protein: 29.0g | carbs: 1.0g | fiber: 0g | sodium: 175mg

Steamed Trout with Lemon Herb Crust

Prep time: 10 minutes | Cook time: 15 minutes | Serves 2

3 tablespoons olive oil
3 garlic cloves, chopped
2 tablespoons fresh lemon juice
1 tablespoon chopped fresh mint
1 tablespoon chopped fresh parsley
¼ teaspoon dried ground thyme
1 teaspoon sea salt
1 pound (454 g) fresh trout (2 pieces)
2 cups fish stock

1. Stir together the olive oil, garlic, lemon juice, mint, parsley, thyme, and salt in a small bowl. Brush the marinade onto the fish. Insert a trivet in the Instant Pot. Pour in the fish stock and place the fish on the trivet.
2. Secure the lid. Select the Steam mode and set the cooking time for 15 minutes at High Pressure. Once cooking is complete, do a quick pressure release. Carefully open the lid. Serve warm.

Per Serving
calories: 477 | fat: 29.6g | protein: 51.7g | carbs: 3.6g | fiber: 0.2g | sodium: 2011mg

Tomato Tuna Melts

Prep time: 5 minutes | Cook time: 3 to 4 minutes | Serves 2

1 (5-ounce / 142-g) can chunk light tuna packed in water, drained
2 tablespoons plain Greek yogurt
2 tablespoons finely chopped celery
1 tablespoon finely chopped red onion
2 teaspoons freshly squeezed lemon juice
Pinch cayenne pepper
1 large tomato, cut into ¾-inch-thick rounds
½ cup shredded cheddar cheese

1. Preheat the broiler to High. Stir together the tuna, yogurt, celery, red onion, lemon juice, and cayenne pepper in a medium bowl. Place the tomato rounds on a baking sheet. Top each with some tuna salad and cheddar cheese.
2. Broil for 3 to 4 minutes until the cheese is melted and bubbly. Cool for 5 minutes before serving.

Per Serving
calories: 244 | fat: 10.0g | protein: 30.1g | carbs: 6.9g | fiber: 1.0g | sodium: 445mg

Hazelnut Crusted Sea Bass

Prep time: 10 minutes | Cook time: 15 minutes | Serves 2

2 tablespoons almond butter
2 sea bass fillets
⅓ cup roasted hazelnuts
A pinch of cayenne pepper

1. Preheat the oven to 425ºF (220ºC). Line a baking dish with waxed paper. Brush the almond butter over the fillets.
2. Pulse the hazelnuts and cayenne in a food processor. Coat the sea bass with the hazelnut mixture, then transfer to the baking dish. Bake in the preheated oven for about 15 minutes.
3. Cool for 5 minutes before serving.

Per Serving
calories: 468 | fat: 30.8g | protein: 40.0g | carbs: 8.8g | fiber: 4.1g | sodium: 90mg

Crispy Sardines

Prep time: 5 minutes | Cook time: 5 minutes | Serves 4

Avocado oil, as needed
1½ pounds (680 g) whole
fresh sardines, scales
removed

1 teaspoon freshly ground
black pepper
2 cups flour
1 teaspoon salt

1. Preheat a deep skillet over medium heat.
2. Pour in enough oil so there is about 1 inch of it in the pan. Season the fish with the salt and pepper.
3. Dredge the fish in the flour so it is completely covered. Slowly drop in 1 fish at a time, making sure not to overcrowd the pan.
4. Cook for about 3 minutes on each side or just until the fish begins to brown on all sides. Serve warm.

Per Serving
calories: 794 | fat: 47g | protein: 48g | carbs: 44 g | fiber: 2g | sodium: 1441mg

Shrimp with Garlic and Mushrooms

Prep time: 10 minutes | Cook time: 15 minutes | Serves 4

1 pound (454 g) peeled and
deveined fresh shrimp
1 teaspoon salt
1 cup extra-virgin olive oil
8 large garlic cloves, thinly
sliced
Zucchini noodles or riced
cauliflower, for serving

4 ounces (113 g) sliced
mushrooms (shiitake, baby
bella, or button)
½ teaspoon red pepper
flakes
¼ cup chopped fresh flat-
leaf Italian parsley

1. Rinse the shrimp and pat dry. Place in a small bowl and sprinkle with the salt.
2. In a large rimmed, thick skillet, heat the olive oil over medium-low heat. Add the garlic and heat until very fragrant, 3 to 4 minutes, reducing the heat if the garlic starts to burn.
3. Add the mushrooms and sauté for 5 minutes, until softened. Add the shrimp and red pepper flakes and sauté until the shrimp begins to turn pink, another 3 to 4 minutes.
4. Remove from the heat and stir in the parsley. Serve over zucchini noodles or riced cauliflower.

Per Serving
calories: 620 | fat: 56g | protein: 24g | carbs: 4g | fiber: 0g | sodium: 736mg

Tuna Sandwiches

Serves: 4

3 Tablespoons Lemon Juice,
Fresh
2 Tablespoons Olive Oil
Sea Salt & Black Pepper to
Taste 1 Clove Garlic, Minced

5 Ounces Canned Tuna,
Drained Ounce Canned
Olives, Sliced
½ Cup Fennel, Fresh &
Chopped 8 Slices Whole
Grain Bread

1. Whisk your lemon juice, garlic, pepper, and oil before adding in your fennel, olive sand tuna. Separate it into chunks before mixing everything.
2. Divide this between four slices of bread, and serve.

Trout with Lemon

Prep time: 5 minutes | Cook time: 15 minutes | Serves 4

4 trout fillets
2 tablespoons olive oil
½ teaspoon salt

1 teaspoon black pepper
2 garlic cloves, sliced
1 lemon, sliced, plus
additional wedges for serving

1. Preheat the air fryer to 380ºF (193ºC).
2. Brush each fillet with olive oil on both sides and season with salt and pepper. Place the fillets in an even layer in the air fryer basket.
3. Place the sliced garlic over the tops of the trout fillets, then top the garlic with lemon slices and cook for 12 to 15 minutes, or until it has reached an internal temperature of 145ºF (63ºC).
4. Serve with fresh lemon wedges.

Per Serving
calories: 231 | fat: 12g | protein: 29g | carbs: 1g | fiber: 0g | sodium: 341mg

Kale & Tuna Bowl

Serves: 6

1 lb. Kale, Chopped
3 Tablespoons Olive Oil
2.25 Ounces Olives, Canned
& Drained
3 Cloves Garlic, Minced
1/2 Cup Onion, Chopped

¼ Cup Capers
¼ Teaspoon Crushed Red
Pepper
2 Teaspoons Sugar Cans
6 Ounces Tuna in Olive Oil,
Undrained
1 15-Ounce Can Cannellini
Beans, Drained & Rinsed
Sea Salt & Black Pepper to
Taste

1. Get out a large stockpot and fill it three-quarters full of water.
2. Bring it to a boil and cook the kale for two minutes. Drain in a colander before setting it aside. Place your empty pot over medium heat, and then add in the oil. Add in the onion, and cook for four minutes. Stir often and cook the garlic for a minute more. Stir often, add the olives, crushed red pepper, capers, and cook for a full minute. Stir often, and add the kale and sugar in. stir well, and cook for eight minutes covered.
3. Remove from heat, and mix in your tuna, pepper, salt, and beans. Serve warm.

Salmon Salad Wraps

Serves: 6

1 lb. Salmon Fillet, Coked &
Flaked
½ Cup Carrots, Diced
½ Cup Celery, Diced
3 Tablespoons Red Onion,
Diced 3 Tablespoons Dill,
Fresh & Diced
2 Tablespoons, Capers

1 Tablespoon Aged
Balsamic Vinegar
1 ½ Tablespoons Olive Oil
Sea Salt & Black Pepper to
Taste
4 Whole Wheat Flatbread
Wraps

1. Get out a bowl and mix your carrots, dill, celery, salmon, red onions, oil, vinegar, pepper, capers, and salt.
2. Divide between flatbread, and fold up to serve.

Chapter 8
Fruits and Desserts

Cherry Walnut Brownies

Prep time: 10 minutes | Cook time: 20 minutes | Serves 9

2 large eggs
½ cup 2% plain Greek yogurt
½ cup sugar
⅓ cup honey
¼ cup extra-virgin olive oil
1 teaspoon vanilla extract
½ cup whole-wheat pastry flour
⅓ cup unsweetened dark chocolate cocoa powder
¼ teaspoon baking powder
¼ teaspoon salt
⅓ cup chopped walnuts
9 fresh cherries, stemmed and pitted
Cooking spray

1. Preheat the oven to 375ºF (190ºC) and set the rack in the middle of the oven. Spritz a square baking pan with cooking spray. In a large bowl, whisk together the eggs, yogurt, sugar, honey, oil and vanilla.
2. In a medium bowl, stir together the flour, cocoa powder, baking powder and salt. Add the flour mixture to the egg mixture and whisk until all the dry ingredients are incorporated. Fold in the walnuts.
3. Pour the batter into the prepared pan. Push the cherries into the batter, three to a row in three rows, so one will be at the center of each brownie once you cut them into squares. Bake the brownies for 20 minutes, or until just set. Remove from the oven and place on a rack to cool for 5 minutes. Cut into nine squares and serve.

Per Serving (1 tablespoon
calories: 154 | fat: 6.0g | protein: 3.0g | carbs: 24.0g | fiber: 2.0g | sodium: 125mg

Peanut Butter and Chocolate Balls

Prep time: 45 minutes | Cook time: 0 minutes | Serves 15 balls

¾ cup creamy peanut butter
¼ cup unsweetened cocoa powder
2 tablespoons softened almond butter
½ teaspoon vanilla extract
1¾ cups maple syrup

1. Line a baking sheet with parchment paper.
2. Combine all the ingredients in a bowl. Stir to mix well. Divide the mixture into 15 parts and shape each part into a 1-inch ball.
3. Arrange the balls on the baking sheet and refrigerate for at least 30 minutes, then serve chilled.

Per Serving (1 ball)
calories: 146 | fat: 8.1g | protein: 4.2g | carbs: 16.9g | fiber: 1.0g | sodium: 70mg

Strawberries with Balsamic Vinegar

Prep time: 5 minutes | Cook time: 0 minutes | Serves 2

2 cups strawberries, hulled and sliced
2 tablespoons sugar
2 tablespoons balsamic vinegar

Place the sliced strawberries in a bowl, sprinkle with the sugar, and drizzle lightly with the balsamic vinegar. Toss to combine well and allow to sit for about 10 minutes before serving.

Per Serving
calories: 92 | fat: 0.4g | protein: 1.0g | carbs: 21.7g | fiber: 2.9g | sodium: 5mg

Grilled Stone Fruit with Honey

Prep time: 8 minutes | Cook time: 6 minutes | Serves 2

3 apricots, halved and pitted
2 plums, halved and pitted
2 peaches, halved and pitted
½ cup low-fat ricotta cheese
2 tablespoons honey
Cooking spray

1. Preheat the grill to medium heat. Spray the grill grates with cooking spray.
2. Arrange the fruit, cut-side down, on the grill, and cook for 2 to 3 minutes per side, or until lightly charred and softened.
3. Serve warm with a sprinkle of cheese and a drizzle of honey.

Per Serving
calories: 298 | fat: 7.8g | protein: 11.9g | carbs: 45.2g | fiber: 4.3g | sodium: 259mg

Spiced Sweet Pecans

Prep time: 4 minutes | Cook time: 17 minutes | Serves 4

1 cup pecan halves
3 tablespoons almond butter
1 teaspoon ground cinnamon
½ teaspoon ground nutmeg
¼ cup raw honey
¼ teaspoon sea salt

1. Preheat the oven to 350ºF (180ºC). Line a baking sheet with parchment paper.
2. Combine all the ingredients in a bowl. Stir to mix well, then spread the mixture in the single layer on the baking sheet with a spatula. Bake in the preheated oven for 16 minutes or until the pecan halves are well browned.
3. Serve immediately.

Per Serving
calories: 324 | fat: 29.8g | protein: 3.2g | carbs: 13.9g | fiber: 4.0g | sodium: 180mg

Orange Mug Cakes

Prep time: 10 minutes | Cook time: 3 minutes | Serves 2

6 tablespoons flour
2 tablespoons sugar
1 teaspoon orange zest
½ teaspoon baking powder
Pinch salt

2 tablespoons olive oil
2 tablespoons unsweetened almond milk
2 tablespoons freshly squeezed orange juice
½ teaspoon orange extract
½ teaspoon vanilla extract

1. Combine the flour, sugar, orange zest, baking powder, and salt in a small bowl. In another bowl, whisk together the egg, olive oil, milk, orange juice, orange extract, and vanilla extract. Add the dry ingredients to the wet ingredients and stir to incorporate. The batter will be thick.
2. Divide the mixture into two small mugs. Microwave each mug separately. The small ones should take about 60 seconds; large ones should take about 90 seconds, but microwaves can vary. Cool for 5 minutes before serving.

Per Serving
calories: 303 | fat: 16.9g | protein: 6.0g | carbs: 32.5g | fiber: 1.0g | sodium: 118mg

Fruit and Nut Chocolate Bark

Prep time: 15 minutes | Cook time: 2 minutes | Serves 2

2 tablespoons chopped nuts
3 ounces (85 g) dark chocolate chips

¼ cup chopped dried fruit (blueberries, apricots, figs, prunes, or any combination of those)

1. Line a sheet pan with parchment paper and set aside. Add the nuts to a skillet over medium-high heat and toast for 60 seconds, or just fragrant. Set aside to cool.
2. Put the chocolate chips in a microwave-safe glass bowl and microwave on High for 1 minute.
3. Stir the chocolate and allow any unmelted chips to warm and melt. If desired, heat for an additional 20 to 30 seconds.
4. Transfer the chocolate to the prepared sheet pan. Scatter the dried fruit and toasted nuts over the chocolate evenly and gently pat in so they stick.
5. Place the sheet pan in the refrigerator for at least 1 hour to let the chocolate harden. When ready, break into pieces and serve.

Per Serving (1 tablespoon)
calories: 285 | fat: 16.1g | protein: 4.0g | carbs: 38.7g | fiber: 2.0g | sodium: 2mg

Apple Compote

Prep time: 15 minutes | Cook time: 10 minutes | Serves 4

6 apples, peeled, cored, and chopped
¼ cup raw honey

1 teaspoon ground cinnamon
¼ cup apple juice
Sea salt, to taste

Put all the ingredients in a stockpot. Stir to mix well, then cook over medium-high heat for 10 minutes or until the apples are glazed by honey and lightly saucy. Stir constantly. Serve immediately.

Per Serving
calories: 246 | fat: 0.9g | protein: 1.2g | carbs: 66.3g | fiber: 9.0g | sodium: 62mg

Crunchy Almond Cookies

Prep time: 5 minutes | Cook time: 5 to 7 minutes | Serves 4 to 6

½ cup sugar
8 tablespoons almond butter
1 large egg
½ cup tahini

1½ cups all-purpose flour
1 cup ground almonds
¼ cup extra-virgin olive oil
¼ cup freshly squeezed lemon juice

1. Preheat the oven to 375ºF (190ºC). Line a baking sheet with parchment paper.
2. Using a mixer, whisk together the sugar and butter. Add the egg and mix until combined. Alternately add the flour and ground almonds, ½ cup at a time, while the mixer is on slow.
3. Drop 1 tablespoon of the dough on the prepared baking sheet, keeping the cookies at least 2 inches apart.
4. Put the baking sheet in the oven and bake for about 5 to 7 minutes, or until the cookies start to turn brown around the edges.
5. Let it cool for 5 minutes before serving.

Per Serving
calories: 604 | fat: 36.0g | protein: 11.0g | carbs: 63.0g | fiber: 4.0g | sodium: 181mg

Apple and Berry Ambrosia

Prep time: 15 minutes | Cook time: 0 minutes | Serves 4

2 cups unsweetened coconut milk, chilled
2 tablespoons raw honey

1 apple, peeled, cored, and chopped
2 cups fresh raspberries
2 cups fresh blueberries

1. Stir milk and honey in a large bowl and mix well.
2. Then mix in the remaining ingredients. Stir to coat the fruits well and serve immediately.

Per Serving (2 tablespoons)
calories: 386 | fat: 21.1g | protein: 4.2g | carbs: 45.9g | fiber: 11.0g | sodium: 16mg

Chocolate, Almond, and Cherry Clusters

Prep time: 15 minutes | Cook time: 3 minutes | Makes 10 clusters

1 cup dark chocolate (60% cocoa or higher), chopped
1 tablespoon coconut oil

½ cup dried cherries
1 cup roasted salted almonds

1. Line a baking sheet with parchment paper.
2. Melt the chocolate and coconut oil in a saucepan for 3 minutes. Stir constantly.
3. Turn off the heat and mix in the cherries and almonds. Drop the mixture on the baking sheet with a spoon. Place the sheet in the refrigerator and chill for at least 1 hour or until firm.
4. Serve chilled.

Per Serving
calories: 197 | fat: 13.2g | protein: 4.1g | carbs: 17.8g | fiber: 4.0g | sodium: 57mg

Chocolate and Avocado Mousse

Prep time: 40 minutes | Cook time: 5 minutes | Serves 4 to 6

8 ounces (227 g) dark chocolate (60% cocoa or higher), chopped
¼ cup unsweetened coconut milk
2 tablespoons coconut oil

2 ripe avocados, pitted ¼ cup raw honey
Sea salt, to taste

1. Put the chocolate in a saucepan. Pour in the coconut milk and add the coconut oil.
2. Cook for 3 minutes or until the chocolate and coconut oil melt. Stir constantly.
3. Put the avocado in a food processor, then drizzle with honey and melted chocolate. Pulse to combine until smooth.
   Pour the mixture in a serving bowl, then sprinkle with salt.
4. Refrigerate to chill for 30 minutes and serve.

Per Serving (¼ cup)
calories: 654 | fat: 46.8g | protein: 7.2g | carbs: 55.9g | fiber: 9.0g | sodium: 112mg

Lemony Tea and Chia Pudding

rep time: 30 minutes | Cook time: 0 minutes | Serves 3 to 4

2 teaspoons matcha green tea powder (optional)
2 tablespoons ground chia seeds

1 to 2 dates
2 cups unsweetened coconut milk
Zest and juice of 1 lime

1. Put all the ingredients in a food processor and pulse until creamy and smooth.
2. Pour the mixture in a bowl, then wrap in plastic. Store in the refrigerator for at least 20 minutes, then serve chilled.

Per Serving
calories: 225 | fat: 20.1g | protein: 3.2g | carbs: 5.9g | fiber: 5.0g | sodium: 314m g

Watermelon and Blueberry Salad

Prep time: 5 minutes | Cook time: 0 minutes | Serves 6 to 8

1 medium watermelon
1 cup fresh blueberries
⅓ cup honey

2 tablespoons lemon juice
2 tablespoons finely chopped fresh mint leaves

1. Cut the watermelon into 1-inch cubes. Put them in a bowl.
2. Evenly distribute the blueberries over the watermelon. In a separate bowl, whisk together the honey, lemon juice and mint.
3. Drizzle the mint dressing over the watermelon and blueberries. Serve cold.

Per Serving
calories: 287 | fat: 26.7g | protein: 1.2g | carbs: 12.0g | fiber: 2.1g | sodium: 592mg

Mint Banana Chocolate Sorbet

Prep time: 4 hours 5 minutes | Cook time: 0 minutes Serves 1

1 frozen banana
1 tablespoon almond butter
2 tablespoons minced fresh mint

2 to 3 tablespoons dark chocolate chips (60% cocoa or higher)
2 to 3 tablespoons goji (optional)

1. Put the banana, butter, and mint in a food processor. Pulse to purée until creamy and smooth.
2. Add the chocolate and goji, then pulse for several more times to combine well. Pour the mixture in a bowl or a ramekin, then freeze for at least 4 hours before serving chilled.

Per Serving (2 tablespoons)
calories: 213 | fat: 9.8g | protein: 3.1g | carbs: 2.9g | fiber: 4.0g | sodium: 155mg

Raspberry Yogurt Basted Cantaloupe

Prep time: 15 minutes | Cook time: 0 minutes | Serves 6

2 cups fresh raspberries, mashed
1 cup plain coconut yogurt
½ teaspoon vanilla extract

1 cantaloupe, peeled and sliced
½ cup toasted coconut flakes

1. Combine the mashed raspberries with yogurt and vanilla extract in a small bowl. Stir to mix well.
2. Place the cantaloupe slices on a platter, then top with raspberry mixture and spread with toasted coconut.
3. Serve immediately.

Per Serving (¼ cup)
calories: 75 | fat: 4.1g | protein: 1.2g | carbs: 10.9g | fiber: 6.0g | sodium: 36mg

Coconut Blueberries with Brown Rice

Prep time: 55 minutes | Cook time: 10 minutes | Serves 4

1 cup fresh blueberries
2 cups unsweetened coconut milk
1 teaspoon ground ginger

¼ cup maple syrup Sea salt, to taste
2 cups cooked brown rice

1. Put all the ingredients, except for the brown rice, in a pot. Stir to combine well.
2. Cook over medium-high heat for 7 minutes or until the blueberries are tender.
3. Pour in the brown rice and cook for 3 more minute or until the rice is soft. Stir constantly.
   Serve immediately.

Per Serving
calories: 470 | fat: 24.8g | protein: 6.2g | carbs: 60.1g | fiber: 5.0g | sodium: 7 5mg

Walnut and Date Balls

Prep time: 5 minutes | Cook time: 8 to 10 minutes | Serves 6 to 8

1 cup walnuts
1 cup unsweetened shredded coconut
14 medjool dates, pitted
8 tablespoons almond butter

1. Preheat the oven to 350ºF (180ºC).
2. Put the walnuts on a baking sheet and toast in the oven for 5 minutes.
3. Put the shredded coconut on a clean baking sheet. Toast for about 3 to 5 minutes, or until it turns golden brown. Once done, remove it from the oven and put it in a shallow bowl.
4. In a food processor, process the toasted walnuts until they have a medium chop. Transfer the chopped walnuts into a medium bowl. Add the dates and butter to the food processor and blend until the dates become a thick paste. Pour the chopped walnuts into the food processor with the dates and pulse just until the mixture is combined, about 5 to 7 pulses.
5. Remove the mixture from the food processor and scrape it into a large bowl.
6. To make the balls, spoon 1 to 2 tablespoons of the date mixture into the palm of your hand and roll around between your hands until you form a ball. Put the ball on a clean, lined baking sheet. Repeat until all the mixture is formed into balls.
7. Roll each ball in the toasted coconut until the outside of the ball is coated. Put the ball back on the baking sheet and repeat.
8. Put all the balls into the refrigerator for 20 minutes before serving. Store any leftovers in the refrigerator in an airtight container.

Per Serving (1 tablespoon)
calories: 489 | fat: 35.0g | protein: 5.0g | carbs: 48.0g | fiber: 7.0g | sodium: 114mg

Glazed Pears with Hazelnuts

Prep time: 10 minutes | Cook time: 20 minutes | Serves 4

4 pears, peeled, cored, and quartered lengthwise
1 cup apple juice
1 tablespoon grated fresh ginger
½ cup pure maple syrup
¼ cup chopped hazelnuts

1. Put the pears in a pot, then pour in the apple juice. Bring to a boil over medium-high heat, then reduce the heat to medium-low. Stir constantly.
2. Cover and simmer for an additional 15 minutes or until the pears are tender.
3. Meanwhile, combine the ginger and maple syrup in a saucepan. Bring to a boil over medium-high heat. Stir frequently. Turn off the heat and transfer the syrup to a small bowl and let sit until ready to use.
4. Transfer the pears in a large serving bowl with a slotted spoon, then top the pears with syrup.
5. Spread the hazelnuts over the pears and serve immediately.

Per Serving
calories: 287 | fat: 3.1g | protein: 2.2g | carbs: 66.9g | fiber: 7.0g | sodium: 8mg

Sweet Spiced Pumpkin Pudding

Prep time: 2 hours 10 minutes | Cook time: 0 minutes | Serves 6

1 cup pure pumpkin purée
2 cups unsweetened coconut milk
1 teaspoon ground cinnamon
¼ teaspoon ground nutmeg
½ teaspoon ground ginger
Pinch cloves
¼ cup pure maple syrup
2 tablespoons chopped pecans, for garnish

1. Combine all the ingredients, except for the chopped pecans, in a large bowl. Stir to mix well.
2. Wrap the bowl in plastic and refrigerate for at least 2 hours. Remove the bowl from the refrigerator and discard the plastic.
3. Spread the pudding with pecans and serve chilled.

Per Serving
calories: 249 | fat: 21.1g | protein: 2.8g | carbs: 17.2g | fiber: 3.0g | sodium: 46mg

Bulgur Pilaf with Almonds

Cook time: 20 minutes | Serves 4

⅔ cup uncooked bulgur
1⅓ cups water
¼ cup sliced almonds
1 cup small diced red bell pepper
⅓ cup chopped fresh cilantro
1 tablespoon olive oil
¼ teaspoon salt

1. Place the bulgur and water in a saucepan and bring the water to a boil. Once the water is boiling, cover the pot with a lid and turn off the heat. Let the covered pot stand for 20 minutes.
2. Transfer the cooked bulgur to a large mixing bowl and add the almonds, peppers, cilantro, oil, and salt. Stir to combine. Place about 1 cup of bulgur in each of 4 containers.
3. STORAGE: Store covered containers in the refrigerator for up to 5 days.
4. Bulgur can be either reheated or eaten at room temperature.

Per Serving
calories: 17 Total fat: 7g; Saturated fat: 1g; Sodium: 152mg; Carbohydrates: 25g; Fiber: 6g; Protein: 4g

Lemony Blackberry Granita

Prep time: 10 minutes | Cook time: 0 minutes | Serves 4

1 pound (454 g) fresh blackberries
1 teaspoon chopped fresh thyme
½ cup raw honey
½ cup water
¼ cup freshly squeezed lemon juice

1. Put all the ingredients in a food processor, then pulse to purée.
2. Pour the mixture through a sieve into a baking dish. Discard the seeds remaining in the sieve.
3. Put the baking dish in the freezer for 2 hours. Remove the dish from the refrigerator and stir to break any frozen parts. Return
4. the dish back to the freezer for an hour, then stir to break any frozen parts again.
5. Return the dish to the freezer for 4 hours until the granita is completely frozen.
6. Remove it from the freezer and mash to serve.
   Per Serving
   calories: 183 | fat: 1.1g | protein: 2.2g | carbs: 45.9g | fiber: 6.0g | sodium: 6mg

Raspberry Red Wine Sauce

Cook time: 20 minutes | Serves 1 Cup

2 teaspoons olive oil
2 tablespoons finely chopped shallot
1½ cups frozen raspberries
1 cup dry, fruity red wine

1 teaspoon honey
¼ teaspoon kosher salt
½ teaspoon unsweetened cocoa powder
1 teaspoon thyme leaves, roughly chopped

1. In a skillet, heat the oil over medium heat. Add the shallot and cook until soft, about 2 minutes.
2. Add the raspberries, wine, thyme, and honey and cook on medium heat until reduced, about 15 minutes. Stir in the salt and cocoa powder.
3. Transfer the sauce to a blender and blend until smooth. Depending on how much you can scrape out of your blender, this recipe makes ¾ to 1 cup of sauce. Scoop the sauce into a container and refrigerate.

Per Serving
107; Total fat: 3g; Saturated fat: <1g; Sodium: 14 8mg; Carbohydrates: 1g; Fiber: 4g; Protein: 1g

Crispy Sesame Cookies

Prep time: 5 minutes | Cook time: 8 to 10 minutes | Serves 14 to 16

1 cup hulled sesame seeds
1 cup sugar

8 tablespoons almond butter
2 large eggs
1¼ cups flour

1. Preheat the oven to 350ºF (180ºC).
2. Toast the sesame seeds on a baking sheet for 3 minutes.
3. Set aside and let cool. Using a mixer, whisk together the sugar and butter. Add the eggs one at a time until well blended.
4. Add the flour and toasted sesame seeds and mix until well blended. Drop spoonfuls of cookie dough onto a baking sheet and form them into round balls, about 1 inch in diameter, similar to a walnut.
5. Put in the oven and bake for 5 to 7 minutes, or until golden brown. Let the cookies cool for 5 minutes before serving.

Per Serving
calories: 218 | fat: 12.0g | protein: 4.0g | carbs: 25.0g | fiber: 2.0g | sodium: 58mg

Mascarpone Baked Pears

Prep time: 10 minutes | Cook time: 20 minutes | Serves 2

2 ripe pears, peeled
1 tablespoon plus 2 teaspoons honey, divided
1 teaspoon vanilla, divided
¼ teaspoon ground coriander

¼ teaspoon ginger
¼ cup minced walnuts
¼ cup mascarpone cheese
Pinch salt
Cooking spray

1. Preheat the oven to 350ºF (180ºC). Spray a small baking dish with cooking spray.
2. Slice the pears in half lengthwise. Using a spoon, scoop out the core from each piece. Put the pears, cut-side up, in the baking dish.
3. Whisk together 1 tablespoon of honey, ½ teaspoon of vanilla, ginger, and coriander in a small bowl. Pour this mixture evenly over the pear halves.
4. Scatter the walnuts over the pear halves.
5. Bake in the preheated oven for 20 minutes, or until the pears are golden and you're able to pierce them easily with a knife.
6. Meanwhile, combine the mascarpone cheese with the remaining 2 teaspoons of honey, ½ teaspoon of vanilla, and a pinch of salt. Stir to combine well.
7. Divide the mascarpone among the warm pear halves and serve.

Per Serving
calories: 308 | fat: 16.0g | protein: 4.1g | carbs: 42.7g | fiber: 6.0g | sodium: 88mg

Banana, Cranberry, and Oat Bars

Prep time: 15 minutes | Cook time: 40 minutes | Makes 16 bars

2 tablespoon extra-virgin olive oil
2 medium ripe bananas, mashed
½ cup almond butter
½ cup maple syrup
⅓ cup dried cranberries
1½ cups old-fashioned rolled oats

¼ cup oat flour
¼ cup ground flaxseed
¼ teaspoon ground cloves
½ cup shredded coconut
½ teaspoon ground cinnamon
1 teaspoon vanilla extract

1. Preheat the oven to 400ºF (205ºC). Line an 8-inch square pan with parchment paper, then grease with olive oil.
2. Combine the mashed bananas, almond butter, and maple syrup in a bowl. Stir to mix well.
3. Mix in the remaining ingredients and stir to mix well until thick and sticky.
4. Spread the mixture evenly in the pan with a spatula, then bake in the preheated oven for 40 minutes or until a toothpick inserted in the center comes out clean.
5. Remove them from the oven and slice into 16 bars to serve.

Per Serving
calories: 145 | fat: 7.2g | protein: 3.1g | carbs: 18.9g | fiber: 2.0g | sodium: 3mg

Mango and Coconut Frozen Pie

Prep time: 1 hour 10 minutes | Cook time: 0 minutes
Serves 8

For Crust:
1 cup cashews
½ cup rolled oats
1 cup soft pitted dates

For Filling:
2 large mangoes, peeled and chopped
½ cup unsweetened shredded coconut
1 cup unsweetened coconut milk
½ cup water

1. Combine the ingredients for the crust in a food processor. Pulse to combine well.
2. Pour the mixture in an 8-inch springform pan, then press to coat the bottom. Set aside.
3. Combine the ingredients for the filling in the food processor, then pulse to purée until smooth.
4. Pour the filling over the crust, then use a spatula to spread the filling evenly. Put the pan in the freezer for 30 minutes.
5. Remove the pan from the freezer and allow to sit for 15 minutes at room temperature before serving.

Per Serving :(, cup)
calories: 426 | fat: 28.2g | protein: 8.1g | carbs: 14.9g | fiber: 6.0g | sodium: 174mg

Rice Pudding with Roasted Oranges

Prep time: 10 minutes | Cook time: 19 to 20 minutes | Serves 6

2 medium oranges
2 teaspoons extra-virgin olive oil
⅛ teaspoon kosher salt
2 large eggs
2 cups unsweetened almond milk

1 cup orange juice
1 cup uncooked instant brown rice
¼ cup honey
½ teaspoon ground cinnamon
1 teaspoon vanilla extract
Cooking spray

1. Preheat the oven to 450ºF (235ºC). Spritz a large, rimmed baking sheet with cooking spray. Set aside. Slice the unpeeled oranges into ¼-inch rounds. Brush with the oil and sprinkle with salt.
2. Place the slices on the baking sheet and roast for 4 minutes. Flip the slices and roast for 4 more minutes, or until they begin to brown. Remove from the oven and set aside.
3. Crack the eggs into a medium bowl. In a medium saucepan, whisk together the milk, orange juice, rice, honey and cinnamon. Bring to a boil over medium-high heat, stirring constantly. Reduce the heat to medium- low and simmer for 10 minutes, stirring occasionally.
4. Using a measuring cup, scoop out ½ cup of the hot rice mixture and whisk it into the eggs. While constantly stirring the mixture in the pan, slowly pour the egg mixture back into the saucepan.
5. Cook on low heat for 1 to 2 minutes, or until thickened, stirring constantly. Remove from the heat and stir in the vanilla. Let the pudding stand for a few minutes for the rice to soften. The rice will be cooked but slightly chewy. For softer rice, let stand for another half hour. Top with the roasted oranges. Serve warm or at room temperature.

Per Serving:
calories: 204 | fat: 6.0g | protein: 5.0g | carbs: 34.0g | fiber: 1.0g | sodium: 14 8mg

Citrus, Cranberry and Quinoa Energy Bites

Prep time: 25 minutes | Cook time: 0 minutes |Makes 12 bites

2 tablespoons almond butter
2 tablespoons maple syrup
¾ cup cooked quinoa
1 tablespoon dried cranberries
1 tablespoon chia seeds

¼ cup ground almonds
¼ cup sesame seeds, toasted
Zest of 1 orange
½ teaspoon vanilla extract

1. Line a baking sheet with parchment paper.
2. Combine the butter and maple syrup in a bowl. Stir to mix well.
3. Fold in the remaining ingredients and stir until the mixture holds together and is smooth.
4. Divide the mixture into 12 equal parts, then shape each part into a ball.
5. Arrange the balls on the baking sheet, then refrigerate for at least 15 minutes.
6. Serve chilled.

Per Serving
calories: 110 | fat: 10.8g | protein: 3.1g | carbs: 4.9g | fiber: 3.0g | sodium: 211mg

Grape Stew

Preparation time: 10 minutes Cooking time: 10 minutes
Portions: 4

2/3 cup of stevia
1 tablespoon olive oil
1/3 cup coconut water

1 teaspoon of vanilla extract
1 teaspoon lemon zest, grated
2 cups red grapes, halved

1. Heat a skillet with coconut water over medium heat, add the oil, stevia and the rest of the ingredients; stir, then simmer for 10 minutes, divide into cups and serve.

Per Serving :
calories 122, fat 3.7, fiber 1.2, carbohydrates 2.3, protein 0.4

Papaya Cream

Preparation time: 10 minutes Cooking time: 0 minutes
Portions: 2

1 cup papaya, peeled and chopped
1 cup heavy cream

1 tablespoon of stevia
½ teaspoon of vanilla extract

1. In a blender, combine the cream with the papaya and other ingredients; pulse well, divide into cups and serve cold.

Per Serving :
calories 182, fat 3.1, fiber 2.3, carbohydrates 3.5, protein 2

Cinnamon and Banana cupcakes

Preparation time: 10 minutes Cooking time: 20 minutes
Portions: 4

4 tablespoons avocado oil
4 eggs
½ cup of orange juice
2 teaspoons of cinnamon powder

1 teaspoon of vanilla extract
4 bananas, peeled and chopped
¾ cup almond flour
½ teaspoon baking powder
Cooking spray

1. In a bowl, combine oil with eggs, orange juice and remaining ingredients except cooking spray, whisk well, pour into cupcake pan greased with cooking spray, place in 350 °F oven and bake for 20 minutes.
2. Cool the cupcakes and serve.

Per Serving
calories 142, fat 5.8, fiber 4.2, carbohydrates 5.7, protein 1.6

Oranges and Apricots Cake

Preparation time: 10 minutes Cooking time: 20 minutes
Portions: 8

¾ cup of stevia
2 cups of almond flour
¼ cup olive oil
½ cup of almond milk

1 teaspoon of baking powder
2 eggs
½ teaspoon vanilla extract
Juice and zest of 2 oranges
2 cups apricots, chopped

1. In a bowl, mix the stevia with the flour and the rest of the ingredients; whisk and pour into a cake pan lined with baking paper.
2. Place in 375 °F oven, bake for 20 minutes, cool, slice and serve.

Per Serving:
calories 221, fat 8.3, fiber 3.4, carbohydrates 14.5, protein 5

Lemon Cream

Preparation time: 1 hour Cooking time: 10 minutes
Portions: 6

2 eggs, beaten
1 and ¼ cup of stevia
10 tablespoons avocado oil

1 cup heavy cream Juice of 2 lemons
Peel of 2 lemons, grated

1. In a skillet, combine cream with lemon juice and remaining ingredients; whisk well, cook for 10 minutes, divide into cups and refrigerate for 1 hour before serving.

Per Serving:
calories 200, fat 8.5, fiber 4.5, carbohydrates 8.6, protein 4.5

Tangerine Cream

Preparation time: 20 minutes Cooking time: 0 minutes
Portions: 8

4 mandarins, peeled and cut into wedges
Juice of 2 mandarins
2 tablespoons of stevia

4 eggs, beaten
¾ cup of stevia
¾ cup almonds, ground

1. In a blender, combine mandarins with mandarin juice and other ingredients; whisk well, divide into cups and refrigerate for 20 minutes before serving.

Per Serving
calories 106, fat 3.4, fiber 0, carbohydrates 2.4, protein 4

Cocoa Brownies

Preparation time: 10 minutes Cooking time: 20 minutes
Portions: 8

30 ounces canned lentils, rinsed and drained
1 tablespoon honey
1 banana, peeled and chopped

½ teaspoon of baking soda
4 tablespoons almond butter
2 tablespoons cocoa powder
Cooking spray
⅓ cup rolled oats

1. In a food processor, combine the lentils with the honey and other ingredients except the cooking spray and give it a good pulse.
2. Pour into a baking dish greased with cooking spray, spread evenly, place in 375 °F oven and bake for 20 minutes. Cut
3. the brownies and serve them cold.

Per Serving
calories 200, fat 4.5, fiber 2.4 carbohydrates 8.7, protein 4.3

Strawberry Cream

Preparation time: 10 minutes Cooking time: 20 minutes
Portions: 4

½ cup of stevia
2 pounds of strawberries, chopped
1 cup almond milk

2 tablespoons milk
Peel of 1 lemon, grated
½ cup heavy cream
3 egg yolks, beaten

1. Heat a saucepan with the milk over medium-high heat, add the stevia and the rest of the ingredients; whisk well, simmer for 20 minutes, divide into cups and serve cold.

Per Serving
calories 152, fat 4.4, fiber 5.5, carbohydrates 5.1, protein 0.8

Chapter 9
Sauces, Dips, and Dressings

Not Old Bay Seasoning

Prep time: 10 minutes | Cook time: 0 minutes | Makes about ½ cup

3 tablespoons sweet paprika
1 tablespoon mustard seeds
2 tablespoons celery seeds
2 teaspoons freshly ground black pepper
1½ teaspoons cayenne pepper

1 teaspoon red pepper flakes
½ teaspoon ground ginger
½ teaspoon ground nutmeg
½ teaspoon ground cinnamon
¼ teaspoon ground cloves

1. Mix together all the ingredients in an airtight container until well combined.
2. You can store it in a cool, dry, and dark place for up to 3 months.

Per Serving (1 tablespoon)
calories: 26 | fat: 1.9g | protein: 1.1g | carbs: 3.6g | fiber : 2.1g | sodium: 3mg

Harissa Sauce

Prep time: 10 minutes | Cook time: 20 minutes | Makes 3 to 4 cups

1 large red bell pepper, deseeded, cored, and cut into chunks
1 yellow onion, cut into thick rings
4 garlic cloves, peeled
1 cup vegetable broth

2 tablespoons tomato paste
1 tablespoon tamari
1 teaspoon ground cumin
1 tablespoon Hungarian paprika

1. Preheat the oven to 450ºF (235ºC). Line a baking sheet with parchment paper.
2. Place the bell pepper on the prepared baking sheet, flesh-side up, and space out the onion and garlic around the pepper.
3. Roast in the preheated oven for 20 minutes. Transfer to a blender.
4. Add the vegetable broth, tomato paste, tamari, cumin, and paprika. Purée until smooth. Served chilled or warm.

Per Serving (¼ cup)
calories: 15 | fat: 1.0g | protein: 1.0g | carbs: 3.0g | fiber : 1.0g | sodium: 201mg

Aioli

Prep time: 5 minutes | Cook time: 0 minutes | Makes ½ cup

½ cup plain Greek yogurt
2 teaspoons Dijon mustard

½ teaspoon hot sauce
¼ teaspoon raw honey
Pinch salt

1. In a small bowl, whisk together the yogurt, mustard, hot sauce, honey, and salt.
2. Serve immediately or refrigerate in an airtight container for up to 3 days.

Per Serving
calories: 47 | fat: 2.5g | protein: 2.1g | carbs: 3.5g | fiber : 0g | sodium: 231mg

Hot Pepper Sauce

Prep time: 10 minutes | Cook time: 20 minutes | Makes 4 cups

1 red hot fresh chiles, deseeded
2 dried chiles
2 garlic cloves, peeled

½ small yellow onion, roughly chopped
2 cups water
2 cups white vinegar

Place all the ingredients except the vinegar in a medium saucepan over medium heat. Allow to simmer for 20 minutes until softened. Transfer the mixture to a food processor or blender. Stir in the vinegar and pulse until very smooth. Serve immediately or transfer to a sealed container and refrigerate for up to 3 months.

Per Serving (2 tablespoons)
calories: 20 | fat: 1.2g | protein: 0.6g | carbs: 4.4g | fiber : 0.6g | sodium: 12mg

Peanut Sauce with Honey

Prep time: 5 minutes | Cook time: 0 minutes | Serves 4

¼ cup peanut butter
1 tablespoon peeled and grated fresh ginger
1 tablespoon honey

1 tablespoon low-sodium soy sauce
1 garlic clove, minced
Juice of 1 lime
Pinch red pepper flakes

1. Whisk together all the ingredients in a small bowl until well incorporated. Transfer to an airtight container and refrigerate for up to 5 days.

Per Serving
calories: 117 | fat: 7.6g | protein: 4.1g | carbs: 8.8g | fiber : 1.0g | sodium: 136mg

Peri-Peri Sauce

PPrep time: 10 minutes | Cook time: 5 minutes | Serves 4

1 tomato, chopped
1 red onion, chopped
1 red bell pepper, deseeded and chopped
1 red chile, deseeded and chopped
4 garlic cloves, minced

2 tablespoons extra-virgin olive oil
Juice of 1 lemon
1 tablespoon dried oregano
1 tablespoon smoked paprika

1. Process all the ingredients in a food processor or a blender until smooth. Transfer the mixture to a small saucepan over medium-high heat and bring to a boil, stirring often.
2. Reduce the heat to medium and allow to simmer for 5 minutes until heated through. You can store the sauce in an airtight container in the refrigerator for up to 5 days.

Per Serving
calories: 98 | fat: 6.5g | protein: 1.0g | carbs: 7.8g | fiber : 3.0g | sodium: 295mg

Ginger Teriyaki Sauce

Prep time: 5 minutes | Cook time: 0 minutes | Serves 2

¼ cup pineapple juice
¼ cup low-sodium soy sauce
2 tablespoons packed coconut sugar

1 tablespoon grated fresh ginger
1 tablespoon arrowroot powder or cornstarch
1 teaspoon garlic powder

1. Whisk the pineapple juice, soy sauce, coconut sugar, ginger, arrowroot powder, and garlic powder together in a small bowl.
2. Store in an airtight container in the fridge for up to 5 days.

Per Serving
calories: 37 | fat: 0.1g | protein: 1.1g | carbs: 12.0g | fiber: 0g | sodium: 881mg

Homemade Blackened Seasoning

Prep time: 10 minutes | Cook time: 0 minutes | Makes about ½ cup

2 tablespoons smoked paprika
2 tablespoons garlic powder
2 tablespoons onion powder
1 tablespoon sweet paprika

1 teaspoon dried dill
1 teaspoon freshly ground black pepper
½ teaspoon ground mustard
¼ teaspoon celery seeds

1. Add all the ingredients to a small bowl and mix well.
2. Serve immediately, or transfer to an airtight container and store in a cool, dry and dark place for up to 3 months.

Per Serving (1 tablespoon)
calories: 22 | fat: 0.9g | protein: 1.0g | carbs: 4.7g | fiber: 1.0g | sodium: 2mg

Tzatziki

Prep time: 15 minutes | Cook time: 0 minutes | Serves 4 to 6

½ English cucumber, finely chopped
1 teaspoon salt, divided
1 cup plain Greek yogurt
8 tablespoons olive oil, divided

1 garlic clove, finely minced
1 to 2 tablespoons chopped fresh dill
1 teaspoon red wine vinegar
½ teaspoon freshly ground black pepper

1. In a food processor, pulse the cucumber until puréed. Place the cucumber on several layers of paper towels lining the bottom of a colander and sprinkle with ½ teaspoon of salt.
2. Allow to drain for 10 to 15 minutes. Using your hands, squeeze out any remaining liquid. In a medium bowl, whisk together the cucumber, yogurt, 6 tablespoons of olive oil, garlic, dill, vinegar, the remaining ½ teaspoon of salt, and pepper until very smooth.
3. Drizzle with the remaining 2 tablespoons of olive oil. Serve immediately or refrigerate until ready to serve.

Per Serving
calories: 286 | fat: 29.0g | protein: 3.0g | carbs: 5.0g | fiber: 0g | sodium: 615mg

Garlic Lemon-Tahini Dressing

Prep time: 5 minutes | Cook time: 0 minutes | Serves 8 to 10

½ cup tahini
¼ cup extra-virgin olive oil
¼ cup freshly squeezed lemon juice

1 garlic clove, finely minced
2 teaspoons salt

1. In a glass mason jar with a lid, combine the tahini, olive oil, lemon juice, garlic, and salt. Cover and shake well until combined and creamy.
2. Store in the refrigerator for up to 2 weeks.

Per Serving
calories: 121 | fat: 12.0g | protein: 2.0g | carbs: 3.0g | fiber: 1.0g | sodium: 479mg

Ranch-Style Cauliflower Dressing

Prep time: 10 minutes | Cook time: 0 minutes | Serves 8

2 cups frozen cauliflower, thawed
½ cup unsweetened plain almond milk
2 tablespoons apple cider vinegar
2 tablespoons extra-virgin olive oil
1 garlic clove, peeled
2 teaspoons finely chopped fresh parsley

2 teaspoons finely chopped scallions (both white and green parts)
1 teaspoon finely chopped fresh dill
½ teaspoon onion powder
½ teaspoon Dijon mustard
½ teaspoon salt
¼ teaspoon freshly ground black pepper

1. Place all the ingredients in a blender and pulse until creamy and smooth.
2. Serve immediately, or transfer to an airtight container to refrigerate for up to 3 days

Per Serving (2 tablespoons)
calories: 41 | fat: 3.6g | protein: 1.0g | carbs: 1.9g | fiber: 1.1g | sodium: 148mg

Cheesy Pea Pesto

Prep time: 5 minutes | Cook time: 0 minutes | Serves 4

½ cup fresh green peas
½ cup grated Parmesan cheese
¼ cup extra-virgin olive oil

¼ cup pine nuts
¼ cup fresh basil leaves
2 garlic cloves, minced
¼ teaspoon sea salt

1. Add all the ingredients to a food processor or blender and pulse until the nuts are chopped finely.
2. Transfer to an airtight container and refrigerate for up to 2 days. You can also store it in ice cube trays in the freezer for up to 6 months

Per Serving
calories: 247 | fat: 22.8g | protein: 7.1g | carbs: 4.8g | fiber: 1.0g | sodium: 337mg

Lentil-Tahini Dip

Prep time: 10 minutes | Cook time: 15 minutes | Makes 3 cups

1 cup dried green or brown lentils, rinsed
2½ cups water, divided

⅓ cup tahini
1 garlic clove
½ teaspoon salt, plus more as needed

1. Add the lentils and 2 cups of water to a medium saucepan and bring to a boil over high heat.
2. Once it starts to boil, reduce the heat to low, and then cook for 14 minutes, stirring occasionally, or the lentils become tender but still hold their shape. You can drain any excess liquid.
3. Transfer the lentils to a food processor, along with the remaining water, tahini, garlic, and salt and process until smooth and creamy.
4. Taste and adjust the seasoning if needed. Serve immediately.

Per Serving (¼ cup)
calories: 100 | fat: 3.9g | protein: 5.1g | carbs: 10.7g | fiber: 6.0g | sodium: 106mg

Creamy Cider Yogurt Dressing

Prep time: 5 minutes | Cook time: 0 minutes | Serves 2

1 cup plain, unsweetened, full-fat Greek yogurt
½ cup extra-virgin olive oil
½ lemon, juiced
1 tablespoon chopped fresh oregano

½ teaspoon dried parsley
½ teaspoon kosher salt
¼ teaspoon garlic powder
¼ teaspoon freshly ground black pepper

1. In a large bowl, whisk all ingredients to combine.
2. Serve chilled or at room temperature.

Per Serving
calories: 407 | fat: 40.7g | protein: 8.3g | carbs: 3.8g | fiber: 0.5g | sodium: 382mg

Orange-Garlic Dressing

Prep time: 5 minutes | Cook time: 0 minutes | Serves 2

¼ cup extra-virgin olive oil
1 orange, zested
2 tablespoons freshly squeezed orange juice
¾ teaspoon za'atar seasoning

1 teaspoon garlic powder
½ teaspoon salt
¼ teaspoon Dijon mustard
Freshly ground black pepper, to taste

Whisk together all ingredients in a bowl until well combined. Serve immediately or refrigerate until ready to serve.

Per Serving
calories: 287 | fat: 26.7g | protein: 1.2g | carbs: 12.0g | fiber: 2.1g | sodium: 592mg

Mascarpone with Strawberries

Cook time: 10 minutes | Serves 4

1 (8-ounce) container mascarpone cheese
2 teaspoons honey
¼ teaspoon ground cardamom

2 tablespoons milk
1 pound strawberries (should be 24 strawberries in the pack)

1. Combine the mascarpone, honey, cardamom, and milk in a medium mixing bowl.
2. Mix the ingredients with a spoon until super creamy, about 30 seconds.
3. Place 6 strawberries and 2 tablespoons of the mascarpone mixture in each of 4 containers.
4. STORAGE: Store covered containers in the refrigerator for up to 5 days.

Per Serving
289; Total fat: 2; Saturated fat: 10g; Sodium: 26mg; Carbohydrates: 11g; Fiber: 3g; Protein: 1g

Creamy Cucumber Dip

Prep time: 10 minutes | Cook time: 0 minutes | Serves 6

1 medium cucumber, peeled and grated
¼ teaspoon salt
1 cup plain Greek yogurt
2 garlic cloves, minced

1 tablespoon extra-virgin olive oil
1 tablespoon freshly squeezed lemon juice
¼ teaspoon freshly ground black pepper

1. Place the grated cucumber in a colander set over a bowl and season with salt. Allow the cucumber to stand for 10 minutes.
2. Using your hands, squeeze out as much liquid from the cucumber as possible. Transfer the grated cucumber to a medium bowl.
3. Add the yogurt, garlic, olive oil, lemon juice, and pepper to the bowl and stir until well blended.
4. Cover the bowl with plastic wrap and refrigerate for at least 2 hours to blend the flavors.
Serve chilled.

Per Serving (¼ cup)
calories: 47 | fat: 2.8g | protein: 4.2g | carbs: 2.7g | fiber: 0g | sodium: 103mg

Parsley Vinaigrette

Prep time: 5 minutes | Cook time: 0 minutes | Makes about ½ cup

½ cup lightly packed fresh parsley, finely chopped
⅓ cup extra-virgin olive oil
1 garlic clove, minced

3 tablespoons red wine vinegar
¼ teaspoon salt, plus additional as needed

1. Place all the ingredients in a mason jar and cover. Shake vigorously for 1 minute until completely mixed.
2. Taste and add additional salt as needed.
3. Serve immediately or serve chilled.

Per Serving (1 tablespoon)
calories: 92 | fat: 10.9g | protein: 0g | carbs: 0g | fiber: 0g | sodium: 75mg

Blueberry, Flax, and Sunflower Butter Bites

Cook time: 10 minutes | Serves 6

¼ cup ground flaxseed
½ cup unsweetened
sunflower butter, preferably
unsalted
⅓ cup dried blueberries

2 tablespoons all-fruit
blueberry preserves
Zest of 1 lemon
2 tablespoons unsalted
sunflower seeds

1. Mix all the Shopping List: in a medium mixing bowl until well combined.
2. Form balls, slightly smaller than a golf ball, from the mixture and place on a plate in the freezer for about 20 minutes to firm up.
3. Place 2 bites in each of 6 containers and refrigerate.
4. STORAGE: Store covered containers in the refrigerator for up to 5 days. Bites may also be stored in the freezer for up to 3 months.

Per Serving
229; Total fat: 14g; Saturated fat: 1g; Sodium: 1mg;
Carbohydrates: 26g; Fiber: 3g;

Romesco Sauce

Cook time: 10 minutes | Serves 1 Cups

½ cup raw, unsalted
almonds
4 medium garlic cloves (do
not peel)
(12-ounce) jar of roasted
red peppers, drained

½ cup canned diced
fire-roasted tomatoes,
drained
1 teaspoon smoked paprika
½ teaspoon kosher salt
Pinch cayenne pepper
teaspoons red wine vinegar
2 tablespoons olive oil

1. Preheat the oven to 350°F.
2. Place the almonds and garlic cloves on a sheet pan and toast in the oven for 10 minutes. Remove from the oven and peel the garlic when cool enough to handle.
3. Place the almonds in the bowl of a food processor. Process the almonds until they resemble coarse sand, to 45 seconds.
4. Add the garlic, peppers, tomatoes, paprika, salt, and cayenne. Blend until smooth. Once the mixture is smooth, add the vinegar and oil and blend until well combined.
5. Taste and add more vinegar or salt if needed. Scoop the romesco sauce into a container and refrigerate.
6. STORAGE: Store the covered container in the refrigerator for up to 7 days.

Per Serving
158; Total fat: 13g; Saturated fat: 1g; Sodium: 292mg; Carbohydrates: 10g; Fiber: 3g; Protein: 4g

Antipasti Shrimp Skewers

Cook time: 10 minutes | Serves 4

16 pitted kalamata or
green olives
16 fresh mozzarella balls
(ciliegine)

16 medium (41 to 50 per
pound) precooked peeled,
deveined shrimp
8 (8-inch) wooden or metal
skewers

1. Alternate 2 olives, 2 mozzarella balls, 2 cherry tomatoes, and 2 shrimp on 8 skewers.
2. Place skewers in each of 4 containers.
3. STORAGE: Store covered containers in the refrigerator for up to 4 days.

Per Serving
108; Total fat: 6g; Saturated fat: 1g; Sodium: 328mg; Carbohydrates: ; Fiber: 1g; Protein: 9g

Candied Maple-Cinnamon Walnuts

Cook time: 15 minutes | Serves 4

1 cup walnut halves
½ teaspoon ground
cinnamon

2 tablespoons pure
maple syrup

1. Preheat the oven to 325°F. Line a baking sheet with a silicone baking mat or parchment paper.
2. In a small bowl, mix the walnuts, cinnamon, and maple syrup until the walnuts are coated.
3. Pour the nuts onto the baking sheet, making sure to scrape out all the maple syrup. Bake for 15 minutes. Allow the nuts to cool completely.
4. Place ¼ cup of nuts in each of containers or resealable sandwich bags.
5. STORAGE: Store covered containers at room temperature for up to 7 days.

Per Serving
190; Total fat: 17g; Saturated fat: 2g; Sodium: 2mg; Carbohydrates: 10g; Fiber: 2g;

Chermoula Sauce

Cook time: 10 minutes | Serves 1 Cups

1 cup packed parsley leaves
1 cup cilantro leaves
½ cup mint leaves
1 teaspoon chopped garlic
½ teaspoon ground cumin
½ teaspoon ground
coriander

½ teaspoon smoked
paprika
⅛ teaspoon cayenne
pepper
⅛ teaspoon kosher salt
3 tablespoons freshly
squeezed lemon juice
3 tablespoons water
½ cup extra-virgin olive oil

1. Place all the ingredients in a blender or food processor and blend until smooth.
2. Pour the chermoula into a container and refrigerate.
3. STORAGE: Store the covered container in the refrigerator for up to 5 days.

Per Serving :(¼ cup)
257; Total fat: 27g; Saturated fat: ; Sodium: 96mg; Carbohydrates: 4g; Fiber: 2g; Protein: 1g

Artichoke-Olive Compote

Cook time: 15 minutes | Serves 1 Cups

1 (6-ounce) jar marinated artichoke hearts, chopped
⅓ cup chopped pitted green olives (8 to 9 olives)
3 tablespoons chopped fresh basil
½ teaspoon freshly squeezed lemon juice
2 teaspoons olive oil

1. Place all the ingredients in a medium mixing bowl and stir to combine.
2. Place the compote in a container and refrigerate.
3. STORAGE: Store the covered container in the refrigerator for up to 7 days.

Per Serving :(, cup)
8 Total fat: 7g; Saturated fat: 1g; Sodium: 350mg; Carbohydrates: 5g; Fiber: <1g; Protein: <1g

Green Olive and Spinach Tapenade

Cook time: 20 minutes | Serves 1½ C ups

1 cup pimento-stuffed green olives, drained
3 packed cups baby spinach
teaspoon chopped garlic
½ teaspoon dried oregano
⅓ cup packed fresh basil
2 tablespoons olive oil
teaspoons red wine vinegar

1. Place all the ingredients in the bowl of a food processor and pulse until the mixture looks finely chopped but not puréed.
2. Scoop the tapenade into a container and refrigerate.
3. STORAGE: Store the covered container in the refrigerator for up to 5 days.

Per Serving:(¼ cup)
80; Total fat: 8g; Saturated fat: 1g; Sodium: 6mg; Carbohydrates: 1g; Fiber: 1g; Protein: 1g

Garlic Yogurt Sauce

Cook time: 5 minutes | Serves 1 Cups

1 cup low-fat (2%) plain Greek yogurt
1 tablespoon freshly squeezed lemon juice
1 tablespoon olive oil
¼ teaspoon kosher salt
½ teaspoon garlic powder

1. Mix all the ingredients in a medium bowl until well combined. Spoon the yogurt sauce into a container and refrigerate.
2. STORAGE: Store the covered container in the refrigerator for
3. up to 7 days.

Per Serving: (¼ cup)
75; Total fat: 5g; Saturated fat: 1g; Sodium: 173mg; Carbohydrates: 3g; Fiber: 0g; Protein: 6g.

Honey-Lemon Vinaigrette

Cook time: 5 minutes | Serves ½ C up

¼ cup freshly squeezed lemon juice
1 teaspoon honey
2 teaspoons Dijon mustard
⅛ teaspoon kosher salt
¼ cup olive oil

1. Place the lemon juice, honey, mustard, and salt in a small bowl and whisk to combine.
2. Whisk in the oil, pouring it into the bowl in a thin stream.
3. Pour the vinaigrette into a container and refrigerate.

4. STORAGE: Store the covered container in the refrigerator for up to 2 weeks. Allow the vinaigrette to come to room temperature and shake before serving.

Per Serving:(2 tablespoons)
131; Total fat: 14g; Saturated fat: 2g; Sodium: 133mg; Carbohydrates: 3g; Fiber: <1g; Protein: <1g

Smoked Paprika and Olive Oil–Marinated Carrots

Cook time: 5 minutes | Serves 4

(1-pound) bag baby carrots (not the petite size)
2 tablespoons olive oil
2 tablespoons red wine vinegar
¼ teaspoon garlic powder
¼ teaspoon ground cumin
¼ teaspoon smoked paprika
⅛ teaspoon red pepper flakes
¼ cup chopped parsley
¼ teaspoon kosher salt

1. Pour enough water into a saucepan to come ¼ inch up the sides. Turn the heat to high, bring the water to a boil, add the carrots, and cover with a lid. Steam the carrots for 5 minutes, until crisp tender.
2. After the carrots have cooled, mix with the oil, vinegar, garlic powder, cumin, paprika, red pepper, parsley, and salt.
3. Place ¾ cup of carrots in each of 4 containers. STORAGE: Store covered containers in the refrigerator for up to 5 days.

Per Serving
109; Total fat: 7g; Saturated fat: 1g; Sodium: 234mg; Carbohydrates: 11g; F iber: 3g; Protein: 2g

Basil, Almond, and Celery Heart Pesto

Cook time: 10 minutes | Serves 1

½ cup raw, unsalted almonds
2 cups fresh basil leaves, (about 1½ ounces)
½ cup chopped celery hearts with leaves
¼ teaspoon kosher salt
1 tablespoon freshly squeezed lemon juice
¼ cup olive oil
3 tablespoons water

1. Place the almonds in the bowl of a food processor and process until they look like coarse sand.
2. Add the basil, celery hearts, salt, lemon juice, oil and water and process until smooth. The sauce will be somewhat thick. If you would like a thinner sauce, add more water, oil, or lemon juice, depending on your taste preference.
3. Scoop the pesto into a container and refrigerate.
4. STORAGE: Store the covered container in the refrigerator for up to 2 weeks. Pesto may be frozen for up to 6 months.

Per Serving : (¼ cup)
231; Total fat: 22g; Saturated fat: 3g; Sodium: 178mg; Carbohydrates: 6g; Fiber: 3g; Protein: 4 g

 # Favorite Italian Recipes

MEATBALLS IN TOMATO SAUCE

Prep Time: 30 mins   Cooking Time: 20 mins
Servings: 4
Ingredients:
For the meatballs:
  350 gr – 13 oz ground beef
  30 gr – 1 oz Parmigiano
  ½ egg
  1 slice of white bread
  1 or 2 tsp of milk
  Chopped parsley
  Salt and pepper
For the sauce:
  500 gr – 15 oz tomato sauce
  3 garlic cloves
  ¼ onion
  Salt and pepper
  Extra virgin olive oil

Directions
1. Mix ground beef, ½ egg, Parmigiano, chopped parsley, salt, pepper, and the slice of bread soaked in milk. Form meatballs (about 25g – 0.8 oz each, yielding about 18 meatballs).
2. In a pan, place olive oil, garlic, and chopped onion. When golden, add meatballs and brown on each side.
3. Add tomato sauce, salt, pepper, basil, and parsley. Cook on low heat for 45 minutes.
4. Serve the Meatballs in Tomato Sauce hot!
   Per serving: Calories: 492, Carbs: 20.7g, Protein: 23.7g, Fat: 34.9g, Fiber: 3.1g, Sodium: 1001mg

CHICKEN THIGHS WITH PEPPERS AND THYME

Prep Time: 15 mins   Cook Time: 35 mins
Servings: 4
Ingredients:
4 chicken thighs
3 peppers
3 tbsp tomato sauce
Garlic
Olive oil
Salt and pepper
Fresh thyme
White wine (if available)

Directions:
1. Broil whole peppers in the oven until each side is darkened. Place them in a plastic bag, let cool for 20 minutes, then peel off the skin and cut them into pieces.
2. Tie chicken thighs with kitchen twine, then insert a small piece of fresh thyme inside.
3. In a pan, sauté garlic with olive oil over medium heat until golden brown. Add chicken thighs and brown on all sides.
4. Add white wine (if available), tomato sauce, and water as needed. Season with salt and pepper. Let thighs cook. When almost ready, add the peeled peppers and finish cooking.
5. Serve with fresh thyme.
   Per serving: Calories: 378, Carbs: 14g, Protein: 38g, Fat: 18.2g, Fiber: 3.1g, Sodium: 355mg

HEIRLOOM BEAN BLEND SOUP

Prep Time: 15 mins   Cooking Time: 1hr 55 mins
Servings: 4
Ingredients:
2 cups of a mix of dry beans, peas, chickpeas, and lentils
1 large potato (diced)
1 carrot (chopped)
1 celery stick (chopped)
1/2 onion (chopped)
3 tbsp tomato paste
Salt & pepper
Extra virgin olive oil
Water
Basil

Directions:
1. Soak the dry legumes overnight.
2. Sauté the chopped onion in extra virgin olive oil over medium heat.
3. Add diced potatoes, chopped carrots, and celery to the pan. Then, introduce the rinsed legume mix and tomato paste. Mix well.
4. Add water, salt, pepper, and basil. Let it cook on medium/low heat. Serve immediately
   Per serving Calories: 251.3, Carbohydrates: 40.4g, Protein: 18.7g, Fat: 1.7g, Sodium: 138.6mg

SPAGHETTI CARBONARA (Spaghetti with Guanciale and Eggs)

Prep Time: 10 mins   Cooking Time: 10 mins
Servings: 4
Ingredients:
Spaghetti: 1/2 pounds (325 g)
Guanciale (pork rind): 5 oz (155 g)
Egg yolks: 6 (average size)
Pecorino Romano cheese: ½ cup (50 g)
Black pepper: to taste

Directions:
1. Put a pot of salted water on the burner to cook the pasta.
2. Remove the pork rind from the guanciale, cut it into slices, then into strips about 1/2" (1cm) thick.
3. Put the guanciale pieces into a non-stick pan and brown over medium heat for about 15 minutes, being careful not to burn it.
4. Meanwhile, cook the spaghetti in boiling water for the time indicated on the package.
5. In a bowl, combine egg yolks, most of the Pecorino cheese, and black pepper. Whip the mixture by hand and add a tablespoon of cooking water to dilute it.
6. Once the guanciale is cooked, set it aside. Drain the pasta al dente directly into the pan with the guanciale and stir briefly.
7. Remove from heat and quickly pour the egg and Pecorino cheese mixture into the pan. Mix quickly to combine.
8. For extra creaminess, add a little cooking water if necessary. Serve immediately with the remaining Pecorino cheese and ground black pepper on top.
Per serving: Calories: 680, Carbs: 66.9g, Protein: 19.3g, Fats: 37.2g, Fiber: 2.2g, Sodium: 586mg

SPAGHETTI CACIO E PEPE (Pecorino and Black Pepper Spaghetti)

Prep Time: 10 mins   Cook Time: 10 mins
Servings: 4

Ingredients:
Spaghetti: 1/2 pounds (320 g)
Black pepper: to taste (corns)
Pecorino Romano cheese: 7 oz (200 g) (medium seasoning), grated
Fine salt: to taste

Directions:
1. Grate the Pecorino cheese.
2. Boil water in a pan (use about half of the usual amount for pasta, making it richer in starch). Add salt to taste.
3. Cook the spaghetti in the salted boiling water.
4. Crush the black peppercorns on a cutting board with a meat pestle or grinder to release more flavor.
5. Pour half of the crushed pepper into a large non-stick pan, toast over low heat, then add a couple of ladles of cooking water.
6. Drain the spaghetti very al dente and add it directly to the pan with the toasted pepper; it will continue cooking with the seasoning.
7. Stir the pasta continuously with kitchen tongs, adding a ladle of water if needed.
8. Prepare the Pecorino cream: Pour about half of the grated Pecorino cheese into a bowl. Add a ladle of cooking water and stir vigorously with a whisk, adding more water when needed.
9. Add the remaining half of the Pecorino cheese, keeping some aside for garnish. Adjust the Pecorino-to-water ratio for a creamy consistency without lumps.
10. Finish cooking the pasta, stirring and adding hot water if necessary.
11. Before adding the Pecorino cream, briefly stir the cream over steam to adjust its temperature.
12. Turn off the heat, pour in the Pecorino cream, stir continuously, and sauté the pasta.
13. Transfer the spaghetti cacio e pepe to a plate, season with the remaining pepper, garnish with Pecorino, and enjoy immediately.
Per serving: Calories: 490, Carbs: 66.9g, Protein: 24.4g, Fats: 15g, Fiber: 2.2g, Sodium: 1229mg

PASTA ALLA GRICIA

Prep Time: 10 mins   Cook Time: 15 mins
Servings: 4
Ingredients:
0.5 lb (320 g) Rigatoni
0.5 lb (250 g) Guanciale (pork rind) (already peppered)
½ cup (60 g) Pecorino Romano cheese (grated) Fine salt (to taste)

Directions:
1. Place a pot of water on the burner for the pasta. Cut guanciale into 1/2" (1 cm) thick slices. Separate any rind and cut into strips about 1/8" (1/2 cm) thick. In a hot pan, add guanciale without additional fat. Let it sizzle on medium heat for about 10 minutes until golden and crisp, avoiding burning.
2. When the water boils, add salt and cook the rigatoni. While cooking, grate Pecorino cheese. Two minutes before the pasta is done, slow down guanciale cooking by adding a ladle of pasta cooking water. Stir to create a creamy texture.
3. Drain the pasta and add it directly to the guanciale sauce, preserving some cooking water. Stir for about 1 minute, remove from heat, sprinkle with a third of grated Pecorino cheese, and add more cooking water if necessary.
4. Stir and toss the pasta to create a creamy consistency. Serve Pasta alla Gricia, garnishing each plate with the remaining Pecorino cheese.
Per Serving: Calories: 565, Carbs: 65.3g, Protein: 24.9g, Fats: 22.1 g, Fiber: 2.1 g, Sodium: 2849 mg

ARANCINI (FRIED RICE BALLS)

Prep Time: 60 mins   Cook Time: 45 mins
Serving: 4
Ingredients:
Arborio rice: 750g (26 oz)
Saffron: 2 small bags (0.6g / 0.021 oz)
Parmigiano cheese: 80g (2.8 oz), grated
Eggs: 5 (2 for rice, 3 for breading)
Ground beef: 250g (9 oz)
Peas: 100g (3.5 oz)
Onion: 1/2
Celery stick: 1
Carrot: 1
Vegetable broth: 1 mug
White wine: 1 glass
Tomato paste: 1 full tablespoon
Mozzarella: 150g (5 oz)
Extra virgin olive oil
Parsley
Basil
Breadcrumbs
Flour
Salt and pepper

Directions:
1. Saute chopped onion, celery, and carrot in a pan with olive oil. Add ground beef, white wine, peas, vegetable broth, chopped parsley, basil, salt, and pepper. Cook for 40 minutes to an hour, adding water if needed.
2. Boil rice in little water. Mix with grated parmigiano, 2 eggs, and saffron mixed with beaten eggs. Let it cool for 2 hours.
3. Cut mozzarella into small cubes.
4. Take a full tablespoon of rice, form a ball, create a small hole, fill it with sauce and a mozzarella cube. Close the hole with more rice, forming a ball (the size of a small orange).
5. Cover arancini with flour, dip in beaten eggs, and coat with breadcrumbs.
6. Deep fry and serve hot or warm.

Per serving: Calories: 628, Carbs: 55.1g, Protein: 13.8g, Fats: 38.8g, Fiber: 1.7g, Sodium: 635mg

MEDITERRANEAN MEAL PLAN

Meal	Food Choices	Portion
Breakfast		
	Bakery Products or Cereals	40g - 1.4 oz
	Skimmed Milk or Fruit Yogurt	150ml -5.1 fl oz or 1 serving
	Coffee or Tea	
Lunch/Dinner		
	Choice of First Course	
	Bread / Pasta / Barley / Farro / Corn Flour / Semolina	90g - 3.2 oz
	Gnocchi or Potatoes	300g - 10.6 oz
	Stuffed Pasta	200g - 7 oz
	Rotating Second Course	
	Meat (3 times a week)	100g - 3.5 oz
	Fish (3 times a week)	120g - 4.2 oz
	Fresh Cheese (or 50g of aged cheese) (3 times a week)	100g - 3.5 oz
	Lean Cold Cuts (Bresaola, Speck, Cooked Ham, Raw Ham) (2 times a week)	50g - 1.8 oz
	Dried Legumes or 125g of Fresh/Frozen Legumes (2 times a week)	50g- 1.8 oz
	Eggs (2 times a week)	
Every Day		
	Vegetables (As Desired)	

Meal	Food Choices	Portion
	Jam or Honey	15g - 0.5 oz
	Olive Oil	25g- 0.9 oz (replaceable with butter or mayonnaise once a week)
	Fresh Fruit	350g - 12.3 oz (with meals or as a snack)
	Crackers or Biscuits or Bread	30g or 50g - 1.1 oz o 1.8 oz (as a snack)
	Once a week, replace a meal with a Margherita or Vegetarian Pizza	
	Drink at least 1.5 liters of water per day	

Proteine 62 gr 17%   *Grassi* 43 gr 26%   *Carboidrati* 234 gr 57%   *Calorie* 1550

These are the guideline for the Mediterranean diet. The table provides a dietary plan with adequate energy intake, nutrient balance, and excellent satiety. Starting from this weekly schedule, everyone can vary their menu by drawing from the chapters with various recipes. It would be wrong to offer a rigid diet plan because everyone has their own calorie needs and tastes. Therefore, consider this guideline and adapt the hundreds of recipes in the book to the table. You will create healthy and delicious daily menus and eat in a balanced manner.

INDEX OF RECIPES

Made in the USA
Las Vegas, NV
08 September 2024

94972656R00063